interactive
SCIENCE

A fast sprinter, the Eastern Collared Lizard can run on its large hind legs, using its long tail for balance.

SAVVAS
LEARNING COMPANY

You are an author!

You are one of the authors of this book. You can write in this book! You can take notes in this book! You can draw in it too! This book will be yours to keep.

Fill in the information below to tell about yourself. Then write your autobiography. An autobiography tells about you and the kinds of things you like to do.

My Photo

Name ....

School ....

Town, State ....

Autobiography ....

ON THE COVER
A fast sprinter, the Eastern Collared Lizard can run on its large hind legs, using its long tail for balance.

ISBN-13: 978-0-328-87141-4
ISBN-10: 0-328-87141-9
17 2021

Program Authors

DON BUCKLEY, M.Sc.
Director of Technology & Innovation,
The School at Columbia University, New York, New York
Don Buckley has transformed learning spaces, textbooks, and media resources so that they work for students and teachers. He has advanced degrees from leading European universities, is a former industrial chemist, published photographer, and former consultant to MOMA's Education Department. He also teaches a graduate course at Columbia Teacher's College in Educational Technology and directs the Technology and Innovation program at the school. He is passionate about travel, architecture, design, change, the future, and innovation.

ZIPPORAH MILLER, M.A.Ed.
Coordinator for K-12 Science Programs, Anne Arundel County Public Schools.
Mrs. Zipporah Miller served as a reviewer during the development of Next Generation Science Standards and provides national training to teachers, administrators, higher education staff and informal science stakeholders on the Next Generation Science Standards. Prior to her appointment in Anne Arundel, Mrs. Miller served as the Associate Executive Director for Professional Development Programs and Conferences at the National Science Teachers Association (NSTA).

MICHAEL J. PADILLA, Ph.D.
Eugene P. Moore School of Education, Clemson University,
Clemson, South Carolina
A former middle school teacher and a leader in middle school science education, Dr. Michael Padilla has served as president of the National Science Teachers Association and reviewed the Next Generation Science Standards. He is a former professor of science education at Clemson University. As lead author of the *Science Explorer* series, Dr. Padilla has inspired the team in developing a program that promotes student inquiry and meets the needs of today's students.

KATHRYN THORNTON, Ph.D.
Professor, Mechanical & Aerospace Engineering,
University of Virginia,
Charlottesville, Virginia
Selected by NASA in May 1984, Dr. Kathryn Thornton is a veteran of four space flights. She has logged more than 975 hours in space, including more than 21 hours of extravehicular activity. As an author on the *Scott Foresman Science* series, Dr. Thornton's enthusiasm for science has inspired teachers around the globe.

MICHAEL E. WYSESSION, Ph.D.
Associate Professor of Earth and Planetary Science,
Washington University, St. Louis, Missouri
An author on more than 50 scientific publications, Dr. Wysession was awarded the prestigious Packard Foundation Fellowship and Presidential Faculty Fellowship for his research in geophysics. Dr. Wysession is an expert on Earth's inner structure and has mapped various regions of Earth using seismic tomography. He is known internationally for his work in geoscience education and research, and was an author of the Next Generation Science Standards.

Instructional Design Author

GRANT WIGGINS, Ed.D.
President, Authentic Education,
Hopewell, New Jersey
Dr. Wiggins is a co-author with Jay McTighe of *Understanding by Design, 2nd Edition* (ASCD 2005). His approach to instructional design provides teachers with a disciplined way of thinking about curriculum design, assessment, and instruction that moves teaching from covering content to ensuring understanding.
UNDERSTANDING BY DESIGN® and UbD™ are trademarks of ASCD, and are used under license.

Activities Author

KAREN L. OSTLUND, Ph.D.
Past President, National Science Teachers Association, Arlington, Virginia
Dr. Ostlund has over 40 years of experience teaching at the elementary, middle school, and university levels. She was Director of WINGS Online (Welcoming Interns and Novices with Guidance and Support) and the Director of the UTeach/Dell Center for New Teacher Success with the UTeach program in the College of Natural Sciences at the University of Texas at Austin. She also served as Director of the Center for Science Education at the University of Texas at Arlington, as President of the Council of Elementary Science International, and as a member of the Board of Directors of the National Science Teachers Association. As an author of Scott Foresman Science, Dr. Ostlund was instrumental in developing inquiry activities.

ELL Consultant

JIM CUMMINS, Ph.D.
Professor and Canada Research Chair,
Curriculum, Teaching and Learning Department at the University of Toronto
Dr. Cummins's research focuses on literacy development in multilingual schools and the role technology plays in learning across the curriculum. *Interactive Science* incorporates research-based principles for integrating language with the teaching of academic content based on Dr. Cummins's work.

Reviewers

Program Consultants

William Brozo, Ph.D.
Professor of Literacy, Graduate School of Education, George Mason University, Fairfax, Virginia.
Dr. Brozo is the author of numerous articles and books on literacy development. He co-authors a column in The Reading Teacher and serves on the editorial review board of the Journal of Adolescent & Adult Literacy.

Kristi Zenchak, M.S.
Biology Instructor, Oakton Community College, Des Plaines, Illinois
Kristi Zenchak helps elementary teachers incorporate science, technology, engineering, and math activities into the classroom. STEM activities that produce viable solutions to real-world problems not only motivate students but also prepare students for future STEM careers. Ms. Zenchak helps elementary teachers understand the basic science concepts, and provides STEM activities that are easy to implement in the classroom.

Content Reviewers

Brad Armosky, M.S.
Texas Advanced Computing Center
University of Texas at Austin
Austin, Texas

Alexander Brands, Ph.D.
Department of Biological Sciences
Lehigh University
Bethlehem, Pennsylvania

Paul Beale, Ph.D.
Department of Physics
University of Colorado
Boulder, Colorado

Joy Branlund, Ph.D.
Department of Earth Science
Southwestern Illinois College
Granite City, Illinois

Constance Brown, Ph.D
Atmospheric Science Program
Geography Department
Indiana University
Bloomington, Indiana

Dana Dudle, Ph.D.
Biology Department
DePauw University
Greencastle, Indiana

Rick Duhrkopf, Ph. D.
Department of Biology
Baylor University
Waco, Texas

Mark Henriksen, Ph.D.
Physics Department
University of Maryland
Baltimore, Maryland

Andrew Hirsch, Ph.D.
Department of Physics
Purdue University
W. Lafayette, Indiana

Linda L. Cronin Jones, Ph.D.
School of Teaching & Learning
University of Florida
Gainesville, Florida

T. Griffith Jones, Ph.D.
College of Education
University of Florida
Gainesville, Florida

Candace Lutzow-Felling, Ph.D.
Director of Education
State Arboretum of Virginia & Blandy Experimental Farm
Boyce, Virginia

Cortney V. Martin, Ph.D.
Virginia Polytechnic Institute
Blacksburg, Virginia

Sadredin Moosavi, Ph.D.
University of Massachusetts Dartmouth
Fairhaven, Massachusetts

Klaus Newmann, Ph.D.
Department of Geological Sciences
Ball State University
Muncie, Indiana

Scott M. Rochette, Ph.D.
Department of the Earth Sciences
SUNY College at Brockport
Brockport, New York

Ursula Rosauer Smedly, M.S.
Alcade Science Center
New Mexico State University
Alcade, New Mexico

Frederick W. Taylor, Ph.D.
Jackson School of Geosciences
University of Texas at Austin
Austin, Texas

Chapter 1

Properties of Matter

What are the properties of matter? 1

Try It! How are weight and volume affected when
objects are combined? 2

Let's Read
Science! **Compare and Contrast** 3

STEM Activity Trap and Store 4

Lesson 1
What makes up matter? 8
MY PLANET DiaRY Fun Fact 8

Lesson 2
How can matter be described? 16
Explore It! What are some properties of solids? 16

Lesson 3
What are solids, liquids, and gases? 22
Explore It! How can water change state? 22
math! Ranges 26

Lesson 4
What are mixtures and solutions? 28
Explore It! How can a mixture be separated? 28

Lesson 5
How does matter change? 34
Explore It! What happens when air heats up? 34

Investigate It! What are some ways to separate
a mixture? 40

Science in Your Backyard Sidewalks & Playgrounds 42

Vocabulary Smart Cards 43

Study Guide and Chapter Review 47

Benchmark Practice 50

Go Green! Aerogels 51

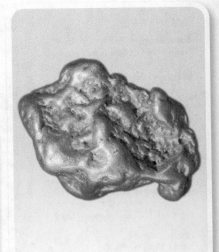

*Gold has properties that
determine how it can be used.*

SavvasRealize.com

**Go online for engaging
videos, interactivities,
and virtual labs.**

Forces and Motion

What affects the motion of objects? 53

Try It! How can you make a paper helicopter
drop slowly? 54

Let's Read
Science! ◉ **Main Idea and Details** 55

STEM Activity Watch It Fly! 56

Lesson 1
What are forces? 60
 MY PLANET DIARY Misconception 60

Lesson 2
What are Newton's laws? 66
 Explore It! How can forces affect motion? 66
 math! Using Formulas 72

Lesson 3
How are forces combined? 74
 Explore It! How do forces combine? 74

Lesson 4
How are shadows formed? 78
 Explore It! What can cause the size and
 shape of a shadow to change? 78

Investigate It! What forces affect the motion of
a rocket? 82

Biography Isaac Newton 84

Vocabulary Smart Cards 85

Study Guide and Chapter Review 89

Benchmark Practice 92

NASA **Field Trip** NASA's Space Centers 93

Apply It! How is motion affected by mass? 94

Performance-Based Assessment 98

Forces and motion can be
used for recreation.

SavvasRealize.com

**Go online for engaging
videos, interactivities,
and virtual labs.**

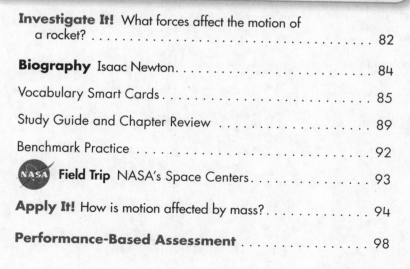

Growth and Survival

How do plants and animals grow and change? . . .101

Try It! How can temperature affect seed growth? 102

Let's Read
Science! Cause and Effect 103

STEM Activity Come in Out of Nature! 104

Lesson 1
What are some physical structures in living things? 108
MY PLANET DIARY Connections 108

Lesson 2
How do adaptations help plants? 114
Explore It! How can plants survive in the desert? 114

Lesson 3
How do adaptations help animals? 120
Explore It! Which bird beak can crush seeds? 120

Lesson 4
What are the life cycles of some animals? . . 126
Explore It! How do butterflies grow and change? 126

Investigate It! How do seeds grow? 132

Science Careers Zoologist 134

Vocabulary Smart Cards 135

Study Guide and Chapter Review 137

Benchmark Practice 140

Biography Charles Darwin 141

As a tadpole grows into a frog, its tail becomes smaller.

SavvasRealize.com

Go online for engaging videos, interactivities, and virtual labs.

Chapter 4

Ecosystems

How do living things interact with their environments? 143

Try It! What is in a local ecosystem? 144

Let's Read Science! Main Idea and Details 145

STEM Activity Let It Self-Water! 146

Lesson 1
How do plants get and use energy? 150
my planet diary Discovery 150
math! Analyze Data 152

Lesson 2
How do organisms interact in ecosystems? 158
Explore It! What do some molds need to grow? 158
math! Read a Graph 164

Lesson 3
How do ecosystems change? 166
my planet diary Fun Fact 166
math! Subtracting Fractions 172

Lesson 4
How do humans impact ecosystems? 174
Explore It! Which materials break down fastest in soil? . . 174

Investigate It! What heats up air? 178

STEM Tracking Migrations 180

Vocabulary Smart Cards 181

Study Guide and Chapter Review 185

Benchmark Practice 188

Go Green! Create a Compost Pile 189

Apply It! How can salt affect the hatching of brine shrimp eggs? 190

Performance-Based Assessment 194

An organism can play different roles in an ecosystem.

SavvasRealize.com

Go online for engaging videos, interactivities, and virtual labs.

Chapter 5

The Water Cycle and Weather

How does water move through the environment? 197

Try It! How can water move in the water cycle? 198

Let's Read Science! ◉ Draw Conclusions 199

STEM Activity Filter It Out! 200

Lesson 1
What is the water cycle? 204
MY PLANET DIARY Connections 204
math! Estimating Area 209

Lesson 2
What are the spheres of Earth? 210
MY PLANET DIARY Fun Fact 210
math! Read a Circle Graph 213

Lesson 3
What is weather? 216
Explore It! How accurate are weather forecasts? 216
math! Line Graphs 219

Lesson 4
How do clouds and precipitation form? 224
Explore It! Does a cloud form? 224

Lesson 5
What is climate? 230
Explore It! How does a thermometer work? 230

Lesson 6
What are erosion and deposition? 236
Explore It! How does melting ice cause erosion? 236
math! Calculate Rates 239

Investigate It! Where is the hurricane going? 242
STEM Predicting Tsunamis 244
Vocabulary Smart Cards 245
Study Guide and Chapter Review 251
Benchmark Practice 254
Science in Your Backyard Keep a Weather Journal 255

The water in this river may have been part of the air or the ocean before.

SavvasRealize.com

Go online for engaging videos, interactivities, and virtual labs.

Chapter 6

Earth and Space

How do objects move in space? 257

STEM Quest Plan a Trip Around the World of Patterns xxii

Try It! What does a spiral galaxy look like from
different angles? 258

Let's Read
Science! Compare and Contrast 259

STEM Activity Breathe Deeply! 260

Lesson 1
How does Earth move? 264
Explore It! How does sunlight strike Earth's surface? 264

Lesson 2
What is a star? 270
my planet diary Misconception 270

Lesson 3
What are the inner planets? 276
Explore It! How does distance affect orbiting time? 276
math! Analyze a Bar Graph 280

Lesson 4
What are the outer planets? 284
Explore It! How are the sizes of the inner and outer
planets different? 284

Lesson 5
**What are asteroids, meteors, comets,
and moons?** 290
Explore It! How does a meteoroid fall through
Earth's atmosphere? 290

Investigate It! How can spinning affect a planet's shape? . 296

Science in Your Backyard Planet Hunting 298

Vocabulary Smart Cards 299

Study Guide and Chapter Review 303

Benchmark Practice 306

Field Trip Green Bank Observatory 307

Apply It! How does the speed of a meteorite
affect the crater it makes? 308

Performance-Based Assessment 312

Earth is warmer near the tropics, where sunlight is direct.

SavvasRealize.com

Go online for engaging videos, interactivities, and virtual labs.

The Nature of Science

What is science? 315

Try It! What questions do scientists ask? 316

Let's Read Science! **Text Features** 317

STEM Activity Where's the Wind Going? 318

Lesson 1
What do scientists do? 322
MY PLANET DIARY Fun Fact 322

Lesson 2
How do scientists investigate? 328
Explore It! Which method keeps bread freshest? 328

Lesson 3
How do scientists collect and interpret data? 336
Explore It! Why do scientists use thermometers? 336

Lesson 4
How do scientists support their conclusions? . 344
Explore It! Which towel absorbs the most water? 344

Investigate It! How does a banana slice change over time? 348

math! Interpret Graphs 350

Vocabulary Smart Cards 351

Study Guide and Part 1 Review 355

Benchmark Practice 358

STEM Flight Simulators 359

Scientists use different methods to collect information.

SavvasRealize.com

Go online for engaging videos, interactivities, and virtual labs.

Skills Handbook
Part 2

Design and Function

How does technology affect our lives? 361

Try It! How can you design a strong glue? 362

Let's Read **Science!** ⊙ **Main Idea and Details** 363

STEM Activity Is Your Arm a Simple Machine? 364

Lesson 1
What is technology? 368
Explore It! Which transport system works best? 368

Lesson 2
How does technology mimic living things? . . 374
MY PLANET DIARY Did You Know? 374

Lesson 3
What is the design process? 380
Explore It! How can the design of a model arm help you learn about how your arm works? 380
math! Ordered Pairs 386

Investigate It! How can you make and redesign a model of a robotic arm? 388

Go Green! Denim Insulation 390

Vocabulary Smart Cards 391

Study Guide and Part 2 Review 393

Benchmark Practice 396

NASA **Big World, My World** Infrared Technology 397

Design It! How much weight can a model arm support? 398

Performance-Based Assessment 404

Measurements EM1

English/Spanish Glossary EM2

Index EM12

Technology can make work easier and solve problems.

SavvasRealize.com

Go online for engaging videos, interactivities, and virtual labs.

interactive SCIENCE

Big Question

At the start of each chapter you will see two questions—
an **Engaging Question** and a **Big Question.**
Just like a scientist, you will predict an answer to the
Engaging Question. Each Big Question will help you
start thinking about the Big Ideas of science. Look for the
symbol throughout the chapter!

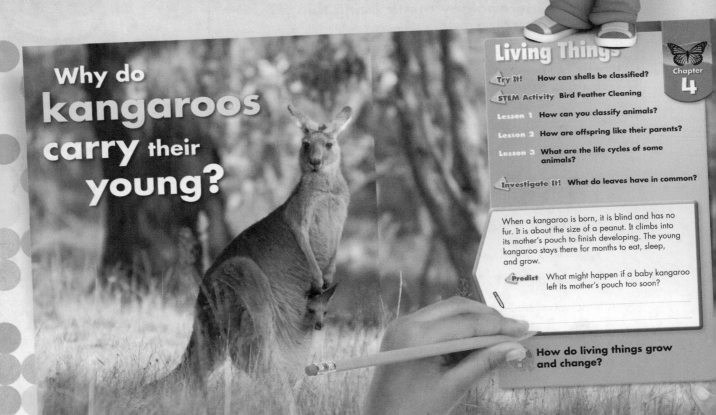

Why do kangaroos carry their young?

Living Things

Try It! How can shells be classified?

STEM Activity Bird Feather Cleaning

Lesson 1 How can you classify animals?

Lesson 2 How are offspring like their parents?

Lesson 3 What are the life cycles of some animals?

Investigate It! What do leaves have in common?

Chapter 4

When a kangaroo is born, it is blind and has no fur. It is about the size of a peanut. It climbs into its mother's pouch to finish developing. The young kangaroo stays there for months to eat, sleep, and grow.

Predict What might happen if a baby kangaroo left its mother's pouch too soon?

How do living things grow and change?

PearsonRealize.com

152

Interact with your book!   Interact with inquiry!   Interact online!

Let's Read Science!

You will see a page like this toward the beginning of each chapter. It will show you how to use a reading skill that will help you understand what you read.

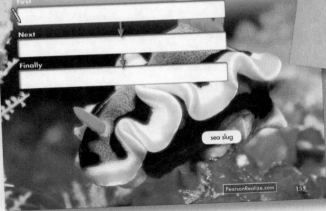

◉ **Sequence**
- **Sequence** is the order in which events take place.
- Clue words such as *first, next, then,* and *finally* can help you figure out the sequence of events.

Let's Read Science!

Classify Animals

Scientists can classify animals according to their behaviors, such as how they act, and their physical characteristics, such as hair. Scientists may classify a slug such as the one below. Scientists may first identify whether or not the slug has a backbone. Next, they can find out what the slug eats. Finally, scientists can compare and contrast the slug to other animals.

Practice It!

Complete the graphic organizer to show the sequence of classifying animals.

First

Next

Finally

sea slug

PearsonRealize.com   155

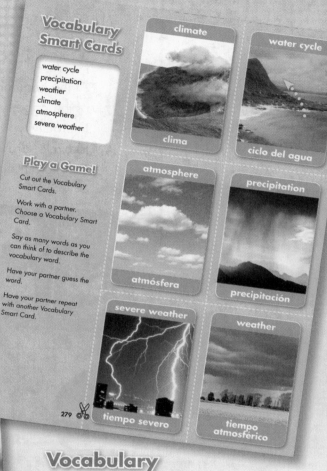

Vocabulary Smart Cards

water cycle
precipitation
weather
climate
atmosphere
severe weather

Play a Game!

Cut out the Vocabulary Smart Cards.

Work with a partner. Choose a Vocabulary Smart Card.

Say as many words as you can think of to describe the vocabulary word.

Have your partner guess the word.

Have your partner repeat with another Vocabulary Smart Card.

279 ✂

climate / clima
water cycle / ciclo del agua
atmosphere / atmósfera
precipitation / precipitación
severe weather / tiempo severo
weather / tiempo atmosférico

Vocabulary Smart Cards

Go to the end of the chapter and cut out your own set of **Vocabulary Smart Cards.** Draw a picture to learn the word. Play a game with a classmate to practice using the word!

Savvas Realize.com

Go to **SavvasRealize.com** for a variety of digital activities.

"Engage with the page!"

interactive SCIENCE

Envision It!

At the beginning of each lesson, at the top of the page, you will see an **Envision It!** interactivity that gives you the opportunity to circle, draw, write, or respond to the Envision It! question.

Lesson 2

How are offspring like their parents?

Envision It!

Circle the two pictures that show behaviors an animal must learn.

Draw an ✗ on the pictures that show behaviors an animal is born knowing how to do.

I will know that some characteristics and behaviors are inherited and some are learned or acquired.

Words to Know

inherit
instinct

MY PLANET DIARY   DISCOVERY

Karl von Frisch

A honey bee scout flies out of the hive to look for food. It finds flowers full of sweet nectar. How can the scout communicate to the other bees where the food is? Beginning in the 1920s, Karl von Frisch studied bee behavior. He discovered that the scout bee performs a dance. The dance tells other bees where to find the food. The bees in the hive are born knowing what the dance means.

What do you think the bees will do after they see the scout's dance?

Both Alike and Different

Why do kittens look like cats and not like dogs? Why does a corn seed grow into a corn plant and not a tomato plant? Most young plants and animals grow to look like their parents. Some plants and animals look like their parents even when they are very young.

The young antelope in the picture shares many characteristics with its parent. For example, the young antelope has the same body shape as its parent. Its fur is about the same length too.

The young antelope is also different in some ways. For example, its horns are much smaller than its parent's horns. The young antelope's horns will grow larger as it gets older. But even then, its horns may not have the exact shape or size of its parent's horns.

1. **Compare and Contrast** Describe other ways in which the young antelope and its parent are alike and different.

PearsonRealize.com   169

168

MY PLANET DIARY

My Planet Diary will introduce you to amazing scientists, fun facts, and important discoveries in science. They will also help you to overcome common misconceptions about science concepts.

Read See DO!

After reading small chunks of information, stop to check your understanding. The visuals help teach about what you read. Answer questions, underline text, draw pictures, or label models.

Do the math!

Scientists commonly use math as a tool to help them answer science questions. You can practice skills that you are learning in math class right in your *Interactive Science* Student Edition!

Got it?

At the end of each lesson you will have a chance to evaluate your own progress! At this point you can stop or go on to the next lesson.

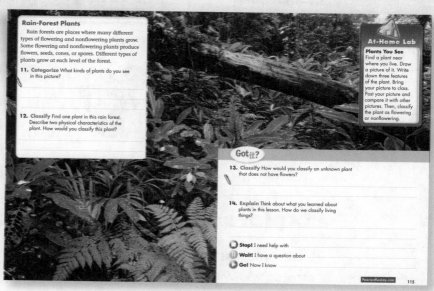

"Have fun! Be a scientist!"

interactive SCIENCE

Try It!

At the start of every chapter, you will have the chance to do a hands-on inquiry activity. The activity will provide you with experiences that will prepare you for the chapter lessons or may raise a new question in your mind.

Lesson 2

How do plants use leaves to make food?

Envision It!

Tell how you think leaves help plants.

I will know that leaves help plants live, grow, and make food.

Words to Know

photosynthesis
carbon dioxide
oxygen

Inquiry **Explore It!**

How does sunlight affect plant survival?

☐ **1. Observe** a green leaf on a plant. Gently fold a piece of foil completely around the whole leaf. Be sure the foil cannot fall off.

☐ **2.** Place the plant near a sunny window. Wait one week.

☐ **3.** Take off the foil. Observe. Compare what you observed before and after the leaf was covered.

Materials

plant

foil

Be careful! Wash your hands when finished.

Explain Your Results

4. Infer What do you think happened to the leaf? Explain.

What Plants Need

Plants need food, air, water, and space to live and grow. Many plants live and grow in soil. The four main parts of a flowering plant are leaves, roots, stems, and flowers. In different kinds of plants, these parts may look alike. They may also look different.

Unlike animals, plants make their own food. Plants need energy from the sun to make food. Food is made in a plant's leaves, using the sun's energy. This food helps plants grow.

1. Text Features Look at the text features on this page. Identify one text feature and the clue it gives you.

Text feature	Clue
Heading	It tells me that I'll read about what plants need.

Bromeliad plants are like other plants. They use energy from the sun to make food.

PearsonRealize.com

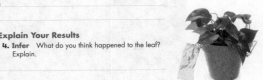

Explore It!

Before you start reading the lesson, **Explore It!** activities provide you with an opportunity to first explore the content!

Design It!

STEM activities are found throughout core and ancillary materials.

The **Design It!** activity has you use the engineering design process to find solutions to problems. By finding a problem and then planning, drawing, and choosing materials, you will make, test, and evaluate a solution for a real world problem. Communicate your evidence through drawings and prototypes and identify ways to make your solution better.

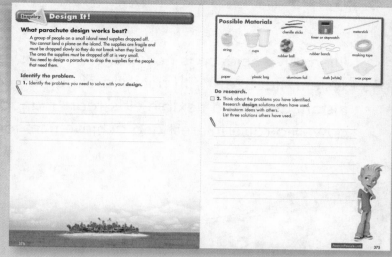

Investigate It!

At the end of every chapter, a Directed Inquiry activity gives you a chance to put together everything you've learned in the chapter. Using the activity card, apply design principles in the Guided version to Modify Your Investigation or the Open version to Develop Your Own Investigation. Whether you need a lot of support from your teacher or you're ready to explore on your own, there are fun hands-on activities that match your interests.

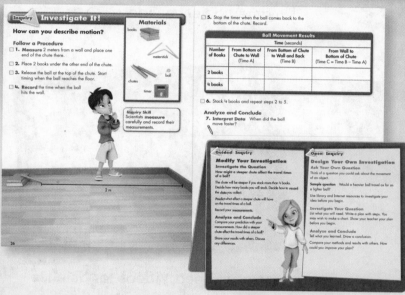

Apply It!

These Open Inquiry activities give you a chance to plan and carry out investigations.

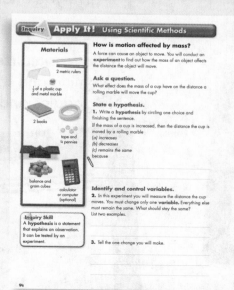

What is Savvas Realize?

Interactive Science is now part of Savvas' brand-new learning management system, Realize! With rich and engaging content, embedded assessment with instant data, and flexible classroom management tools, Realize gives you the power to raise interest and achievement for every student in your classroom.

Engaging Videos

Engage with science topics through videos! Start each chapter with an Untamed Science video.

Savvas Flipped Videos for Science give you another way to learn.

Interactivities and Virtual Labs

Practice science content with engaging online activities.

At **SavvasRealize.com** go online and conduct labs virtually! No goggles and no mess.

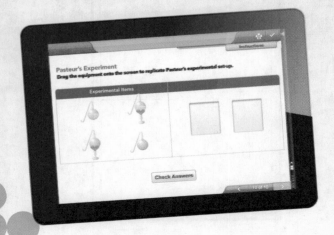

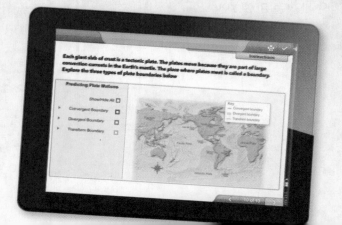

Connect to What You Know

Check what you know at the end of each lesson and chapter.

Get More Practice on skills and content, based on your performance.

Predict your exam readiness with benchmark assessments.

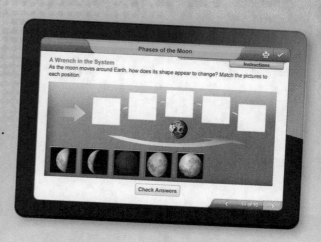

Savvas Realize offers powerful classroom management functionality, including:

Standards-aligned content — search by standard

Powerful Search tools — search by keyword, topic or standards

Customizable curriculum — reorder the table of contents, uploadfiles and media, add links and create custom lessons and assessments

Flexible class management tools — create classes, organize students, and create assignments targeted to students, groups of students, or the entire class.

Tracks student progress — instantly access student and class data that shows standards mastery on assessments, online activity and overall progress.

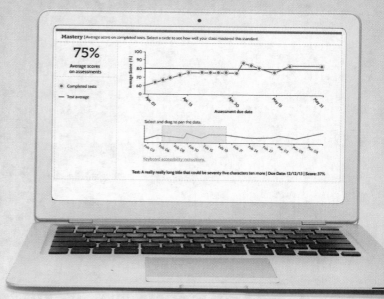

Track Your Learning Online.

SavvasRealize.com

Plan a Trip Around the World of Patterns

Your Quest is to plan an "Earth's Patterns" trip around the world. You will analyze sunrise and sunset data and positions of the Earth relative to the sun and moon. You will predict what the sky will look like at each location. As the trip's tour guide, you will explain Earth's patterns to the tour guests. At the end of the Quest, you will make a travel brochure for your trip.

Quest Kick-Off
Plan a Trip Around the World of Patterns
Predict and sketch what Earth looks like on the other side. Watch a video on the Earth patterns of solar and lunar eclipses.

Quest Check-In 1
Earth's Rotation Day and Night
Research sunrise and sunset data for your town. Think about how night and day will affect your travel plans.

Quest Check-In 2
Gravity and the Moon's Orbit
In this hands-on lab, you will model how Earth's gravity causes the moon to orbit Earth.

Quest Check-In 3
Moon Phases
Complete an interactivity to learn about the order of the phases of the moon.

Quest Check-In 4
Shadows and the Sun
Manipulate a simulation of the Earth rotating around the sun.

Quest Findings
Travel the World of Patterns
Get your travel destination and make your travel brochure.

SavvasRealize.com   Go online for all Quest digital interactivities and hands-on labs

What makes up these GIANT crystals?

Properties of Matter

Chapter 1

Try It! How are weight and volume affected when objects are combined?

STEM Activity Trap and Store

Lesson 1 What makes up matter?

Lesson 2 How can matter be described?

Lesson 3 What are solids, liquids, and gases?

Lesson 4 What are mixtures and solutions?

Lesson 5 How does matter change?

Investigate It! What are some ways to separate a mixture?

You see small crystals, such as sugar or salt, every day. But have you ever seen crystals like these? These giant crystals are in a cave in the Chihuahuan Desert.

Predict This cave was once filled with water that had minerals dissolved in it. How do you think the crystals formed?

....

....

THE BIG ? What are the properties of matter?

SavvasRealize.com

1

Materials

graduated cylinder

beads

plastic cup

plastic spoon

spring scale with bag

sand

How are weight and volume affected when objects are combined?

☐ **1.** Fill a graduated cylinder with 25 mL of beads. **Record** the volume on the chart.

☐ **2.** Hold up the spring scale with the bag. Set the scale to zero. Now the spring scale will only show the weight of what is in the bag.

☐ **3.** Put the beads in the bag and weigh them. Record. Pour the beads into a cup.

☐ **4.** Repeat Step 1 and Step 3 with sand. Pour the sand into the cup with the beads.

☐ **5.** Mix the beads and sand with a spoon. Repeat Step 1 and Step 3 with the mixture of beads and sand.

Inquiry Skill
When you interpret data, you can make an **inference.**

Measurements of Matter		
Objects	Volume (mL)	Weight (g)
beads		
sand		
beads and sand		

Explain Your Results

6. Interpret Data   Did the total volume or weight change after mixing? Explain.

....

....

7. UNLOCK THE BIG ? **Infer**   What did you learn about volume?

....

....

◉ Compare and Contrast

- You **compare** when you tell how things are alike.
- You **contrast** when you tell how things are different.

Copper and Malachite

Copper is a very useful metal. It has a reddish color. It can be formed into sheets and wires without breaking. Malachite is a green mineral. It breaks if you try to change its shape. Malachite and copper are solid and durable. They are often used for decoration.

This jewelry box is carved from malachite. The legs are made from copper.

Practice It!

Complete the graphic organizer below to compare and contrast copper and malachite.

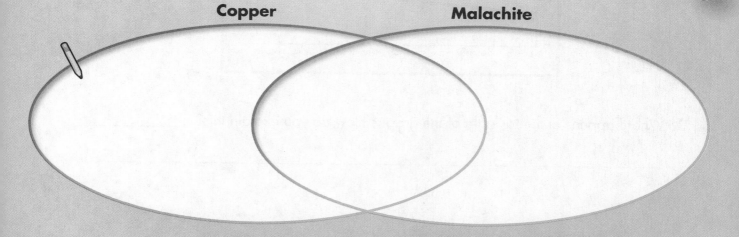

Copper   Malachite

Trap and Store

Burning fossil fuels—such as coal, oil, and natural gas—is a major source of energy for humans. However, this process releases carbon dioxide (CO_2) into Earth's atmosphere. Evidence suggests that this extra carbon dioxide builds up and keeps thermal energy from radiating out into space. As a result, Earth's temperature rises. Some energy plants use devices that trap carbon dioxide before it is released into the atmosphere. They store this trapped carbon dioxide deep underground. Engineers are looking for more ways to trap carbon dioxide gas before it enters the atmosphere because if less carbon dioxide enters the atmosphere, less heat will be trapped. This could be of great help with the problem of global warming. A manufacturing company has hired you to design a carbon dioxide trap.

Identify the Problem

☐ **1.** What problem will your carbon trap help solve? _____

_____

☐ **2.** Why is there a need to solve this problem? _____

Do Research

Examine the graph of carbon dioxide levels in Earth's atmosphere since 1870.

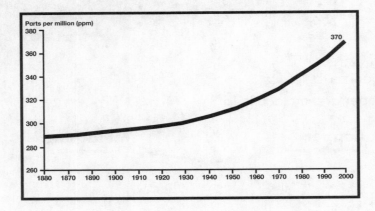

☐ **3.** What happens at the far right of the graph? How do you explain this? _____

_____

When vinegar and baking soda are combined, carbon dioxide is a product of the chemical reaction. To build a model smoke stack, gather one 500 mL plastic bottle containing two tablespoons of vinegar and one teaspoon of baking soda in a small cup. Place the bottle in the center of your desk and pour the baking soda into the vinegar.

☐ **4. Describe** the results. _____

_____

☐ **5.** The carbon dioxide produced by this reaction is heavier than air. **Conclude** what gases, therefore, came out of the bottle during the reaction and what remains in the bottle at the end.

_____

_____

Go to the materials station(s). Pick up each material one at a time. Think about how it may or may not be useful in your carbon trap design. Leave the materials where they are.

☐ **6.** What are your design constraints? _____

_____

Develop Possible Solutions

☐ **7. Describe** two ways that you could trap the carbon dioxide from the vinegar and baking soda reaction, and remove it from the bottle. _____

_____

_____

_____

Choose One Solution

☑ **8. Describe** your carbon trap and how you will build it. _____
_____
_____

_____

☑ **9. List** the materials that you will need. _____
_____

☑ **10.** Why did you choose these materials? _____

_____

_____

Design and Construct a Prototype

Gather your materials plus another cup of baking soda. Rinse out your plastic bottle, and have your teacher replenish the vinegar. Build your carbon trap.

☑ **11. Record** these specific details about your prototype. _____

_____

_____

Test the Prototype

Test your carbon trap. See if you can capture the carbon dioxide and remove it from the bottle without any leaking out.

Communicate Results

☐ **12.** Did your design work? Rate your carbon trap on a scale of 1 to 3 where 1 — little or no CO_2 trapped, 2 — some CO_2 trapped and 3 — all CO_2 trapped.

Explain why you gave your design this rating. _____

_____

_____

_____

Evaluate and Redesign

☐ **13.** What changes could you make to your design to make it work better? _____

_____

_____

☐ **14.** **Record** the new design plans, then make your changes. _____

_____

_____

☐ **15.** How well did your revised prototype work? Explain. _____

_____

_____

What makes up matter?

Stand back and look at this picture from a distance. Tell what colors you see.

MY PLANET DIARY

FunFact

Have you ever noticed how nice it smells when you walk into some buildings? There is a type of air freshener that comes in solid lumps, about the size of a soap bar. These scented lumps do not melt at room temperature, but microscopic particles of them become loose and are released into the air, where we can enjoy their fragrance. If you keep these particles in a closed container, they will slowly collect on the sides, forming beautiful crystals. The shape of the crystals changes from one week to the next, depending on the temperature of the room.

Describe what you think would happen over time to this air freshener if you left the container open.

....

....

....

....

Now look at the dots closely. **Tell** what colors you see.

UNLOCK THE BIG ?

I will know that all things are made of very small particles called atoms and molecules, which cannot be seen without magnifying instruments.

Words to Know

atom   compound
atomic theory   molecule

(handwritten: I need own woon oh'on)

Matter

Like ice, water, and air, you are made of matter. All living and nonliving things are made of matter. Matter is anything that has mass and takes up space. Mass is the amount of matter in an object. Matter includes the food we eat, our homes, our furniture, the sun, the moon, and this book.

A large sand sculpture is made of matter. It takes up a lot of space. It has a large mass. But if you look at it closely, you will see that it is made of tiny sand grains. A sand grain is also made of matter. It is gritty and tan colored, like the sculpture. But unlike the sculpture, a sand grain has a small mass and it does not take up a lot of space. All matter is made of tiny parts.

1. **Compare and Contrast** Use the graphic organizer below to describe how a sand sculpture and a grain of sand are alike and different.

Sand Sculpture   **Grain of Sand**

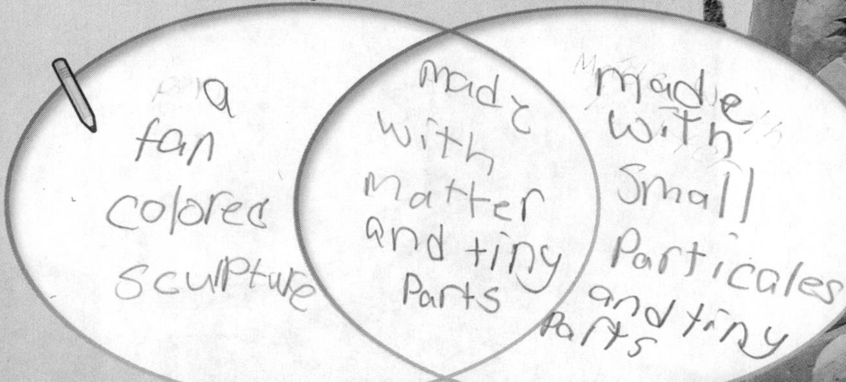

(handwritten Venn diagram: a tan colored sculpture | made with matter and tiny parts | "made" with small particales and tiny parts)

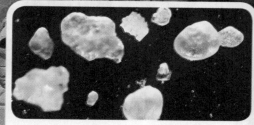

These sand grains are small particles. They are easy to see under a microscope. They are made of even smaller particles, too small to see with a regular microscope.

SavvasRealize.com

Elements

You can probably think of many kinds of food, many different medicines, or several types of fabric. Have you ever wondered how many different kinds of matter exist?

The world around you is made of thousands of materials, but all these materials are made of the same basic kinds of matter, called elements. Elements are the ingredients that make up all the other substances. Elements cannot be broken down into other substances with ordinary physical or chemical processes.

There are over 100 elements. Each element has specific characteristics. Each element will react in its own way with other elements.

Metals

Most elements are metals. Metals are good conductors of electricity and heat. They can be shaped into sheets or wires that can bend without breaking. Most metals, such as iron, are solids and have a gray color. Smooth metal surfaces can reflect light, which makes them appear shiny.

Aluminum *is light and strong. It is used to make ladders, airplane parts, and other items that need to be strong without being heavy.*

3. Identify What metal properties can you see in this ladder?

- Not heavey
- Strong

Calcium *is important for strong bones. You get calcium from food, but pure calcium is a metal! The calcium in food is combined with other elements. Dairy products can be good sources of calcium.*

2. List Write one food that is probably rich in calcium.

Mercury *is a liquid metal. It has many uses. For example, it can be used in thermometers and in energy-saving light bulbs. Mercury is toxic and must be handled with care.*

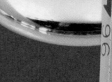

Nonmetals and Semimetals

Elements that do not conduct heat or electricity very well are called nonmetals. Some nonmetals are gases. One example is the oxygen you breathe. Other nonmetals, such as carbon, are solid.

Semimetals are elements that are sometimes like metals and sometimes like nonmetals. For example, they may conduct electricity, but only when light is shining on them. One of the most useful semimetals is silicon.

Silicon can be obtained from sand. The rod on the right is made of purified silicon. It will be used to make chips for electronic devices such as pocket calculators and computers.

4. **Give an Example** What other electronic devices might have silicon chips inside?

Computers, Cars, Phone, TouchScreens, tablets, IPads, and IPods

Sulfur is a solid nonmetal. It can be found in nature as a mineral. Sulfur is brittle and burns easily. Sulfur compounds are used to make matches.

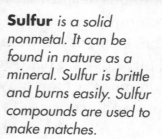

5. **Interpret** What would happen if you tried to break down a sample of sulfur?

Sulfur is an element it can not be broken down.

Neon belongs to a group of elements called the noble gases. These gases usually do not combine with other elements. Neon is used in neon signs.

Atoms

The smallest part of an element that still has the properties of the element is called an **atom.** Atoms are too small to be seen with a regular microscope, but special instruments can show how atoms are arranged.

The atoms of each element are different from the atoms of other elements. However, the atoms of all elements have something in common. They are made of the same three types of particles—protons, neutrons, and electrons.

The number of protons determines what element an atom will be. For example, an atom of carbon always has six protons. No other element has atoms with six protons. Carbon atoms usually have six neutrons and six electrons as well, but some atoms of carbon may have different numbers of electrons and neutrons. As long as an atom has exactly six protons, it will be an atom of carbon.

Since all substances are made of elements and all elements are made of atoms, all the matter around you is made of atoms. The idea that everything is made of small particles is known as the **atomic theory.**

Gold is a pure element. All gold is made of the same type of atoms. Every atom of gold has exactly 79 protons.

6. List What types of particles make up a carbon atom?

....

....

7. CHALLENGE Draw what you think a carbon atom might look like. Use the gold atom below as a model.

This image shows how atoms in a solid are tightly packed.

Protons and neutrons cluster at the center of the atom. This cluster is called the nucleus. Electrons move around the nucleus.

Atomic Arrangement

Atoms are often connected to other atoms in specific ways. The way atoms are connected affects the properties of an element. For example, when carbon atoms are connected as flat sheets, the carbon is soft and black. This form of carbon is called graphite. If the same carbon atoms are connected as pyramids, they form diamonds. Unlike graphite, diamonds are transparent and very hard. However, diamonds and graphite are both made of carbon atoms.

8. **◉ Compare and Contrast** Tell how a diamond and a piece of graphite are alike and different.

....

....

....

....

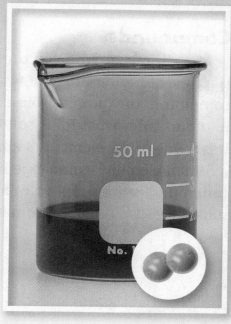

Bromine is an orange-red liquid. It evaporates easily. Its atoms are connected in pairs.

9. **Infer** In the picture above, do you think there are more atoms of bromine in liquid or gas form?

....

Diamonds are used to make jewels. The model below shows how carbon atoms are connected in a diamond.

The "lead" of a pencil is made of graphite. The model on the left shows how carbon atoms are connected in graphite.

Lightning Lab

Letters and Atoms
There are more than 100 kinds of atoms. Most arrangements are not possible, but there still are millions of ways to combine atoms. Write the letters *A, B, C, D,* and cut them out. How many ways can you put them in order? (Examples: *DBCA, CADB*)

Compounds

Most things around you are compounds. A **compound** is a type of matter made of two or more elements. In a compound, the atoms of these elements are joined together in a particular way. Table salt is an example of a compound. It is made of the elements sodium and chlorine.

When elements come together to form a compound, the compound is not simply a mixture of elements. It is a new substance. It is different from its ingredients.

Chlorine *is a poisonous gas. It is greenish-yellow. Chlorine reacts strongly with sodium.*

chlorine molecules

Table salt *is white and solid. It is not poisonous. Chlorine and sodium combine to form ordinary table salt.*

sodium chloride

Sodium *is a soft metal. It can be cut with a knife. It reacts strongly with chlorine.*

sodium atoms

10. Contrast List two ways in which salt is different from chlorine.

....

....

....

The smallest particle of a compound that still has the properties of that compound is called a **molecule.** For example, the smallest particle of water is a water molecule. A water molecule only has three atoms, but other molecules, like those of sugar, may have many atoms.

Changing the number, kind, or position of the atoms in a molecule would result in a molecule of a different substance. For example, a water molecule always has one atom of oxygen and two atoms of hydrogen. Adding an extra oxygen atom would turn a water molecule into a molecule of a different substance.

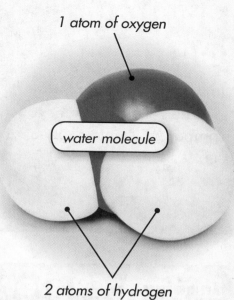

1 atom of oxygen

water molecule

2 atoms of hydrogen

11. **Calculate** Suppose you count all the hydrogen atoms in a group of water molecules. There are 8 hydrogen atoms in total. How many water molecules are in the group?

....

....

Got it?

12. **Explain** What makes up matter? Use the definition of atomic theory to answer.

....

13. A scientist is combining two gray elements. He thinks he will get a gray compound. Use what you learned in this lesson to explain why this prediction may not be correct.

....

....

 Stop! I need help with ....

Wait! I have a question about ....

 Go! Now I know ....

Lesson 2

How can matter be described?

☐ Colorful

☐ Lighter than air

☐ Pointed nose

☐ Smooth surface

Four properties are shown. **Check** the one that you think allows the blimp to float in air.

Inquiry Explore It!

What are some properties of solids?

☐ 1. **Observe** the sand and salt. Use a hand lens.

☐ 2. Put 1 spoonful of sand into both Cup A and Cup B. Put 1 spoonful of salt into both Cup C and Cup D.

☐ 3. Fill each cup halfway with water. Stir only Cup A and Cup C. Observe.

Explain Your Results

4. What properties did you **observe**?

....

....

5. Identify the substance that dissolved. What helped it dissolve? Which substance did not dissolve?

....

....

....

....

Materials

goggles

hand lens

spoon

salt   sand

4 plastic cups

water

masking tape

Be careful! **Wear safety goggles. Do not taste.**

Cup A sand

Cup B sand

Cup C salt

Cup D salt

16

I will know how to compare and contrast solids, liquids, and gases by using their basic properties.

Words to Know
....

mass   temperature
volume

Color

Many solids and liquids have color. Some gases also have color. Color is a physical property of matter. Every solid, liquid, and gas has its own set of physical properties. The physical properties of a material can be observed, described, and measured without changing the material.

Some properties can be measured with tools such as rulers, thermometers, and balances. Color is very useful because you can determine the color of a piece of matter just by looking at it, and color often helps you determine the kind of matter you are looking at, or the state or condition of that piece of matter.

The liquids in this cylinder do not mix. They float on top of each other.

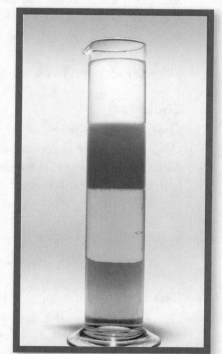

1. **Describe** The glass cylinder to the right contains a column of liquid. What can you learn from looking at the colors?

....

....

....

Solid iodine is dark purple, almost black. Heat turns it into a purple gas. Solid and gaseous iodine have different colors.

Mass

The amount of matter in a solid, liquid, or gas is called its **mass.** Mass is measured by using a balance, often using units of grams or kilograms.

We often weigh objects to get an idea of their mass, but mass and weight are not the same thing. The weight of an object on Earth is different from its weight on Mars, but the mass of the object is the same on both planets.

To find the mass of a solid, such as a toy car, you place the object on one side of a balance. On the other side, you place objects of known mass, such as gram cubes. When the two sides balance each other, the total mass of all the known masses equals the mass of the object.

2. Find Out Look at the balance that has water. Count the cubes. What is the mass of the water inside the container?

....

....

....

....

Solid

The empty container on the left has a mass of 8 g. We know this because it takes 8 cubes to balance it. Each cube has a mass of 1 g.

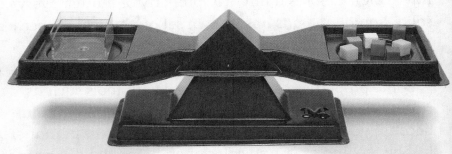

Liquid

Now the container has water. More cubes are needed to balance the extra mass. These extra cubes match the mass of the water.

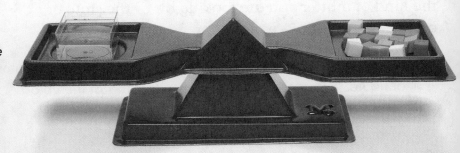

Gas

Gases have mass. This inner tube has more mass when it is pumped full of air than when it is flat.

Volume

The amount of space an object takes up is its **volume**. Volume can be measured in milliliters (mL).

You can use a graduated cylinder to find the volume of a liquid. You just pour the liquid into the cylinder and read the volume off the scale, at the surface.

Solids also have volume. If you put liquid in a graduated cylinder and let a solid object sink in the liquid, the solid takes up some space. The liquid that was in that space is forced to go up. The change in the height of the liquid column tells you the volume of the solid.

Gases have volume. In fact, a small mass of gas can fill a large volume. You can measure the volume of a gas using an upside-down, partially submerged graduated cylinder filled with water. If you blow air into the cylinder with a straw, the bubbles will push some water out. The volume of water pushed out is the same as the volume of the gas.

3. ◎ **Compare and Contrast** Look at the picture below. Explain how the mass and volume of the air in the tube and the water that was pushed down are alike and different.

....

....

....

....

....

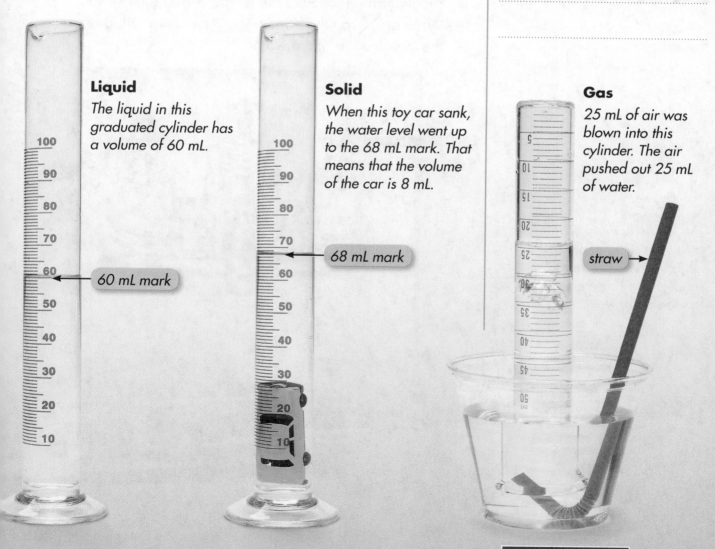

Liquid
The liquid in this graduated cylinder has a volume of 60 mL.

60 mL mark

Solid
When this toy car sank, the water level went up to the 68 mL mark. That means that the volume of the car is 8 mL.

68 mL mark

Gas
25 mL of air was blown into this cylinder. The air pushed out 25 mL of water.

straw

Temperature

The **temperature** of an object is a measure of how fast its particles are moving. The higher the temperature, the faster the particles move. We cannot see the particles that make up the object, but we can tell when they are moving faster because the object becomes hotter.

There are different scales for measuring temperature. In science books, you may find the melting point of a solid in degrees Celsius (°C). In a recipe, you may find a cooking temperature given in degrees Fahrenheit (°F).

Knowing the temperature of solids, liquids, and gases is very useful. For example, the water in a fish tank needs to be kept at the right temperature. A weather report gives us the temperature of the air. And the temperature of your body can help monitor a health problem.

4. **Infer** Look at the sink below. (Circle) the handle that you should turn on to lower the temperature of the water. Write an ✗ on the handle you should turn off to lower the temperature of the water.

The sun heats the solid pavement. The hot pavement heats up the air closest to it, producing a shimmering effect that looks like water.

Texture

When you touch a solid object, you can feel if it is hard, smooth, lumpy, grooved, spongy, or rough. This surface structure that you can feel by touching a material is its texture.

You can also feel the texture of a liquid by rubbing a drop between two fingers. A drop of shampoo may feel soapy. A drop of oil will feel oily. Other liquids may feel slimy, sticky, or thick. For example, people who make soap may use the texture of the liquid mixture of ingredients to decide when it is ready for the next step in the process.

5. List Write two surfaces with a smooth texture and two surfaces with a rough texture.

The rough texture of sandpaper can scratch other materials.

Many stones can be polished to give them a very smooth texture.

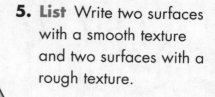
Liquid soap feels slippery.

Got it?

6. Analyze A heavy brick weighs more than a fluffy cushion, but the cushion takes up more space. Which object has more matter? How do you know?

7. UNLOCK THE BIG Which property might be more useful to tell two materials apart: their mass, their temperature, or their color?

■ **Stop!** I need help with

II **Wait!** I have a question about

▶ **Go!** Now I know

Lesson 3

What are solids, liquids, and gases?

Where are some solids, liquids, and gases in the picture? Tell how you know.

Inquiry **Explore It!**

How can water change state?

☐ **1.** Stick a straw halfway inside a bag.
Seal the bag up to the straw.

☐ **2.** Slowly exhale through the straw.
Remove the straw and seal the bag shut.

☐ **3.** Lay the bag on dark paper under bright light.
Use a hand lens to **observe.**

Explain Your Results

4. Communicate What did you **observe**? Explain.

....

....

....

....

Materials

plastic bag

straw

hand lens

dark paper

Be careful! Do not use a straw that someone else has used.

22

UNLOCK
THE BIG
?

I will know some basic
properties of solids, liquids,
and gases.

Words to Know

solid   gas
liquid

States of Matter

Water has three forms. Water is a solid when it is frozen
as ice. Water is a liquid in the ocean. In the air, water can
be a gas. Solid, liquid, and gas are the most familiar states,
or phases, of matter.

The phase of water, or of any material, is due to the
motion and arrangement of its particles—its molecules
or its atoms. The particles are always moving.

Most materials around you are solids, liquids, or gases.
For example, cooking oil is a liquid. Butter is a solid when
it is cold, but butter can turn into a liquid if it gets hot.

1. ◎ **Compare and Contrast** Look at the picture. How
are the solid butter and liquid oil alike and different?

Oil   Butter

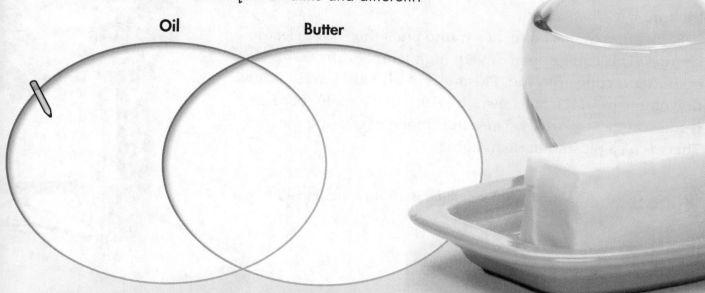

Solids

A **solid** is a substance that has a definite shape and volume. Volume is the amount of space an object takes up. The particles of a solid are very close together. For the most part they stay in the same place. They do not slide easily past each other. However, they vibrate in place.

Liquids

A **liquid** is a substance that has a definite volume but no definite shape. The particles of a liquid can move by gliding past each other. A liquid can take the shape of its container. Forces hold liquid particles together, so a liquid keeps a definite volume.

Gases

A **gas** is a substance without a definite volume or shape. The particles of a gas are far apart compared to the particles of solids and liquids. A gas can be squeezed into a smaller volume. Gas particles only affect one another when they collide as they move. If a gas is placed in an empty container, its particles will spread out evenly. The gas will fill all the space and take the shape of that container.

Plasmas

Sometimes atoms break down into parts that have electric charges. This can happen at very high temperatures. This state of matter is called plasma. Plasma is like a gas because it has no volume or shape of its own. It is also like a metal because it can conduct electricity. The sun is made of gas and plasma. There is also plasma in neon lights.

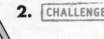

2. CHALLENGE Describe what you think is inside a plasma TV.

....

....

....

Freezing and Melting

As liquids get colder, their particles slow down. At some point they stop gliding past each other and can only vibrate in place. The liquid becomes a solid. The temperature at which a material changes between solid and liquid states has two names. It is called the freezing point when a liquid turns into a solid. It is called the melting point when a solid turns into a liquid. Therefore, the melting point and the freezing point are the same temperature. This temperature is often just referred to as the melting point.

Each material has its own melting point. Therefore, the melting point can be used to help identify a material.

Some materials are more useful in their solid state than in their liquid state. For example, lead is a metal that is dense. Solid lead is used to weigh down or sink fishing hooks.

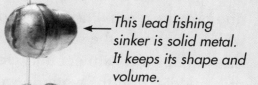

This lead fishing sinker is solid metal. It keeps its shape and volume.

The melting point of lead is 327°C. At this temperature, solid lead becomes liquid and can be poured into molds to give it any shape we want.

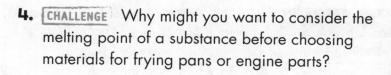

3. **Compare** What is the difference between the melting point and freezing point of a substance?

_____

_____

4. CHALLENGE Why might you want to consider the melting point of a substance before choosing materials for frying pans or engine parts?

_____

_____

_____

5. **Recognize** Water has a melting point of 0°C. What is its freezing point?

_____

Lightning Lab

Wandering Ice
Place an ice cube on a dish and set it in a place where it will not be disturbed. Observe how long it takes for the ice cube to melt. Observe how long it takes for the water to evaporate.

Evaporation

Evaporation takes place when particles leave a liquid and become a gas. Particles evaporate from a liquid when they are at the surface of the liquid and are moving upward with enough speed. This is how rain puddles and the water in wet clothes evaporate.

If the temperature of a liquid is high enough, particles will change to a gas not only at the surface, but also throughout the liquid. As gas particles move quickly upward through a liquid, bubbles of gas form under the surface of the liquid. The boiling point of a liquid is the temperature at which this occurs.

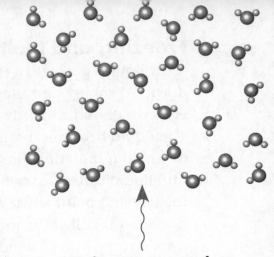

Molecules of water evaporate from the clothes as they dry. In water vapor, the molecules of water are far apart.

6. Explain How can clothes dry without heating them to the boiling point of water?

....

....

....

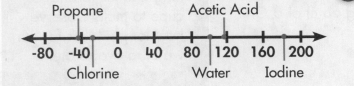

Do the math!

Ranges

The chart shows the temperatures at which 5 different substances change form.

Boiling Points (°C)	
Liquid	**Boiling Point**
Water	100°C
Acetic acid (found in vinegar)	118°C
Chlorine	−34°C
Propane	−42°C
Iodine	185°C

Propane   Acetic Acid

-80 -40 0 40 80 120 160 200

Chlorine   Water   Iodine

1 Which liquid has the highest boiling point?
  A. Water   C. Acetic acid
  B. Iodine   D. Propane

2 In which temperature range is the greatest gap between boiling points?
  F. 185°C to 100°C
  G. −34°C to −42°C
  H. 118°C to −42°C
  I. 100°C to −34°C

CHALLENGE Choose a common substance, such as ammonia or rubbing alcohol. Research its boiling point, and add this information to the chart. Plot the new data point on the number line.

26

Condensation

Condensation occurs when a gas turns into a liquid. This process often occurs when gas particles touch a cold surface and the temperature of the gas drops. Clouds in the sky and dew on the ground form through condensation of water vapor.

As air temperature decreases, the molecules of water vapor come together and condense, forming the liquid water droplets we call dew.

7. Describe What is one thing needed for condensation to occur?

8. Infer The dew on the spider's web formed before sunrise. What might this tell you about the air temperature before sunrise?

Got it?

9. Interpret A substance fills a 1-liter bottle. A scientist transfers the substance to a 2-liter bottle. The substance increases in volume and fills the new space. What is the state of matter of this substance?

10. Why can you use the melting point to help identify a material?

Stop! I need help with

Wait! I have a question about

Go! Now I know

Lesson 4

What are mixtures and solutions?

Once per year, the Chicago River in Illinois is dyed green. What are the parts of the mixture shown in the picture?

Inquiry Explore It!

How can a mixture be separated?

☐ **1.** Place the paper clips and fasteners in a cup. Move the magnet around in the cup slowly. Lift out the magnet. **Observe.**

☐ **2.** Fill the cup with water. Observe.

Explain Your Results

3. Infer What property made it possible to separate the mixture with a magnet?

....

....

4. What property made it possible to use water to separate the mixture?

....

....

Materials

5 brass fasteners

5 metal paper clips

5 plastic paper clips

magnet

water

plastic cup

Words to Know

mixture
solution

Mixtures

In a **mixture,** different materials are placed together but each material in the mixture keeps its own properties. If vegetables are cut and put together to make a mixture, different vegetables do not change their flavors or colors. Most foods that you eat are mixtures of different materials.

Different parts of a mixture can be separated from the rest of the mixture. Suppose your favorite breakfast is a mixture of cereal and raisins. You could easily separate out the raisins with a spoon to eat them first. The parts of a mixture may be combined in different amounts. The bowl of cereal you eat today could have more raisins than the one you ate yesterday.

The bowl of fruit is a mixture. It contains several different parts.

1. **Suggest** What mixture is your favorite to eat? List the parts.

....

....

....

2. **Support** Why is the bowl of beads to the right not a mixture?

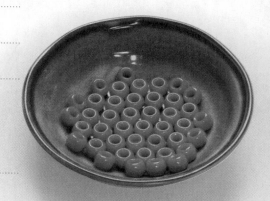

....

....

At-Home Lab

Mixed-Up Foods

Find two different mixtures you eat at home. What are the parts of the mixtures? Tell whether you would ever eat any of the parts separately.

Separating Mixtures

You can use the physical properties of a substance to separate it from a mixture. The materials in a simple mixture can be separated because they have different physical properties. For example, a magnet can separate iron filings from sand. This separation happens because iron has the property of being attracted by magnets. Sand does not have that property. A screen filter can be used to separate a mixture of pebbles and sand. The smaller particles go through the screen but the pebbles do not. Sometimes you can sort the parts of a mixture by hand.

3. **Classify** Complete the chart below. Draw a mixture in the first row. Write how to separate the erasers and screws and the items in the new mixture.

Mixture			
How Can You Separate?	Pour through a strainer.		

4. **CHALLENGE** Suppose you had a mixture of sand and small, hollow beads. How might you separate the mixture?

....

....

....

....

5. Categorize Look at the mixture above. In the boxes provided below, draw four parts of the mixture or write their names.

6. Infer A compound forms when two or more elements combine to form a new substance with new properties. How is a compound different from a mixture?

Solutions

A mixture in which substances are spread out evenly and will not settle is called a **solution.** In a solution, the substance that is dissolved is called the *solute.* The substance in which the solute is being dissolved is called the *solvent.* In a solution of sugar and water, the solute is sugar and the solvent is water. Water is sometimes called a "universal solvent" because it can dissolve many substances.

Solutions of a Solid in a Liquid

When a solid dissolves, individual particles separate from the solid and spread evenly throughout the liquid. You can make solids dissolve in a liquid faster by stirring or heating the solution. Grinding a solid into smaller pieces will also help it dissolve faster.

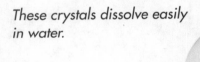

These crystals dissolve easily in water.

7. **Draw** what you think the mixture of purple solid and water will look like after stirring.

Other Solutions

Not all solutions are made by dissolving a solid in a liquid. Two liquids can make a solution. For example, vegetable oils used in cooking might be a solution of soybean and sunflower oils. A gas can also dissolve in a liquid. For example, water can contain dissolved oxygen and carbon dioxide gases.

8. **Infer** Why do you think it is important for sea organisms that some gases dissolve in water?

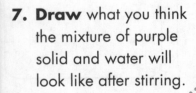

....

....

....

This toy has a colorless liquid floating on a blue-colored liquid. The colorless liquid and the plastic figures will not dissolve in the blue liquid. They are insoluble in it.

Solubility

Many materials can make solutions with water. You can dissolve more of some materials than others in the same amount of water. Some materials will not dissolve in water at all. This describes a material's solubility in water. Different substances can have different solubility in other solvents.

9. [CHALLENGE] The plastic figures in the picture are insoluble in the blue liquid. What else can you tell about their solubility?

....

....

....

Got it?

10. **Predict** To make a gelatin dessert, first you must boil water and then dissolve the gelatin powder in it. What do you think might happen if the water were not hot?

....

....

11. **UNLOCK THE BIG ?** Write one way you can use properties of matter to separate mixtures.

....

....

■ **Stop!** I need help with ....

❚❚ **Wait!** I have a question about ....

▶ **Go!** Now I know ....

Lesson 5

How does matter change?

Envision It!

The pictures above show a possible series of steps in the process of preparing to eat an orange. **Label** the steps.

Inquiry **Explore It!**

What happens when air heats up?

☐ **1.** Stretch a balloon over the top of each bottle.

☐ **2.** Set 1 bottle in each bowl. Wait 1 minute.
Observe. Look closely.

Explain Your Results

3. Compare your **observations** of the balloons.

....

4. Infer How did temperature affect the air in the bottles?

....

....

....

5. Was the change you observed a physical or chemical change? Explain.

....

....

....

Materials

2 balloons

bowl with warm water

bowl with room-temperature water

2 plastic bottles

timer, stopwatch, or clock with second hand

warm water

room-temperature water

34

2 [_____]

3 [_____]

UNLOCK THE BIG ?

I will know that many physical changes are affected by temperature. I will know that many chemical changes are affected by temperature.

Words to Know

physical change
chemical change

Physical Changes

Matter changes all the time. Some changes are physical changes. A **physical change** is a change in some properties of matter without forming a different kind of matter. There are many kinds of physical changes.

When you cut a piece of paper into smaller pieces, you do not produce a new material. You still have paper. The paper has undergone a physical change. Some of its properties have changed, but the properties that make it paper are still there. For example, the cut pieces are smaller than the original sheet and do not have the same shape. However, these pieces can burn or absorb water. They also keep their original color.

Breaking glass and stretching a rubber band are also physical changes. After breaking glass or stretching a rubber band, you still end up with glass or rubber.

1. ◉ **Compare and Contrast** How are the physical properties of a small piece of paper similar to those of a large piece of the same paper? How are they different?

....

....

....

....

When this green slime stretches, it changes shape but does not turn into a new material. The slime keeps its color, its smell, and other properties.

Heated milk dissolves cocoa powder. The cocoa does not stir easily into cold milk.

Temperature and Physical Changes

Physical changes may happen more or less easily depending on the temperature. For example, butter becomes easier to spread as it gets warm, and rubber becomes less elastic as it gets cold. Some physical changes cannot even happen unless the temperature is right. For example, under normal conditions ice does not melt until its temperature rises above its melting point, 0°C.

Melting, freezing, evaporation, and condensation are all physical changes. For example, when water evaporates, it results in water vapor. We may call it water vapor, but it is just water that has gone through a physical change. The total amount of water stays the same when it changes form, even when it seems to disappear through evaporation. Another example is candle wax. The melted wax of a candle still is wax. It hasn't turned into a new substance. It has just become liquid for a while. It becomes solid again as soon as it cools off. The total weight of wax stays the same even when it changes form from solid to liquid and back to solid.

2. **Infer** What physical change do you think is happening to this scented oil below? How does the candle help?

....

....

....

Chemical Changes

To form a new substance, a chemical change has to happen. In a **chemical change,** one or more types of matter change into other types of matter with different properties. When a chemical change occurs, atoms rearrange themselves to form new kinds of matter. In chemical changes, the total amount of the substances involved does not change.

It is not always easy to tell if a substance has changed chemically. Evidence of chemical change may include the release of heat and light, a change in color, a new smell, gas bubbles, or the formation of a solid.

Chemical changes happen all the time around us. The rusting of iron is a familiar chemical change. When you leave an iron object outside, it slowly becomes rusty. Rust is red and brittle. It is a new substance. The process of photosynthesis, in which plants use water and carbon dioxide, is a chemical change because a new substance is made—sugar. When newspapers burn, they also go through a chemical change. They change into ash.

3. ⬤ **Compare and Contrast** How are physical and chemical changes alike? How are they different?

....

....

....

These two solutions have no color. A bright yellow substance forms when we mix them. This suggests that a chemical change has happened.

4. **Describe** Write whether each image below shows a physical change or chemical change.

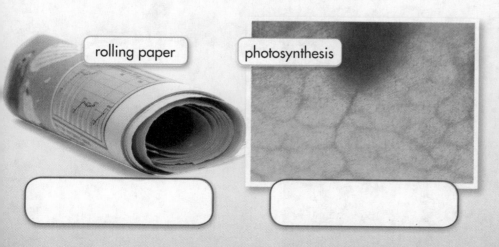

rolling paper

photosynthesis

rusting metal

A chemical reaction inside these glow sticks causes them to glow. The faster the reaction, the brighter the glow.

Temperature and Chemical Changes

When a candle burns, it goes through a chemical change that releases light and heat. But this chemical change cannot start on its own. You need to light the candle with a match. The flame of the match is hot enough to start the burning. After the burning starts, the reaction keeps itself going by the heat it releases.

Many chemical changes can happen without high temperatures, but they often happen faster if the temperature increases. Remember that particles move faster in a material when the temperature rises, so they may have more chances to rearrange themselves into new substances quickly. For example, if you put a fizzy antacid tablet in a glass of water at room temperature, the bubbles will form faster than if you used cold water.

5. **Conclude** The glow sticks to the left were started at the same time, but the one in water glows more brightly. What does this suggest about the water temperature?

....

....

6. **CHALLENGE** Look at the picture below. As a candle burns, it becomes shorter and shorter. Does it disappear? Explain.

....

....

Lightning Lab

Comparing Apples and Lemons

Cut an apple into 6 pieces. Swab 3 pieces with lemon juice. Put these on a plate labeled *Lemon Juice.* Use a new swab. Swab the other 3 pieces with water. Put these on a plate labeled *Water.* Observe the wedges in 15 minutes. Explain what happened.

The tip of this candle is still burning. When a candle burns, the wax and the wick combine with oxygen in the air to become smoke, soot, and hot gas.

Just as higher temperatures can speed up a chemical change, low temperatures can slow it down. When you buy fruit that is not ripe, you can often let it ripen in the kitchen at room temperature. Ripening involves chemical changes that slowly change the color and flavor of a fruit. If you place unripe fruit in a refrigerator, the fruit will often ripen more slowly than if you leave it on the kitchen counter.

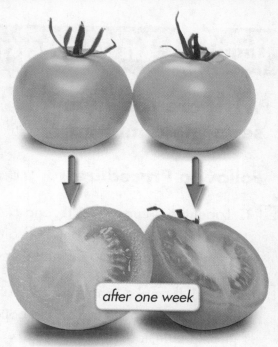

after one week

One of these tomatoes was kept in a refrigerator. The other was kept at room temperature.

7. Look at the pictures to the right. (Circle) the tomato that was stored in the refrigerator. Tell how you know.

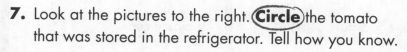

8. **Infer** Why do you think medicine labels usually say, "Store in a cool, dry place"?

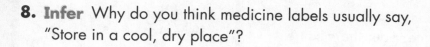

Got it?

9. **Summarize** How can temperature affect many kinds of chemical changes?

10. **UNLOCK THE BIG ?** What properties might change during a chemical reaction?

⬜ **Stop!** I need help with

⏸ **Wait!** I have a question about

▶ **Go!** Now I know

What are some ways to separate a mixture?

Follow a Procedure

☐ **1.** Label the 4 cups A, B, C, and D.
In Cup A place 1 spoonful of salt, 2 spoonfuls of sand, 3 marbles, and 100 mL of water.

☐ **2.** Carefully make 4 holes in the bottom of Cup B by pushing a pencil through the bottom of the cup from the inside.

☐ **3.** Hold Cup B over Cup C. All at once, pour the mixture from Cup A into Cup B. Move Cup B around to clean the marbles. **Record** the part of the mixture that was removed by straining.

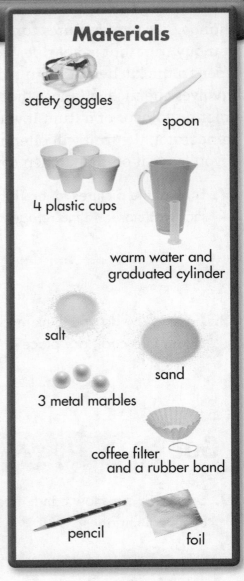

Materials

safety goggles

spoon

4 plastic cups

warm water and graduated cylinder

salt

sand

3 metal marbles

coffee filter and a rubber band

pencil

foil

Be careful! Wear safety goggles.
Do not taste.
Be careful with sharp objects.

Inquiry Skill
Scientists record data on charts and use the data to help **make inferences.**

Results of Separation		
Separating Method	**Part Removed**	**Part Not Removed**
Straining		
Filtering		
Evaporation		

4. Put a coffee filter in Cup D. Slowly pour the mixture from Cup C into Cup D. Record the part of the mixture that was removed by filtering.

5. Remove the filter. Use the spoon to drip 2 drops of the liquid onto the foil. Let the liquid evaporate. Record the results.

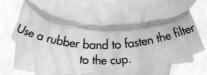

Use a rubber band to fasten the filter to the cup.

Analyze and Conclude

6. Communicate Name a property you used to separate parts of the mixture.

7. **UNLOCK THE BIG ?** **Infer** Describe another mixture. How could the properties of matter help you separate it into its parts?

Sidewalks & Playgrounds

Concrete is everywhere in our world. Highways, skyscrapers, sidewalks, and skate parks are often made of concrete. Ancient Romans used materials similar to concrete to build structures. Some of those structures are still standing today.

Concrete is made of many different materials. The main ingredient is cement—a human-made material. Cement is a fine powder that includes several different minerals. To make concrete, cement is mixed with sand, gravel, crushed rock, and water. Once concrete is set, or hardened, it is very strong and long-lasting.

What makes concrete so strong? One of the materials that makes it so strong is water. Surprised? When workers pour concrete it is very wet, but days later it is dry. The water does not just evaporate—it changes chemically! The water and cement react to form a gel. As the water and cement continue to react, they harden into concrete.

REVIEW THE BIG ?

How does mixing water and cement change their properties?

Vocabulary Smart Cards

atom
atomic theory
compound
molecule
mass
volume
temperature
solid
liquid
gas
mixture
solution
physical change
chemical change

Play a Game!

Cut out the Vocabulary Smart Cards.

Work with a partner.

Player 1 chooses a Vocabulary Smart Card.

Say as many words as you can think of that describe that vocabulary word to Player 2.

Player 2 guesses the word.

molecule

molécula

atom
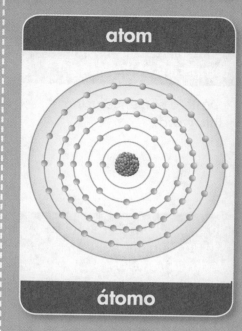
átomo

mass

masa

atomic theory

teoría atómica

volume
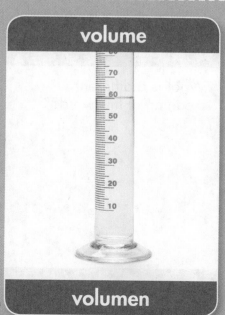
volumen

compound

compuesto

the smallest part of an element that still has the properties of the element

Write a sentence using this word.

....

....

la partícula más pequeña de un elemento, que todavía tiene las propiedades de ese elemento

the smallest particle of a compound that still has the properties of that compound

Draw an example of this word.

la partícula más pequeña de un compuesto, que todavía tiene las propiedades de ese compuesto

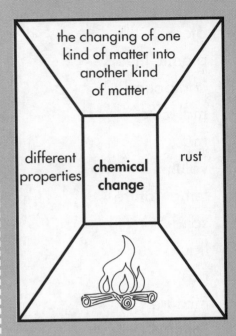

the changing of one kind of matter into another kind of matter

different properties | chemical change | rust

Make a Word Frame!

Choose a vocabulary word and write it in the center of the frame. Write or draw details about the vocabulary word in the spaces around it.

the idea that everything is made of small particles

Write a sentence using this term.

....

....

....

la idea de que la materia está formada por partículas pequeñas

the amount of matter in a solid, liquid, or gas

Write a sentence using this word.

....

....

....

cantidad de materia que tiene un sólido, líquido o gas

a type of matter made of two or more elements

Write a different meaning of this word.

....

....

....

....

tipo de materia formada por dos o más elementos

the amount of space an object takes up

What is a different meaning of this word?

....

....

....

....

el espacio que ocupa un objeto

physical change	gas	temperature

cambio físico	gas	temperatura

chemical change	mixture	solid

cambio químico	mezcla	sólido

	solution	liquid
		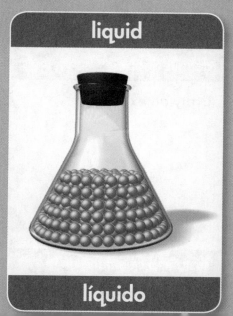
	solución	líquido

a measure of how fast the particles in an object are moving

Write a sentence using this word.

....

....

medida de la rapidez con que se mueven las partículas de un objeto

---

a substance without a definite volume or shape

Write an example of this word.

....

....

....

sustancia que no tiene ni volumen ni forma definidos

---

a change in some properties of matter without forming a different kind of matter

Write an example of this term.

....

....

cambio de algunas de las propiedades de la materia sin que se forme un nuevo tipo de materia

---

a substance that has a definite shape and volume

What are two other meanings of this word?

....

....

....

sustancia que tiene una forma y un volumen definidos

---

different materials placed together, but each material keeps its own properties

Write three other forms of this word.

....

....

unión de materiales diferentes en la cual cada material mantiene sus propiedades

---

a change of one or more types of matter into other types of matter with different properties

Write an example of this term.

....

....

....

cambio de uno o más tipos de materia a otros tipos de materia con propiedades diferentes

---

a substance that has a definite volume but no definite shape

Draw an example.

sustancia que tiene un volumen definido pero no una forma definida

---

a mixture in which substances are spread out evenly and will not settle

What is a different meaning of this word?

....

....

mezcla en la cual una sustancia se dispersa de manera uniforme en otra sustancia y no se asienta

---

....

....

....

....

Study Guide

REVIEW THE BIG ?

What are the properties of matter?

Physical Science

Lesson 1

What makes up matter?

- Matter is made of atoms. Atoms may combine to form molecules.
- Elements are basic kinds of matter. Each element has different atoms.
- Compounds are made up of two or more elements.

Lesson 2

How can matter be described?

- Mass is the amount of matter in an object.
- Volume is the amount of space an object takes up.
- Temperature is a measure of how fast the particles of an object move.

Lesson 3

What are solids, liquids, and gases?

- States of matter include solid, liquid, gas, and plasma.
- Changes in state are caused by changes in the motion of particles.
- Melting, freezing, evaporation, and condensation are state changes.

Lesson 4

What are mixtures and solutions?

- A mixture is made up of two or more materials.
- The parts of a mixture can be separated.
- A solution is a type of mixture. Parts do not settle out of a solution.

Lesson 5

How does matter change?

- Physical changes do not change materials into new materials.
- In a chemical change, one or more new substances form.
- Temperature can affect physical and chemical changes.

Chapter Review

What are the properties of matter?

Lesson 1

What makes up matter?

1. **Summarize** Your classmate has a magnifying glass, and he is looking for atoms. What would you tell him?

2. **Predict** A scientist finds that a sample of matter contains three types of atoms. The sample can be any of the following except
   A. a compound.
   B. a molecule.
   C. an element.

Lesson 2

How can matter be described?

3. **Vocabulary** The amount of matter an object has is its
   A. weight.
   B. volume.
   C. size.
   D. mass.

4. **Describe** What does the property of volume tell you about an object?

Lesson 3

What are solids, liquids, and gases?

5. **Compare and Contrast** Write two ways water and ice are different and two ways they are the same.

6. **Infer** A substance has a melting point of 104°C. Its freezing point will be
   A. lower than 104°C.
   B. higher than 104°C.
   C. 104°C.

Do the math!

7. What is the range of temperature between the boiling points of −42°C to 118°C?
   A. 42°C
   B. 18°C
   C. 118°C
   D. 160°C

8. **Compare** How are liquids and solids alike? How are liquids and gases alike?

Lesson 4

What are mixtures and solutions?

9. Explain Sulfur burns easily. Iron is attracted by magnets. The mineral below is made of sulfur and iron, but it does not burn and it is not attracted by magnets. Is it a mixture? Why or why not?

....

....

....

Lesson 5

How does matter change?

10. Vocabulary In a chemical change
   A. materials retain their properties.
   B. the new material has different properties.
   C. materials always change states.

11. Classify List three examples of physical changes.

....

....

....

12. **APPLY THE BIG ?** **What are the properties of matter?**

....

Think about the materials used to make a car. Some materials are glass, steel, leather, and paint. Choose any three materials. For each one, describe one property that makes it useful in the car. For example, windshield glass is clear so that people can see through it.

....

....

....

....

....

....

....

....

....

....

Benchmark Practice

Read each question and choose the best answer.

1 **A gas**

A does not have a definite volume.

B does not have a definite shape.

C fills its container.

D does all of the above.

2 **Which of the following
statements is true?**

A Atoms are made of molecules.

B Atoms can join to form molecules.

C Atoms contain more than
one element.

D Some atoms do not have protons.

3 **Fill in the blank: When two
materials mix evenly and do not
settle, that mixture is called a**

_____.

A solution

B compound

C sugar

D solute

4 **What can affect the rate of a
chemical change?**

A color

B texture

C temperature

D gas bubbles

5 **Suppose you boil an egg. What
kind of change is taking place?**

A physical and chemical

B chemical

C physical

D No change is occurring.

6 **Describe how you would separate
a mixture of water, sand, pebbles,
and paper clips.**

_____

_____

_____

_____

_____

_____

_____

_____

_____

SavvasRealize.com

Aerogels

aerogel

When many people think of oil polluting the environment, they often think on a large scale, such as an oil tanker spilling millions of gallons of oil into the ocean. Small amounts of oil are deposited every day in sewers and streams and pose a threat to the environment.

One way to clean up oil contamination is with a substance called aerogels. Aerogels are strong solids made from gels. The liquid is removed from a gel and replaced with gas, which changes the properties of the substance. Aerogels are nicknamed "frozen smoke" because they are translucent and can take on either a blue or yellow color, depending on the amount of light present.

Aerogels made from silica gel are especially good at cleaning up spilled oil because they have a low density and are very absorbent. Scientists have been testing the ability of silica aerogel beads to clean up oil by mixing them with water and corn oil. In one investigation, the aerogel absorbed seven times its weight! Because they work so well at removing corn oil from water and are relatively cheap to produce, aerogels may become one of the best methods for removing oil pollution from the environment.

Underline one reason why using silica aerogels may be a good way to clean up oil in the environment.

Which way is he MOVING?

Forces and Motion

Chapter 2

Try It! How can you make a paper helicopter drop slowly?

STEM Activity Watch It Fly!

Lesson 1 What are forces?

Lesson 2 What are Newton's laws?

Lesson 3 How are forces combined?

Lesson 4 How are shadows formed?

Investigate It! What forces affect the motion of a rocket?

Physical Science

Apply It! How is motion affected by mass?

A surfer has to have perfect timing to ride an ocean wave. He has to balance the sideways motion of the water with the upward force of the wave on his board.

Predict Where do you think the surfer will end up after the wave passes? Why?

THE BIG ? What affects the motion of objects?

How can you make a paper helicopter drop slowly?

Materials

scissors

paper clip

heavy paper or card stock (optional)

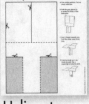

Helicopter Pattern

additional small or large paper clips (optional)

☐ **1.** Use the Helicopter Pattern to **make a model** of a helicopter. Add a paper clip to the bottom.

☐ **2.** Drop the helicopter. **Observe** its motion. Describe how it moves.

....

....

☐ **3.** Modify the design to make the helicopter stay in the air longer.

Explain Your Results

4. What force pulls the helicopter down? What force slows its fall?

....

....

5. UNLOCK THE BIG **?** **Interpret Data** How did your change affect the helicopter's motion?

....

....

....

....

Inquiry Skill
You can **make and use a model** to help explain an object or event.

- Learning to find **main ideas** and **details** can help you understand and remember what you read.

Let's Read
Science!

Small but Strong

Small animals can be very strong for their size. For example, tortoise beetles are the size of a ladybug, but it is very difficult to pull them off a leaf or a stem. These beetles have sticky feet and strong legs that allow them to hold on very tight. Leaf-cutting ants use their strength to carry heavy weights. A leaf-cutting ant can carry a leaf that is many times heavier than the ant itself! A flea is able to jump more than 100 times its own height. That would be like a human jumping from street level to the top of a 50-story building!

Practice It!

Use the graphic organizer below to list the main idea and details from the article shown above.

Detail	**Detail**	**Detail**

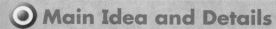

Watch It Fly!

A balloon is a simple rocket—a compartment that holds a gas under pressure. Just like a rocket, the opening at the end of the balloon allows the high-pressure gas inside to escape to an area of lower pressure. As a result, the balloon moves in the direction opposite of the escaping gases. This is an example of Newton's third law of motion, which states that for every action force there is an equal amount of reaction force, but in the opposite direction.

The rocket scientist who lives in your basement needs your help. To help her out, design and build a balloon rocket, and then modify your design to make the fastest balloon rocket possible.

Identify the Problem

☑ **1.** What is your task? _____

_____

Do Research

Examine a photograph or video clip of a rocket launch.

☐ **2. Draw and label** arrows that show the direction that the exhaust gases come out of a rocket and the direction the rocket moves as a result.

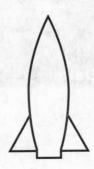

Go to the materials station(s). Gather a balloon. Fill the balloon with air, but don't tie it off. Instead, let go of the balloon and observe its motion. Caution: Wear your goggles.

3. How are the forces acting on the balloon the same as the forces that send a rocket into

space? _____

_____

_____

4. What happens to the shape of the balloon as it deflates?_____

_____

Now half-fill the balloon with air and let it go again.

5. Was the motion of the balloon the same or different than a full balloon? Explain._____

_____

_____

Go to the materials station(s). Pick up each material one at a time. Think about how it may
or may not be useful in your design. Leave the materials where they are.

6. What are your design constraints? _____

_____

Develop Possible Solutions

7. Draw two different shapes of balloons you could use for your rocket.

8. Explain how the string weight and material could affect the speed at which your
balloon rocket travels. _____

_____

_____

☐ **9. Describe** two different ways you could combine materials to make a balloon rocket

that shoots down the string. _____

_____

_____

Choose One Solution

☐ **10. Describe** your balloon rocket and how you will build it. _____

_____

_____

_____

_____

☐ **11. List** the materials that you will need. _____

_____

☐ **12. Describe** how you will determine how many centimeters per second (cm/s) your
balloon rocket travels. _____

_____

_____

Design and Construct a Prototype

Gather your materials. Build your balloon rocket. **Measure** the circumference and the
length of the inflated balloon. Note the measurements and placement of other materials.

☐ **13. Record** the design details of your prototype. _____

_____

_____

_____

Test the Prototype

Test your balloon rocket. Record the distance your rocket traveled, the time it took, and the speed at which it traveled in the table below. Repeat the test three times.

☐ **14.**

Trial	Distance (cm)	Time (s)	Speed (cm/s)
1			
2			
3			

Communicate Results

☐ **15.** Average distance: _____

Average time: _____

Average speed: _____

Evaluate and Redesign

☐ **16. Explain** how you would change your design to make your balloon rocket faster.

_____

_____

_____

_____

☐ **17. Describe** how well your redesigned balloon rocket worked. _____

_____

_____

_____

Lesson 1
What are forces?

Envision It!

Tell why the metal ring on the string does not fall.

my planet diary

//// **MISCONCEPTION** ////

You may have seen video clips of astronauts floating around in a spacecraft. People often think astronauts have no weight at all in space. In fact, they do. Most astronauts work just 300 km above ground. This is relatively close to Earth. At that height, they are only a few pounds lighter. They seem to float because their spacecraft is moving along with them. However, the spacecraft and the astronauts are both in fact falling, just like a skydiver. They don't crash because they are also moving forward fast enough to follow the curvature of the Earth.

Which everyday activities do you think would be easier in orbit?

....

....

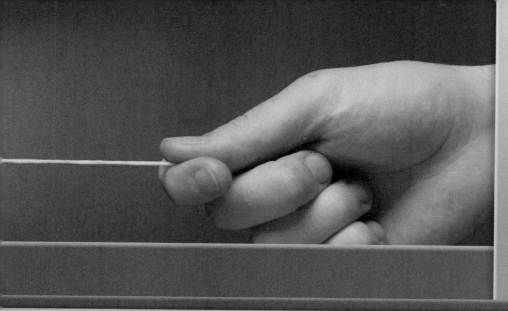

Words to Know

force
contact force
friction
non-contact force
gravity

Forces

When one object pushes or pulls another object, the first object is exerting a force on the second one. A **force** is a push or pull that acts on an object.

Every force has a strength, or magnitude. This strength is measured in units called newtons (N). A force also has a direction. The direction of a force can be described by telling which way the force is acting. The dog is pushing the ball with a force of around 2 N.

Forces can change the way objects move. When an object begins to move, it is because a force has acted on it. When an object is already moving, forces can make it speed up, slow down, or change direction.

1. ◉ **Main Idea and Details** Use the graphic organizer below to list two details and the main idea found in the last paragraph of the text.

The direction of the arrow shows that the dog is pushing, not pulling.

Detail

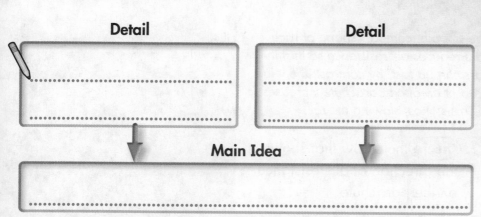

Detail

Main Idea

Contact Forces

Car mechanics use forces to lift tires and pull tool carts. These forces cannot act unless the mechanic touches the object to be moved. The object may be touched directly with a hand or using a handle or a rope, but there must be contact. A force that requires two pieces of matter to touch is called a **contact force.** You exert a contact force when you push or pull a piece of furniture.

One kind of contact force is friction. **Friction** is the force that results when two materials rub against each other or when their contact prevents sliding. Friction makes it harder for one surface to move past another. The amount of friction between two objects may depend on their texture, shape, speed, and weight. It may also depend on whether or not the surfaces are wet.

Solids are not the only materials that can cause friction. Air and water also resist motion when an object pushes against them. Air resistance is a type of friction that is present when particles of air contact a surface. Water causes a similar type of friction. Submarines and ships are designed with shapes that help them reduce friction and move through water easily.

3. **CHALLENGE** Why do you think mechanics need to change tires during races?

....

....

....

....

....

....

The smooth, compact shape of race cars reduces air resistance so that the cars can go fast. By contrast, the wide area of an open parachute increases air resistance, slowing the fall.

2. **Circle** the arrow that shows the direction of air resistance on the parachute.

The large amount of friction between the tires and the track makes it harder for cars to slide out of control. Friction also causes the brakes on the back of inline skates to slow or stop the skater.

4. **Explain** How do brakes help an inline skater stop?

....

....

....

....

This mechanic is pushing on a lever so she can lift one side of the car.

This member of the pit crew is pulling a worn-out tire off the car.

Many shoes have rough soles that increase friction with the ground and prevent slipping.

Non-Contact Forces

For friction to work, two things need to touch. There has to be contact between two surfaces, or contact with a gas or a liquid. But there are forces that can act at a distance. They work even if the object that is pushing or pulling is not touching the object being pushed or pulled! A force that acts at a distance is called a **non-contact force.** Three examples of non-contact forces are gravity, electric forces, and magnetic forces.

Gravity

Every object in the universe exerts a pull on every other object. This force of attraction between any two objects is called **gravity.** Only the gravity of a large object such as Earth is strong enough to cause effects that we can notice easily. Without gravity, things would not fall. Gravity pulls objects toward Earth's center without touching them.

The weight of an object is just the force of Earth's pull on that object. As an object moves away from Earth, the object weighs less and less because the pull of Earth's gravity becomes weaker and weaker with distance.

5. [CHALLENGE] Draw in the box at the right where you think the feather will be by the time the apple has hit the bottom of the box.

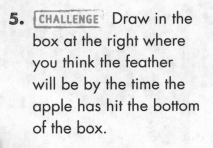

At-Home Lab

Does Gravity Affect You?
Stand. Stretch your left arm overhead. Leave your right arm at your side. Wait for 1 minute. Then compare the color of the palms of your hands. Share what you notice.

Gravity with no Air Resistance

Feathers normally fall slowly. You don't expect a feather to fall as fast as an apple. However, if you pump the air out of a box and drop a feather and an apple inside, they will fall at the same rate!

Gravity with Air Resistance

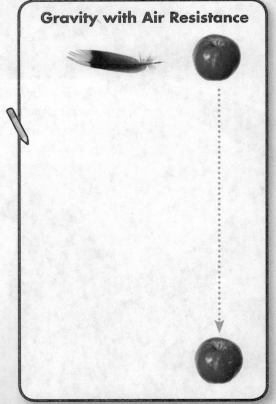

Electric and Magnetic Forces

Electric forces act between objects that are electrically charged. Oppositely charged objects are attracted to each other and tend to move toward each other. Objects with the same charge repel each other and tend to move away from each other.

Magnets will pull strongly on objects made of some metals, such as iron, cobalt, and nickel. Every magnet has a north pole and a south pole. Magnetic force is greatest at a magnet's poles. The north pole of one magnet will pull on the south pole of another magnet. The north poles of two magnets will push away from each other. The south poles of two magnets will act in the same way.

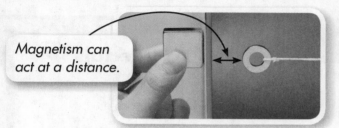

Magnetism can act at a distance.

6. Analyze What is happening to the cat's fur?

....

....

....

Got it?

7. Identify What are some forces that might affect a rock as it tumbles down a hill?

....

....

8. UNLOCK THE BIG ? **Conclude** If Earth is pulling down on you, are you pulling up on Earth? Explain.

....

....

⬛ **Stop!** I need help with ....

⏸ **Wait!** I have a question about ....

▶ **Go!** Now I know ....

What are Newton's laws?

Envision It!

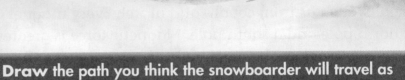

Draw the path you think the snowboarder will travel as she jumps off the slope.

Inquiry **Explore It!**

How can forces affect motion?

☐ **1.** Place the ruler on a flat, level surface.
Put Marble **A** in the groove of the ruler at the 10 cm mark.
Put Marble **B** in the groove at the 20 cm mark.

☐ **2. Predict** What will happen if you push **A** so that it hits **B**?

☐ **3.** Test your prediction. Repeat your test 4 times. Tell your results. Tell whether the results were the same each time.

Explain Your Results

4. Communicate Describe the forces that affected each marble.

....

....

5. Share your results. Discuss why tests should be repeated.
Tell why an **investigation** should be repeatable by others.

Materials

2 metal marbles

metric ruler
with groove

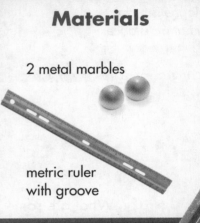

Marble **A**

Marble **B**

I will know that a given object will have more change of motion with a large force. I will know that a given force will cause more change of motion on small masses.

Words to Know

acceleration

inertia

Changes in Motion

Have you ever observed the motion of a car? When the car approaches a red light, the driver steps on the brake pedal. The speed of the car drops to zero. When the light turns green, the driver steps on the gas pedal. The speed climbs from zero. If the car has to turn a corner, the driver turns the steering wheel. The car changes direction.

When an object speeds up, slows down, or changes direction, its motion changes. The rate at which the speed or the direction of motion of an object changes over time is its **acceleration.**

When we speak of acceleration, we usually mean going faster and faster, but in science the word *acceleration* means *any* change in motion. For example, the circular motion of a Ferris wheel is accelerated. Even if the wheel turns with constant speed, the riders change direction all the time. They go up, then forward, then down, and then backward.

An object has no acceleration if it moves in a straight line without changing its speed or direction, or if it is not moving at all. Motion without acceleration is called uniform motion. The word *uniform* tells us that the motion does not change. A train traveling at a steady speed on a straight track has uniform motion. A book sitting on a table also has uniform motion. Its speed is zero.

1. **Explain** What kind of motion do the people on the escalator below have? Why?

....

....

....

....

Newton's First Law

Newton's first law of motion says that an object will stay in uniform motion unless a net force acts on the object. Without that force, an object at rest will stay at rest. An object in motion will keep the same speed and direction. For example, a marble will stay still on the floor unless you push it. If the marble is already moving, it will continue to move at a constant speed in a straight line until a force acts on it.

The tendency of an object to resist any change in motion is known as **inertia**. Objects with a lot of mass have more inertia than objects with less mass. Your body's inertia is what pushes you against the side of a car when the car turns. Your body tends to keep moving in a straight line when the car changes direction. The car must push you as it turns. Inertia is also what makes your body rise up from your seat when the car goes up and over a steep hill. At the top of the hill, your body tends to continue going forward as the car begins to move down the hill.

Things you push or throw eventually will stop. This is because there are other forces acting on these objects. For example, friction and air resistance will slow down a rolling marble until it stops. However, a space probe will keep moving through space because it has no friction to slow it down. Even without fuel, a space probe can travel a long distance by inertia. It only needs fuel to change direction or to slow down.

2. ◉ **Main Idea and Details** Read the second paragraph again. (Circle) the main idea and **underline** two details.

3. **Infer** Why do standing passengers fall forward when a bus stops?

4. [CHALLENGE] Why is fuel needed to change the speed or direction of a probe in space?

A crash-test dummy has inertia. Even if a moving car is stopped in a crash, the inertia of the dummy will keep it moving forward.

The bowling ball has inertia. Inertia will keep it rolling for many meters, even after the player releases it.

5. Use blue to color the part of the arrow where a force is pushing the ball, and red to color the part of the arrow where the ball is moving only by inertia.

The ball is released here.

6. **Suggest** What could prevent the test dummy's inertia from carrying the dummy through the windshield?

....

....

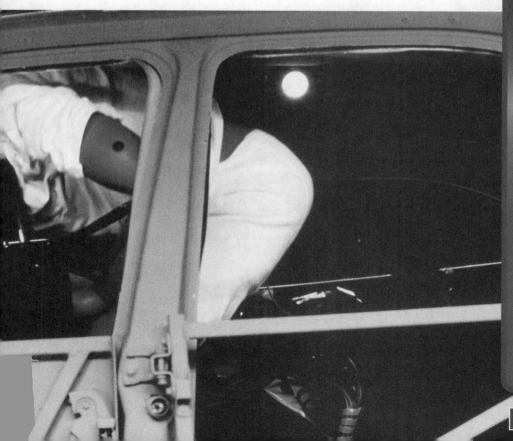

Newton's Second Law

Newton's second law of motion describes how acceleration, mass, and force are related. Force is the product of mass and acceleration. The force acting on an object can cause the object to speed up, slow down, or change direction.

Same Force, Different Masses

Newton's second law says that the greater the mass of the object, the smaller its change in motion will be for a given force. This means that the same force will cause an object with small mass to accelerate more than an object with large mass. Large masses are harder to accelerate and harder to stop. For example, the engine and brakes of a truck provide the same forces whether the truck is empty or loaded. However, the loaded truck has more mass and will accelerate more slowly. It will also take longer to stop. Truck drivers must be aware of Newton's second law in order to drive safely.

7. **Compare** The boats below have no engines. The engine shown can push either boat with the same force. (Circle) the boat that is more likely to experience less acceleration with this engine. Tell why.

Same Mass, Different Forces

Newton's second law of motion also says that the greater the force applied, the greater the change in motion for a given mass. In other words, a large force will produce more acceleration than a small force acting on the same object.

You can see this law at work in the Olympic sport of archery. Archers shoot arrows at targets. The archer must be sure that the arrow starts moving with just the right speed and direction in order to reach the target. The arrow starts at rest. The archer bends the bow by pulling on the bow string. The amount of bending controls the force that will accelerate the arrow. This force changes the motion of the arrow. When the arrow leaves the bow, it is traveling very fast. The same arrow can experience different accelerations depending on the amount of stretching of the bow.

8. **Predict** If the archer pulls the string to B instead of to A, there will be less force on the arrow. How will this affect the acceleration of the arrow?

9. **Infer** Look at the shape of the bow and string to the right. How can you tell that a force will act on the arrow when the string is released?

Using Formulas

The formula that describes the relationship between force, mass, and acceleration is:

Force = Mass × Acceleration

This means that the stronger the force acting on an object, the more that object will accelerate. The formula is often written as follows:

F = m × a

The unit of force in the metric system is called a newton (N). The unit of mass in the metric system is the kilogram (kg).
The unit of acceleration is the meter per second squared $(\frac{m}{s^2})$.

$$1 \text{ N} = 1 \text{ kg} \times \frac{m}{s^2}$$

Example

A block with a mass of 12 kg is being pushed. Its acceleration is $5 \frac{m}{s^2}$. What force is acting on the block?

Solve for the force, F. Use $m = 12$ kg, $a = 5 \frac{m}{s^2}$

$F = m \times a$

$F = 12 \text{ kg} \times 5 \frac{m}{s^2}$

$F = 60 \text{ kg} \times \frac{m}{s^2}$

$F = 60 \text{ N}$

Think I know that $1 \text{ kg} \times \frac{m}{s^2} = 1 \text{ N}$, so $60 \text{ kg} \times \frac{m}{s^2} = 60 \text{ N}$

The force being applied to the block is 60 N.

---

1 A 25 kg block is being pushed and is accelerated at a rate of $6 \frac{m}{s^2}$. What force is being applied to the block? Show your work.

Work Area

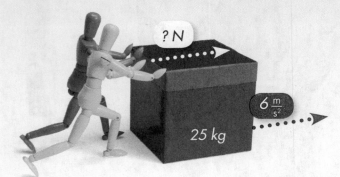

Newton's Third Law

Newton's third law of motion states that when one object exerts a force on a second object, the second object exerts a force on the first. These forces are equal in strength and opposite in direction.

It is impossible to have one force without an equal and opposite force. For example, if you have ever ridden bumper cars, you know that when a moving car collides with a stationary car, both drivers feel the force of the collision. The driver of the stationary car feels a force and starts to move. The driver of the moving car feels an opposite force that slows the moving car.

10. Choose Suppose the girl on the left bumps the car on the right. Which girl feels a bigger bump? Explain.

_____

_____

Got it?

11. Explain What is needed to give a large boulder a large acceleration?

_____

_____

12. UNLOCK THE BIG ? Suppose a train engine is pulling ten cars. The last car becomes separated from the train. What happens to the motion of the rest of the train?

_____

_____

◻ **Stop!** I need help with _____

❚❚ **Wait!** I have a question about _____

▶ **Go!** Now I know _____

How are forces combined?

Tell what forces you think are affecting the gazelle on the left.

Inquiry Explore It!

How do forces combine?

☑ **1.** Tie one end of a thread to a paper clip. Tape the other end to your desk.

☑ **2.** Lift the paper clip straight up.
Observe what happens when you let go.

☑ **3.** Use a magnet to lift the paper clip as high as possible. Then, raise the magnet a little more very slowly. Observe what happens.

Explain Your Results

4. Infer What forces combined to keep the paper clip in place?

....

....

....

....

Materials

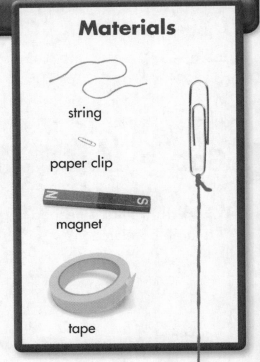

string

paper clip

magnet

tape

I will know that an object will not start moving if the forces acting on it are balanced.

Word to Know

balanced

Adding Forces

Have you ever asked a friend to help you push something heavy? By pushing together, two people can combine their forces into a single force. This combined force can have a bigger effect.

When two forces act on the same object and have the same direction, their strengths can be added together. The combined force will point in the same direction as the two single forces. For example, if two people lift a box together, their forces can be added because both forces point upward. If each person applies a force of 100 N, their combined force will be an upward force with a strength of 100 N + 100 N, or 200 N.

1. **Compute** Suppose the girl on the left is pulling with a force of 350 N. The girl on the right is pushing with a force that is $\frac{3}{5}$ of 350 N. What are the strength and direction of their combined force?

....

....

....

....

The girl on the left is pulling the wagon. The girl on the right is pushing. Their forces act on the same object and point in the same direction. They can be added.

Balanced Forces

When you hold a book in your hand, your hand is pushing the book up. At the same time, the Earth's gravity is pulling the book down. The two forces push against each other just enough to keep the book from moving.

Two forces of equal strength that combine to act on the same object but in opposite directions are **balanced.** Balanced forces cancel each other out and cannot change the motion of the object.

Several forces can be balanced at the same time. For example, several ropes may pull on a camping tent without causing a change in motion. The total of all the forces acting on a body is called the net force. When the forces acting on a body are balanced, the net force is zero.

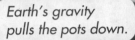

Earth's gravity pulls the pots down.

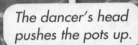

The dancer's head pushes the pots up.

2. **Determine** Think about the two forces acting on the stack of pots to the left. Explain why the pots are not moving. Use the words opposite and balanced.

....

....

....

....

....

....

....

....

3. Diagram The forces acting on this hammock must be balanced because there is no change in motion. **Draw** arrows showing the forces that keep the hammock still.

Got it?

4. Infer The left gazelle on the first pages of this lesson is being pushed to the left by the right gazelle. How can its legs balance the push?

....

....

5. Estimate Suppose it takes 260 N of force to push an object. One person pushes with 140 N of force. A second person helps by pushing in the same direction. How much force does the second person need to apply?

....

 **Stop!** I need help with ....

 **Wait!** I have a question about ....

Go! Now I know ....

Lesson 4

How are shadows formed?

Tell how a shadow and the object that makes the shadow are alike and different.

Inquiry Explore It!

What can cause the size and shape of a shadow to change?

Materials

flashlight   toy car

☐ **1.** Shine a flashlight on a wall.

☐ **2.** Put a toy between the light and the wall. **Observe** the shadow.

☐ **3.** Move the toy and light farther from the wall. Observe. Move them closer to the wall. Tell what happens.

☐ **4.** Move the light farther from the toy. Observe. Move it closer. Observe.

Explain Your Results

5. Find a way to change the shape of the shadow. Describe how you did this.

....

....

6. Communicate How did the shadow change?

....

....

UNLOCK
THE BIG
?

I will know how
shadows form.

Word to Know

shadow

Light Sources

Light is a form of energy. The sun is the primary source of light energy for Earth. A bonfire, a candle, and a street lamp are some other sources of light energy.

Light energy travels as waves in straight lines, as long as nothing is in its way. A **shadow** is an area of partial darkness where light has been blocked by an object.

1. Look at the object shown. **Draw** what the object's shadow might look like if the object were in a path of light.

2. CHALLENGE Do objects such as waxed paper and frosted glass have shadows when they are in the path of light?

....

....

....

....

Lightning Lab

Making Shadows

Shine a flashlight on the wall. Move an object that will absorb light forward and backward in front of the flashlight. Sketch the object's shadow at three different distances. Describe how the size and outline of the object's shadow change.

Shadows

If you hold your hand in front of a wall and then shine a flashlight on your hand, a hand-shaped shadow will show up on the wall. Your hand absorbs or reflects the light and blocks the path of the light rays. A shadow appears where the light rays cannot reach the wall. The size of a shadow can change. If you hold your hand close to the wall and shine the flashlight on it, the shadow will be about the same size as your hand. If you move your hand closer to the flashlight, the shadow will be larger than your hand.

3. **Cause and Effect** Read the paragraph again. (Circle) what causes a shadow to form.

4. **Infer** In which picture is the light source closer to the object? Explain.

....

....

....

The angle at which light strikes an object also affects the size of a shadow. Think of your own shadow on a sunny day. Around noon, when the sun is highest in the sky, your shadow is short. Early in the morning or late in the day, the sun is lower in the sky. Your shadow is longer.

5. **Infer** Do you think it is early morning or noon in this picture? Explain.

....

....

Got it?

6. **Explain** How does changing the position of a light source such as a flashlight affect the size of an object's shadow?

....

....

....

7. **Infer** When light passes through a clear window, does the window have a shadow? Explain.

....

....

◻ **Stop!** I need help with ....

⏸ **Wait!** I have a question about ....

▶ **Go!** Now I know ....

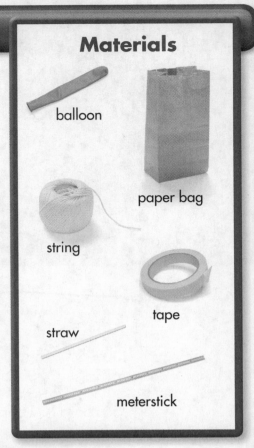

What forces affect the motion of a rocket?

Follow a Procedure

Materials

balloon

paper bag

string

tape

straw

meterstick

☐ **1.** Tie one end of a 10-meter piece of string to a chair. Slide a straw onto the string. Tape a paper bag to the straw. Tie the other end of the string to another chair. Make the string tight by pulling the chairs apart. Slide the bag to the middle of the string.

☐ **2.** Blow up a long balloon. Hold the neck end closed. Put the other end in the bag.

☐ **3. Observe** Let go of the balloon. What happened?

Do not blow up the balloon too much.

☐ **4.** Slide the bag to one end of the string. Blow up the balloon again. Place the balloon in the bag.

☐ **5. Predict** how far the rocket will move.

Inquiry Skill Before you **predict,** think about what you have already observed.

☐ **6.** Let go of the balloon. Use a meterstick to measure how far the rocket moved. Repeat 2 more times.

7. Record your data below. Find the average distance for the 3 trials. Add the 3 distances and divide by 3.

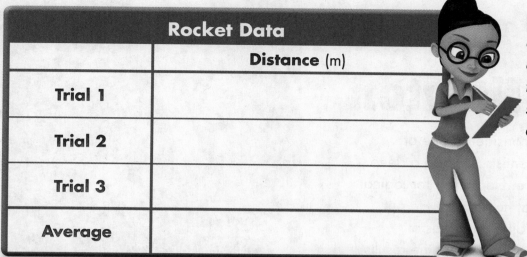

Rocket Data	
	Distance (m)
Trial 1	
Trial 2	
Trial 3	
Average	

Scientists often make observations again and again. Repeating trials helps them be sure what they have observed is accurate.

Analyze and Conclude

8. Observe Compare how far the rocket moved in each trial.

....

....

9. Infer What caused the rocket to move in the direction that it moved?

....

....

....

10. UNLOCK THE BIG ? What made the rocket move? How do you know?

....

....

....

....

Isaac Newton

Isaac Newton is considered one of history's greatest scientists. He had a deep curiosity about nature. He looked for logical ways to explain what he noticed. He put together ideas from different areas of science in creative ways. Among the results were his laws of motion. These laws and his definition of *force* made people think about science in a new way.

Newton graduated from Cambridge University in England in 1665. For more than 30 years, he was a teacher there. Later, he became the head of England's mint, which coined the nation's money. His scientific background helped him catch people making fake money and bring them to justice.

Newton's work gained him the respect of other scientists. His theories still form the basis of our understanding of the universe.

Newton (1642–1727) also studied the sky. He invented a telescope that worked with mirrors instead of lenses.

How do you think understanding Newton's laws of motion can help an engineer design a safer or faster car?

....

....

....

Vocabulary Smart Cards

force
contact force
friction
non-contact force
gravity
acceleration
inertia
balanced
shadow

Play a Game!

Cut out the Vocabulary Smart Cards.

Work with a partner.

Choose a Vocabulary Smart Card.

Say as many words as you can think of that describe that vocabulary word.

Have your partner try to guess the word.

non-contact force

fuerza sin contacto

force

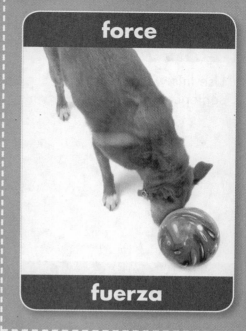

fuerza

gravity

gravedad

contact force

fuerza de contacto

acceleration

aceleración

friction

fricción

a push or pull that acts on an object

Use this word in a sentence.

....

....

....

....

empujón o jalón que se le da a un objeto

---

a force that acts at a distance

Use this word in a sentence.

....

....

....

....

fuerza que actúa a distancia

---

a force that requires two pieces of matter to touch

Draw an example of this word.

fuerza que requiere que dos porciones de materia se toquen

---

the force of attraction between any two objects

Use this word in a sentence.

....

....

....

....

fuerza de atracción entre dos cuerpos cualesquiera

---

the force that results when two materials rub against each other or when their contact prevents sliding

Write an example of this word.

....

fuerza que resulta al frotar un material contra otro o cuando el contacto entre ambos impide el deslizamiento

---

the rate at which the speed or direction of motion of an object changes over time

Write three other forms of this word.

....

....

....

ritmo al cual cambia la rapidez o la dirección del movimiento de un objeto con el tiempo

---

Interactive Vocabulary

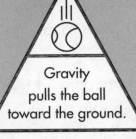

Gravity
pulls the ball
toward the ground.

Gravity is the force of attraction between any two objects.

Make a Word Pyramid!

Choose a vocabulary word and write the definition in the base of the pyramid. Write a sentence in the middle of the pyramid. Draw a picture of an example, or of something related, at the top.

inertia

inercia

balanced

balanceadas

shadow

sombra

the tendency of an object to
resist any change in motion

Write an example of
this word.

....

....

....

tendencia de un cuerpo
a resistirse a cualquier
cambio de movimiento

describes equal forces that
combine to act on an object
in opposite directions

Write a synonym for
this word

....

....

describe fuerzas iguales
que se combinan y
actúan sobre un objeto en
dirección opuestas

an area of partial darkness
where light has been
blocked by an object

Draw an example

región de oscuridad parcial
donde la luz ha sido
bloqueada por un objeto

Lesson 1

What are forces?

- A force is any push or pull.
- Contact forces, such as friction, only happen when objects touch.
- Non-contact forces, such as gravity, can act from a distance.

Lesson 2

What are Newton's laws?

- Due to inertia, objects tend to resist changes in motion.
- Acceleration depends on an object's mass and the force acting on it.
- Every force creates an equal and opposite force.

Lesson 3

How are forces combined?

- Two forces acting on the same object in the same direction can be added together.
- Opposite but equal forces are balanced and cannot change the motion of the object.

Lesson 4

How are shadows formed?

- A shadow is an area of partial darkness where light waves have been blocked by an object.
- The angle at which light strikes an object affects the size of a shadow.

Lesson 1

What are forces?

1. ⊙ **Main Idea and Details** Underline the main idea and circle the details in the following paragraph.

Forces that are applied on objects by other objects can be either contact or non-contact forces. Friction and air resistance are two types of contact forces. Electric forces, gravity, and magnetic forces are non-contact forces.

2. **Interpret** Write a *T* for true or an *F* for false in front of the following statements.

_____ Magnetism is a contact force because magnets make contact.

_____ Friction is a kind of force.

_____ Gravity only acts on heavy objects.

3. **Explain** How can the shapes of a boat and an airplane help them move faster?

....

....

....

Lesson 2

What are Newton's laws?

4. **Synthesize** What laws of motion are demonstrated by a hammer pounding a nail into a board?

....

....

5. **Explain** A batter hits a baseball with a bat. The bat exerts a force on the ball. Does the ball exert a force on the bat?

....

....

6. **Vocabulary** In space, where there is no air and gravity is weak, space probes can travel millions of miles without using any fuel. What allows them to do this? Use the term *inertia* in your answer.

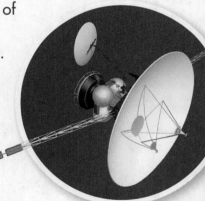

....

....

....

....

Lesson 3

How are forces combined?

7. **Calculate** Gravity pulls downward on a rock with a force of 800 N. If you pull upward on the rock with a force of 400 N, what is the total force acting on the rock?

   A. 400 N downward
   B. 400 N upward
   C. 1200 N downward
   D. 1200 N upward

8. **Explain** Two forces pushing on a toy wagon are balanced. What are balanced forces?

....

....

....

Lesson 4

How are shadows formed?

9. **Synthesize** You have a flashlight in a dark room. Describe what you could do to create a shadow on a wall. What causes the shadow?

....

....

....

....

10. **ANSWER THE BIG ?** **What affects the motion of objects?**

....

A student kicks a soccer ball by applying a force. Describe what happens to the soccer ball.

....

....

....

....

....

What other forces affect the soccer ball after the student's foot stops touching it?

....

....

....

....

....

....

Read each question and choose the best answer.

1 A car runs out of gas while moving forward on a flat, straight road. The car keeps rolling for a while because

A gravity pulls it forward.
B it still has force.
C it has acceleration.
D it has inertia.

2 A force of 20 N accelerates a 2 kg object. How much force is needed to give the same acceleration to a 20 kg object?

A 10 N
B 10 kg
C 200 N
D 400 kg

3 A drummer hits a drum with a drumstick. The drumstick exerts a force on the drum. The reaction

A is stronger than the action.
B changes the motion of the drumstick.
C drives the drum forward.
D creates inertia.

4 You push a large crate with a force of 130 N to the right. What force could your friend apply in order to cause a balanced force on the crate?

A 260 N to the right
B 260 N to the left
C 130 N to the right
D 130 N to the left

5 Which of the following is a contact force?

A friction
B magnetism
C gravity
D electricity

6 Which of the following is <u>not</u> an example of accelerated motion?

A an elevator going up at constant speed
B an elevator slowing down
C an elevator speeding up
D a car taking a curve at constant speed

7 What happens to cause a shadow on the ground when the sun is shining brightly?

....

....

NASA's Space Centers

NASA researches airplane and rocket engines. Scientists at NASA have improved engine design. These engines produce thrust, which is a force that moves an airplane forward or a rocket upward.

The engines on jet airplanes produce more thrust than engines that use propellers. In a jet airplane, a huge fan brings cool air into the front of the engine and compresses it. Then fuel is mixed with the air. After the mixture of fuel and air is burned, the gases that are produced greatly expand. The gases rush out the back of the engine. The force of the gases moving backward pushes the plane forward.

Jet engines produce a great deal of thrust, but they also produce noise. Jet engines can be much more noisy than engines with propellers. NASA has a program that is trying to make jet engines quieter.

A jet airplane is still going very fast when it lands. How do you think the jet could use its engines to help the plane slow down?

....

....

Materials

2 metric rulers

$\frac{1}{2}$ of a plastic cup and metal marble

2 books

tape and 4 pennies

balance and gram cubes

calculator or computer (optional)

Inquiry Skill
A **hypothesis** is a statement that explains an observation. It can be tested by an experiment.

How is motion affected by mass?

A force can cause an object to move. You will conduct an **experiment** to find out how the mass of an object affects the distance the object will move.

Ask a question.

What effect does the mass of a cup have on the distance a rolling marble will move the cup?

State a hypothesis.

1. Write a **hypothesis** by circling one choice and finishing the sentence.

If the mass of a cup is increased, then the distance the cup is moved by a rolling marble

(a) *increases*

(b) *decreases*

(c) *remains the same*

because

....

....

Identify and control variables.

2. In this experiment you will measure the distance the cup moves. You must change only one **variable.** Everything else must remain the same. What should stay the same? List two examples.

....

....

3. Tell the one change you will make.

....

....

....

Design your test.

4. Draw how you will set up your test.

5. List your steps in the order you will do them.

Do your test.

☑ **6.** Follow the steps you wrote.

Use a balance and gram cubes to find the mass of the cup.

☑ **7.** Make sure to **measure** accurately. **Record** your results in a table.

☑ **8.** Scientists repeat their tests to improve their accuracy.

Repeat your test if time allows.

Collect and record your data.

☑ **9.** Fill in the chart.

Work Like a Scientist

Clear and active communication is an essential part of doing science. Talk with your classmates. Compare your methods and results.

Interpret your data.

☑ **10.** Use your data to make a line graph.

☑ **11.** Look at your graph closely. Describe how the distance the cup moved was affected by the mass of the cup. Identify the evidence you used to answer the question.

....

....

....

....

....

> **Technology Tools**
> Your teacher may wish to have you use a computer (with the right software) or a graphing calculator to help collect, organize, analyze, and present your data. These tools can help you make tables, charts, and graphs.

State your conclusion.

12. Communicate your conclusion. Compare your **hypothesis** with your results. Compare your results with those of others.

....

....

....

MATERIALS

- safety goggles
- 2 clear plastic cups
- 2 sheets of paper
- plastic spoon and vinegar
- Compound A and Compound B

Plan an Investigation

Solubility is one physical property of matter. Compare the solubility of materials to determine which material has the highest solubility in water. Choose several substances to compare. Predict which substance will have the highest solubility. Plan an investigation to test your prediction. Your investigation should include the following:

- A testable question
- Written instructions to measure solubility of a substance
- A list of materials and tools to carry out the investigation

Build a Simple Machine

Use common objects to make a machine that will do a simple task such as close a door, water plants, crack an egg, or open a window. Name the machine and design a box or container to package it. Make a diagram with labels to show all the simple machines included in the new machine.

Science and Engineering Practices

1. Ask a question or define a problem.
2. Develop and use models.
3. Plan and carry out investigations.
4. Analyze and interpret data.
5. Use math and computational thinking.
6. Construct explanations or design solutions.
7. Engage in argument from evidence.
8. Obtain, evaluate, and communicate information.

Take the Salt Out

Conduct research on ways to make fresh
water from seawater. Try removing the
salt from saltwater by evaporation and
condensation or by freezing. Draw a
diagram showing your equipment and your
method.

Investigate Mixtures

Remember that when a chemical change
occurs, one or more types of matter changes
into other types of matter with different
properties. Conduct an investigation to
determine whether the mixing of two
substances results in a new substance.
Under the observation of your teacher or an
adult at home, mix 100 grams (g) baking
soda with 100 milliliters (mL) lemon juice
in a clear container. Remember to follow
lab safety rules. Record your observations.
Consider these questions, and draw a
conclusion.

- What properties does the baking soda
  have?

- What properties does the lemon juice
  have?

- Did the mixture result in a new substance?
  Use your observations to explain.

- What properties does the mixture have?

WHAT
is this?

Growth and Survival

Try It!   How can temperature affect seed growth?

STEM Activity   Come in Out of Nature!

Lesson 1   What are some physical structures in living things?

Lesson 2   How do adaptations help plants?

Lesson 3   How do adaptations help animals?

Lesson 4   What are the life cycles of some animals?

Investigate It!   How do seeds grow?

This scaly creature and other species in its family live in warm areas of Asia and Africa.

Predict   What do you think are some advantages of having scales?

....

....

....

THE BIG ?   How do plants and animals grow and change?

How can temperature affect seed growth?

Materials

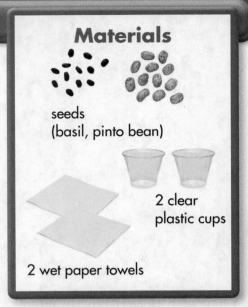

seeds
(basil, pinto bean)

2 clear
plastic cups

2 wet paper towels

☐ **1.** Choose one type of seed to test.
Use the cups and towels to grow the seeds.

☐ **2.** Put one cup in a refrigerator. Put the other cup in a dark place in your classroom.

☐ **3.** **Predict** how temperature will affect the seeds.

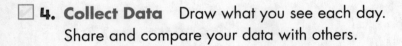

....

....

Inquiry Skill You can **collect data** by drawing what you observe.

☐ **4.** **Collect Data** Draw what you see each day.
Share and compare your data with others.

Seed Observations					
Type of Seed					
Temperature	**Day 1**	**Day 2**	**Day 3**	**Day 4**	**Day 5**
Cold					
Room temperature					

Explain Your Results

5. Compare your results with those of other groups.
How did the seeds respond to temperature?
Infer how this response might help a pinto-bean plant respond to changing seasons.

....

....

....

⊙ Cause and Effect

- A **cause** is why something happens. An **effect** is what happens.
- When you read, sometimes clue words such as *because* and *since* signal a cause-and-effect relationship.

Jellyfish Blooms

Jellyfish are often found in large groups called "blooms." Since jellyfish are poisonous, jellyfish blooms can be a serious problem. In ocean water near Hawaii and Australia and in the Mediterranean Sea, jellyfish blooms can make the water unsafe for swimmers. Some beaches need to be closed to swimmers until the jellyfish are gone. In other places, such as Ireland, fish farms have been wiped out by jellyfish blooms. Fishing nets can be clogged and damaged by the excessive weight of hundreds of jellyfish.

Practice It!

Use the graphic organizer below to list some causes and effects found in the example paragraph.

Cause

Effect

jellyfish bloom

Come in Out of Nature!

Camping is a popular way to spend time enjoying nature. A well designed tent folds easily, keeps people dry during rainstorms, and is made out of a strong material.

When engineers design an object, they usually start by making a drawing. Their drawing includes dimensions. A line has one dimension: length. A flat object, such as a piece of paper, has two dimensions: length and width. A tent, like most objects, has three dimensions: height, width, and length. When engineers make a model, they represent each part of a three-dimensional (3-D) object in two dimensions. Then they assemble their two-dimensional pieces to make a 3-D model.

You have just been promoted to chief tent engineer. As part of your new job, you will draw two-dimensional pattern pieces for each part of a three-dimensional, A-frame tent. You will then build a three-dimensional model of your tent out of your pattern pieces.

Identify the Problem

☐ **1. List** two challenges involved when building a model of a tent.

_____

_____

_____

_____

Do Research

Examine pictures of several tents.

☐ **2.** How do the sizes and shapes of the tents vary? _____

_____

☐ **3.** How do the simplest and most complex tents compare? _____

_____

_____

4. What design constraints must you consider when building a model A-frame tent?

_____

_____

Develop Possible Solutions

5. Sketch different patterns for your tent. **Determine** an appropriate length for each part of the patterns.

Choose One Solution

6. Describe which pattern you will use for your tent. _____

_____

_____

7. Describe how you will make a model tent from this pattern. Include the dimensions of all sides of the tent. Dimensions include length, width, and height. _____

_____

_____

_____

Design and Construct a Prototype

☐ **8.** Use the metric ruler to draw your pattern with the dimensions you chose. Use the ruler to determine the area of the total pattern. **Record** your measurements.

_____

_____

_____

Test the Prototype

Test your design. Use your pattern to make a model tent out of paper.

Communicate Results

☐ **9. Analyze** how well your pattern worked. Summarize how well your tent went together. Share your results with your classmates. _____

_____

_____

_____

Evaluate and Redesign

☐ **10.** What changes could you make to your pattern to make it better? _____

_____

_____

11. Would these changes affect the two-dimensional pattern or the three-dimensional tent? Explain.

_____

_____

_____

_____

12. About how much fabric would it take to build an actual tent from your pattern?

_____

_____

_____

What are some physical structures in living things?

The skin of the glass frog is very translucent. **Circle** the parts of the frog's body that you can see through its skin.

MY PLANET DIARY

Connections

When you admire a work of art, what are some of the things you notice? If it is a sculpture, you may notice its shape or form. You may observe the texture of the art. Brightly-colored paintings can catch your attention.

Color and patterns are two properties we use to distinguish items by sight. Birds and other animals use these properties too. Male painted buntings are some of the most vividly colored birds we see in North America. Their colorful patterned feathers are attractive to birdwatchers, and more importantly, to female painted buntings!

A male painted bunting is much brighter than a female.

Explain Why do you think it is important that male painted buntings are brightly colored?

....

....

I will know similarities and differences in the structures and functions of parts of plants and animals.

Word to Know

exoskeleton

Physical Structures

Some trees shed their bark as a normal part of their growth. The tough outer covering of bark peels away so that new tree growth can expand outward. In a similar way, snakes shed their skins as they grow. All living organisms have structures that help them grow, get energy, and stay healthy. Sometimes structures can be very similar even though the organisms are different.

Other times, physical structures can be very different even if they do similar jobs. For example, an animal egg may be very delicate and may need to be hidden from predators. By contrast, many plant seeds have tough coverings and easily survive being swallowed by an animal. The seeds develop inside tasty fruits that animals like to eat. The seeds benefit because an animal can carry them to places where they may grow better.

paperbark maple tree

garter snake

1. ◉ **Cause and Effect** Use the graphic organizer below to list one cause and one effect from the second paragraph of the section above.

Cause

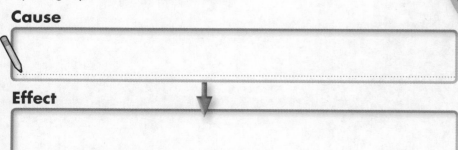

Effect

2. Justify Many stems hold leaves high. Higher leaves are more likely to get sunlight. How is this helpful to a plant?

....

....

The skull is like a strong cage that protects the brain.

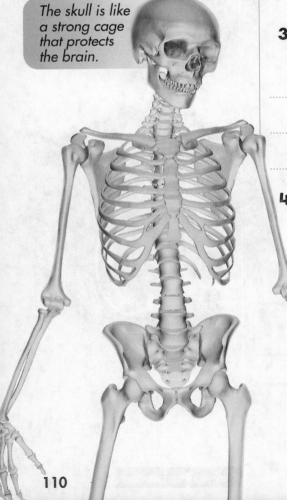

Structures for Support

Some animals, such as fish and humans, have internal skeletons. An internal skeleton supports the body. It also protects organs such as the brain and the heart.

Other animals have **exoskeletons,** which are hard skeletons on the outside of their bodies. Exoskeletons give structure and protection.

Plants have stems that stretch toward the sunlight and can hold the weight of leaves and fruit. Some plants, such as trees, have wood in their stems and branches for additional support.

Insects, such as the cicada, have a hard exoskeleton. In order to grow, insects usually need to shed their old exoskeleton and grow a new one.

3. ◉ Compare and Contrast How is an exoskeleton similar to an internal skeleton? How is it different?

....

....

....

4. Draw some organs that are protected by the rib cage.

Structures for Reproduction

Living things can make other living things similar to themselves. This process is called reproduction.

Many plants reproduce using flowers. For example, when pollen from a cherry flower is carried to another cherry flower, the receiving flower becomes fertilized. It grows into a cherry with a seed inside. The seed has a source of nutrition and a protective covering. If this seed lands on good soil, a new cherry plant may grow.

Animals reproduce in different ways. For example, some female fish lay eggs on underwater rocks. Then the male fertilizes the eggs. The organism grows inside of the egg, which has a source of nutrition and a protective cover. In other animals, such as mammals, males have structures to fertilize eggs within the body of the female.

5. Diagram Read the steps of Flower Fertilization below. Then, on the flower illustration, (circle) where a seed will develop.

seedling

shark egg sac

6. Label Write the correct letter in each circle above.

A organism

B protective cover

C nutrition source

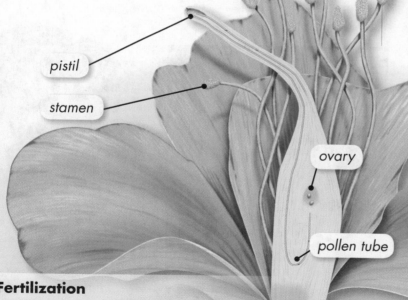
pistil
stamen
ovary
pollen tube

Flower Fertilization

1. Pollen leaves the stamen of a flower.
2. Pollen lands on the pistil of another flower.
3. A pollen tube grows from the pollen grain, and a sperm cell travels down the tube.
4. The sperm cell reaches an egg cell contained in the ovary. Fertilization occurs.
5. The fertilized egg goes on to become a seed.

At-Home Lab

Parts and the Whole
The bones in a skeleton make up a system. A system is a collection of parts that work together. Look at a bicycle. Is it a system? Explain. Think of three other systems that you can find in your home.

7. Draw a picture of one other animal that breathes using lungs and a picture of an animal that breathes with gills. Explain your choices.

Structures for Respiration and Circulation

In order for plants and animals to live, they need to exchange gases with their environments. Animals such as turtles and humans take in air through the mouth or nose and breathe using lungs. Some other animals, such as insects, take air in through structures called spiracles. These are holes in the insect's body. Most fish take in oxygen from water through their gills.

Lungs, spiracles, and gills are three ways animals can get oxygen. A spiracle often allows oxygen to go directly to body tissue. But with lungs and gills, oxygen entering the animal is transported through a circulatory system to the body's cells.

Plants have structures that are similar to spiracles on insects. These microscopic holes are called stomata and are located on the leaves of the plant. The carbon dioxide from the air enters the plant through the stomata. During photosynthesis, a plant uses energy from the sun and carbon dioxide to make sugar, or food. Oxygen is also produced and exits through the stomata.

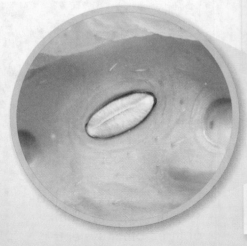

Spiracles on the skin of a caterpillar open up to let gases in or out.

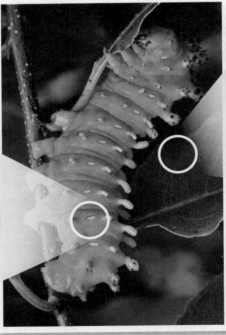

Like the spiracles of insects, stomata on the surface of a leaf open up to let gases in or out.

Some plants also have a circulatory system. These plants are called vascular plants. The tissues in the vascular system act similar to your blood vessels. The plant uses the vascular tissue to transport sugar made in the leaves to the roots for storage.

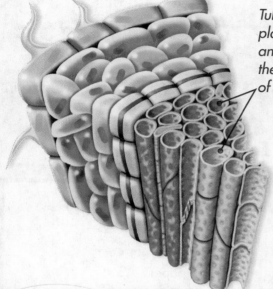

Tube structures within a plant stem transport water and nutrients to and from the leaves, roots, and rest of the plant.

8. **Compare** Blood travels through your body inside arteries and veins. Compare the function of a plant's vascular system to the function of your arteries and veins.

Got it?

9. **Contrast** List two structures that have similar functions in plants and animals. How are they different?

10. **UNLOCK THE BIG ?** What are some structures in plants and animals that serve a similar purpose?

⬜ **Stop!** I need help with

⏸ **Wait!** I have a question about

▶ **Go!** Now I know

Lesson 2

How do adaptations help plants?

Write three things you think these plants are getting from their environment.

How can plants survive in the desert?

☐ **1.** Wet and squeeze out 2 paper towels. Roll up 1 towel. Put the towels on the foil as shown.

☐ **2.** After 1 day unroll the rolled-up towel. **Observe** both towels. Compare. **Record.**

Materials

2 paper towels

plastic container with water

foil

Explain Your Results

3. Infer How does the amount of surface exposed to air affect how fast a leaf loses water?

Roll up one towel.
(model of a needle-like leaf)

Put one towel flat on the foil.
(model of a flat leaf)

I will know plants can
survive in different
environments because of
adaptations.

Word to Know

adaptation

Plant Adaptations

When an environment changes, plants compete to use the same limited resources, such as sunlight. Plants with the best adaptations are more likely to survive. An **adaptation** is a characteristic that increases an organism's ability to survive and reproduce in its environment. Adaptations do not happen quickly. They develop over many generations.

Plants receive genes from their parents. Genes are instructions that determine how the plant grows. Because of these genes, most characteristics of a plant are the same as in its parents. For example, a plant will have the same type of flowers and leaves as its parents.

However, different combinations of genes may cause a plant to be a bit different. Some plants may be a bit taller than their parents or may have different-colored flowers. A plant may also have a mutation, which is a random change in a gene. A mutated gene may cause a plant to grow roots that are a bit longer than average or to become unable to make wax to protect its leaves.

1. **Infer** How do you think the shape of mangrove roots might help the tree during a storm?

....

....

....

....

This mangrove tree can take in gases through its exposed roots. This adaptation helps it survive in its environment.

Natural Selection

If a mutation helps a plant survive in its environment, that plant will have a better chance to live and reproduce. The plant will pass on its genes to its offspring. If the mutation is harmful to the plant, the plant will be less likely to survive or have offspring.

Over many generations, small mutations can add up to surprising adaptations, such as strong roots or bright flowers. This process is called natural selection. It favors useful mutations and reduces harmful mutations. Natural selection helps species develop adaptations to survive in different environments.

Life-Cycle Variations

The life cycles of plants are adapted to their environments. For example, the seeds of a Venus's-flytrap are programmed to germinate, or sprout, after winter. They will not germinate in an indoor pot unless they have been kept in the refrigerator for several weeks. Some plants, like morning glory vines, take advantage of the warm weather and grow very fast, produce flowers and seeds, and then die before the cold arrives again. Other plants live through the winter but do not produce flowers or seeds until spring.

2. **Compare and Contrast** Look at the pictures and read the captions on the right. How are the life cycles of the papaya tree and the cherry tree alike and different?

....

....

....

....

Papaya trees grow in the tropics where the temperature stays more or less the same. They can produce fruit year-round. Each fruit has hundreds of seeds.

Cherry trees grow in regions with cold winters. They produce flowers only in the spring, and the cherries can be harvested in the summer. Each cherry has a single seed.

Physical Characteristics

Changes in the parts of a plant can help it survive in its environment. For example, coconuts are large seeds. If the coconuts from a particular palm tree can float a little better than the average, these coconuts will be more likely to stay afloat when they fall in the water. The floating husk, or outer covering, is a structural adaptation that is helpful when a plant has seeds that are dispersed by water. This type of husk might allow the coconut to travel farther in the ocean than a more dense husk. If the seed travels farther than other seeds, it may have less competition for resources. The seed may then survive and grow into a mature palm tree.

3. **Suggest** Look at the leaves on the plants below. Each leaf is adapted to perform a function. What might be the function of each leaf?

Venus's-flytrap: ....

Prickly pear cactus: ....

Water lily: ....

Coconuts have a lightweight husk that allows them to float for months until they reach a beach where the seed can germinate.

4. **Cause and Effect** Coconut trees grow in tropical regions. What would be an effect of an ocean current that carried coconuts to colder areas?

....

....

....

....

....

prickly pear cactus

Venus's-flytrap

water lily

Succession

When an environment changes, communities of organisms in the environment also change. *Succession* is the predictable order of changes in communities after a change occurs. As communities change, conditions might also change. New conditions allow different communities to move into the environment and grow.

In most cases, succession occurs in stages. If conditions are right, bare land might become grassland. Grassland will give way to shrubs. Shrub land will become a forest. Communities grow and replace one another until there is a stable community with few changes.

5. ◎ **Sequence** The pictures below show the same lake at different times. Write the numbers 1 through 4 on the pictures to show the sequence of succession at the lake.

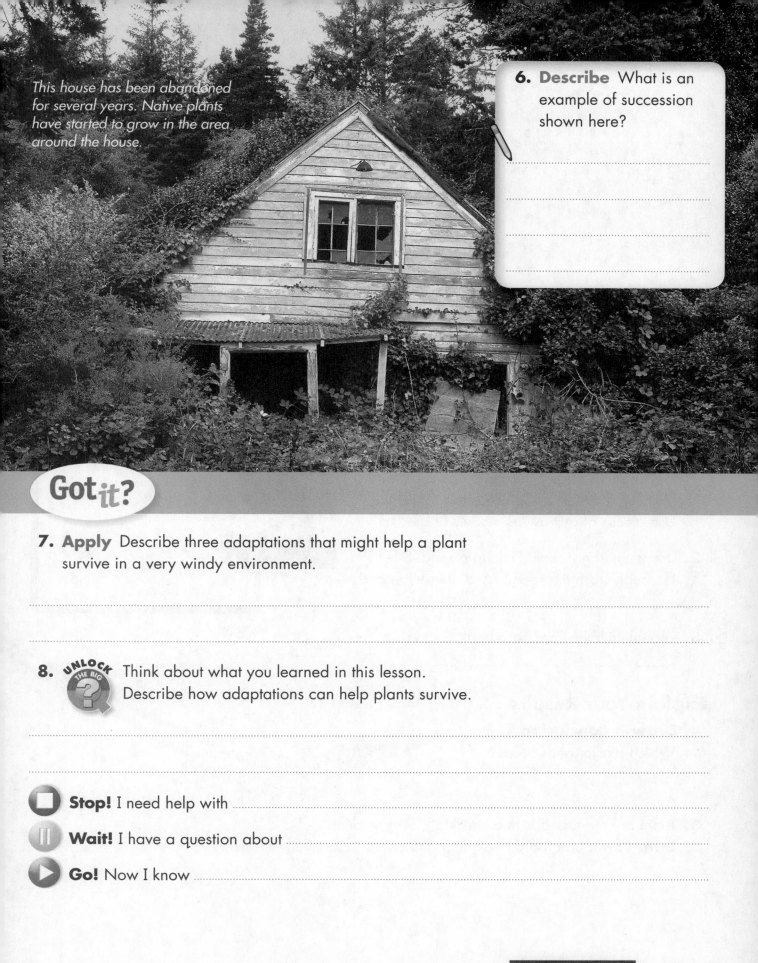

This house has been abandoned for several years. Native plants have started to grow in the area around the house.

6. **Describe** What is an example of succession shown here?

....

....

....

....

Got it?

7. **Apply** Describe three adaptations that might help a plant survive in a very windy environment.

....

....

8. **UNLOCK THE BIG ?** Think about what you learned in this lesson. Describe how adaptations can help plants survive.

....

....

⏹ **Stop!** I need help with ....

⏸ **Wait!** I have a question about ....

▶ **Go!** Now I know ....

How do adaptations help animals?

flying squid

Tell what part of each animal's body you think is adapted for gliding. Explain your answers.

Inquiry ▸ **Explore It!**

Which bird beak can crush seeds?

Materials

4 pieces of straw

2 clothespins

craft sticks

glue

☐ 1. **Make a model** of a heron's beak. Glue 2 craft sticks to a clothespin. Use the other clothespin as a model of a cardinal's beak. Use pieces of a straw as models of seeds.

☐ 2. Use the heron's beak. Pick up a seed. Does the beak crush the seed? Try 5 times. **Record.**

____ ____ ____ ____ ____

☐ 3. Repeat with the cardinal's beak. Record.

____ ____ ____ ____ ____

Explain Your Results

4. **Draw a Conclusion**
   Which bird crushes seeds?

....

5. There are many seeds in a cardinal's environment.
   Infer how a cardinal's beak helps the cardinal survive.

....

....

sugar glider

flying dragon

I will know that animals can survive in different environments because of adaptations.

Word to Know

extinct species

Animal Adaptations

When there is a sudden threat, such as an attack by a predator, an animal such as the blue-ringed octopus may respond by changing color. Animals have physical and behavioral adaptations that help them survive by responding to sudden threats. The blue-ringed octopus is usually pale, but when a predator approaches, it turns a bright yellow color with blue rings. Other animals might respond by running, flying, or using poison.

Changes in an environment, such as an increase in the salt content of the oceans over long periods of time, are too slow to affect individual animals. Animal species, like plant species, change over time to adapt to such slow changes in their environment.

1. **Infer** Read the adaptations listed in the left column of the chart and write a possible function of the adaptation.

Adaptation	Function
fur	
large eyes	
long legs	

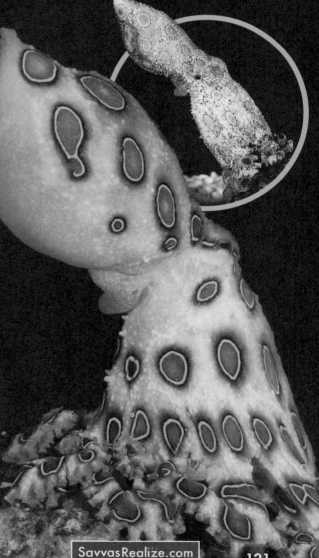

blue-ringed octopus before and after a color change

Swimming Birds

With your fingers spread apart, move your hand through a tub full of water. With your fingers still spread apart, wrap plastic around your hand. Move it through the water again. Ducks have webbing on their feet. Infer how this adaptation helps a duck.

2. **Infer** The pictures below show three structural adaptations. Write what you think the purpose of each one is.

Life-Cycle Variations

Different animals have different life cycles that help them survive in their environment. For example, many birds lay their eggs in the spring, when the weather warms up. The young hatchlings then have several months of good weather when food is available. This makes it easier for them to complete their growth.

Physical Characteristics

The body parts of animals have useful physical characteristics that help the animal survive. Useful changes in the body parts of an animal are called structural adaptations. For example, animals that hunt tend to have eyes on the front of their heads. This makes them better at telling how far away their prey is, and they can pounce or swoop with precision. Animals that are hunted often have eyes on the sides of their heads because that helps them see where a predator might be coming from.

Individual animals do not develop structural adaptations. Instead, animal species develop their physical characteristics through the process of natural selection, just as plant species do. Natural selection affects all species of living things.

gecko foot

sea urchin spines

okapi tongue

The process works in animals as it does in plants. If the genes of a bear give the bear thicker fur, the bear is more likely to survive a cold winter. The bear will pass its genes to its offspring, and the offspring will be likely to inherit the useful structural adaptations of their parent.

3. **◉ Compare and Contrast** What is alike and what is different about the way the two birds below use structural adaptations to find their food?

central shaft——→

4. [CHALLENGE] The large central shaft in a bird's feather is hollow. What advantage might this give to the bird?

finch

owl

Extinction

A species cannot survive if it does not adapt to changes or move to a new environment. Some species cannot move to a new environment. For example, plants cannot pull themselves up by the roots and walk to another place. Also, the changes may be so widespread that there is nowhere left to move. If a species does not adapt to harmful changes or move away from them, its population will decrease. When a species has no members left that are alive, it becomes an **extinct species.**

The dodo was a flightless bird that survived well on an island until sailors brought other animals into its environment. The birds could not defend themselves or fly to safety. They became extinct around 1680.

Behavioral Adaptations

Were you born knowing how to build a house? That is impossible! Atlantic ghost crabs, though, are born knowing how to dig deep holes in the sandy beaches where they live. This behavior is due to genes passed from parent to offspring.

Behavioral adaptations are inherited behaviors that help animals survive. Behavioral adaptations are sometimes called instincts. They affect how an animal behaves around other animals. Some animals, like the ghost crab, have an instinct to burrow into the ground to hide from predators, such as shore birds.

Not all behaviors are instincts. Some behaviors are learned by trial and error or as a result of training. For example, lion cubs learn to hunt by watching their parents and other animals. A lion cub learns to pounce on its prey by pouncing on its mother's twitching tail. When a zebra is separated from the herd, the adult lions will chase it toward a group of lions that are hiding. The lions will then pounce on their prey. The cub learns these behaviors over time.

5. **Infer** Why might lion cubs not need to be born knowing how to hunt?

Atlantic ghost crab

Atlantic ghost crab digging a hole

6. ⊚ **Compare and Contrast** Write two differences between the digging done by an Atlantic ghost crab and the digging done by a farmer.

lion cubs playing

Seasonal Changes

In places with cold winters, there is little food for part of the year. Some animals deal with this food shortage by migrating, or moving. In spring and summer, Canada geese live in Canada and the northern United States. They migrate south to escape cold winter weather and to find food.

Another type of seasonal behavior is hibernation. Hibernation is a state of inactivity that occurs in some animals when it gets cold. These animals slow down or become inactive to conserve energy. Some mammals, reptiles, and amphibians hibernate.

7. ◎ **Cause and Effect** What effect could less winter snow have on the fur of snowshoe hares over many generations?

The snowshoe hare is brown in the summer and white in the winter. This makes it harder for predators to see it.

Got it?

8. **Hypothesize** Do you think that the speed of a change in the environment might affect whether or not a species becomes extinct? Explain.

9. **UNLOCK THE BIG ?** A hedgehog is a small mammal that is covered with sharp spines for protection. How do the offspring of a hedgehog benefit from this adaptation?

◻ **Stop!** I need help with

❚❚ **Wait!** I have a question about

▶ **Go!** Now I know

What are the life cycles of some animals?

Envision It!

This butterfly is coming out of its chrysalis. **Tell** why you think a butterfly needs a chrysalis.

Inquiry **Explore It!**

How do butterflies grow and change?

Over several weeks you will observe the life cycle of a butterfly.

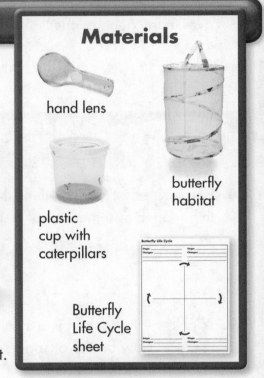

Materials

hand lens

plastic cup with caterpillars

butterfly habitat

Butterfly Life Cycle sheet

☐ 1. **Observe.** Use a hand lens.
Draw what you see.
Use the Butterfly Life Cycle sheet.

☐ 2. **Record** your observations when you see a change.
Draw the changes you see on the Butterfly Life Cycle sheet.

Explain Your Results

3. **Interpret Data** Which stages of the butterfly life cycle did you **observe**? Did you see the complete cycle? Explain.

....

....

....

Word to Know

metamorphosis

Metamorphosis

All animals have a life cycle that is a pattern of birth, growth, and death. When many animals are born, they look similar to their parents. Kittens look like small cats. Turtle hatchlings look like tiny turtles. As they grow, they get bigger. But some animals are born looking different from their parents. They develop in a series of stages. They have different forms in each stage. The process of an animal changing form during its life cycle is called **metamorphosis.** Amphibians and insects grow and develop through metamorphosis.

1. ◉ **Compare and Contrast** Use the graphic organizer to describe how a cat's growth and an insect's growth are alike and different.

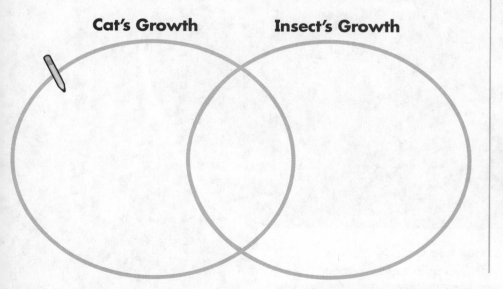

Cat's Growth   **Insect's Growth**

2. **Identify** Do the young bees shown go through metamorphosis? Explain.

....

....

....

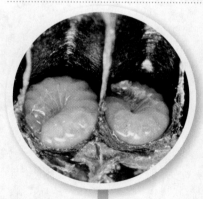

Amphibian Metamorphosis

Frogs, toads, and salamanders develop through metamorphosis. You might be familiar with the stages of the life cycle of a frog. Frogs hatch as tadpoles from eggs laid in water. Tadpoles have gills and a tail. Slowly, the tadpoles grow legs, and their tail shortens. Soon they develop lungs and stop getting oxygen through gills. Then they begin to live on land. As adults, frogs look nothing like they did when they were young.

3. **Describe** How does a frog go through metamorphosis?

....

....

5 adult

bullfrog

The adult frog looks ....
than it does in its tadpole stage.

4. Diagram The diagram numbers stages in a frog's metamorphosis. Fill in the captions to describe each stage.

1 egg

Eggs are laid in
....

2 tadpole

The tadpole has ....
and a tail.

3

The young tadpole grows legs and
its .... shortens.

4

The young tadpole develops lungs and stops getting oxygen

through its ....

129

The diagram shows the four stages in a tiger swallowtail butterfly's metamorphosis.

egg

adult

Complete Metamorphosis

Some insects develop in four stages. This type of development is called complete metamorphosis because there is a complete change from one stage to the next stage. An insect begins its development as an egg. The egg develops into a larva. The larva spends its time feeding and growing. It molts, or sheds, its outer covering a few times and then grows into a pupa. The pupa is inactive while many changes happen in its body. Once these changes are finished, the insect breaks out as an adult. It can now reproduce. Butterflies, ants, bees, flies, and beetles are some insects that go through complete metamorphosis.

5. ◉ **Compare and Contrast** How are a larva and a pupa similar? How are they different?

....

....

....

6. **Identify** Label the larva and the pupa in the diagram.

7. **Infer** During its development, a growing butterfly forms a cocoon called a chrysalis. A chrysalis is another name for the pupa of a butterfly. What does the chrysalis provide the growing butterfly?

....

....

Incomplete Metamorphosis

Insects that have three stages of development go through incomplete metamorphosis. The stages are egg, larva, and adult. In incomplete metamorphosis, the larva is called a nymph. The nymph looks similar to the adult but has no wings. Dragonflies, grasshoppers, and cockroaches go through incomplete metamorphosis.

egg → larva → adult

The diagram shows the three stages in a broad-bodied chaser dragonfly's metamorphosis.

8. **Explain** Why is a dragonfly's metamorphosis considered incomplete?

_____

_____

_____

_____

9. **Identify** (Circle) a difference you see in the body of a nymph dragonfly and an adult dragonfly.

Got it?

10. **Describe** How does a frog change during the stages in its metamorphosis?

....

....

11. **UNLOCK THE BIG ?** How do insects such as butterflies grow and change?

....

....

....

⬜ **Stop!** I need help with ....

⏸ **Wait!** I have a question about ....

▶ **Go!** Now I know ....

How do seeds grow?

Follow a Procedure

☐ **1.** Fold one paper towel. Place it in a cup. Crumple and push a second towel into the cup. Wet both towels.

☐ **2.** Place some bean seeds between the paper towels and the cup.

☐ **3. Observe** the seeds for 5 days.

Materials

paper towels

bean seeds

clear plastic cup

spray bottle with water

Inquiry Skill
Observing a process in the classroom can help you understand what happens when the process occurs in nature.

☐ **4. Record Data**   Draw how the seeds look on each day.
Use the chart to record your drawings.

Seed Changes				
Day 1	**Day 2**	**Day 3**	**Day 4**	**Day 5**

Analyze and Conclude

5. Draw Conclusions   How did the seeds change as they grew?

....

....

6. UNLOCK THE BIG ?   What made it possible for the seeds to grow?

....

....

....

Zoologist

As a zoologist, your job would be to study animals. Zoologists might study different animal characteristics, such as the behaviors or the needs of animals. Often a zoologist picks a specific type of animal to study. For example, an ichthyologist is a zoologist who studies fish, and an ornithologist is a zoologist who studies birds.

Some zoologists work as zookeepers to help keep animals healthy. Other zoologists might work in museums. Still others work at universities where they might teach or do research in labs.

Among other things, zoologists study animal adaptations to specific environments. A zoologist usually has a degree from a university. If you would like to study animals, the field of zoology might be for you!

If you were a zoologist, what animal behavior would you like to learn about?

....

....

....

....

An ichthyologist might study the habits of flying fish.

An ornithologist might study the habits of doves.

Vocabulary Smart Cards

exoskeleton
adaptation
extinct species
metamorphosis

Play a Game!

Cut out the Vocabulary Smart Cards.

Work with a partner. Choose a Vocabulary Smart Card. Do not show the word to your partner.

Say clues to help your partner guess what your word is.

Have your partner repeat with another Vocabulary Smart Card.

135

metamorphosis

metamorfosis

exoskeleton

exoesqueleto

adaptation

adaptación

extinct species

especie extinta

a hard skeleton on the outside of the body of some animals

Write the prefix of this word.

....

Write what the prefix means.

....

esqueleto duro en el exterior del cuerpo de algunos animales

---

the process of an animal changing form during its life cycle

What is the word root of this word?

....

....

....

proceso en el cual cambia la forma de un animal durante su ciclo de vida

---

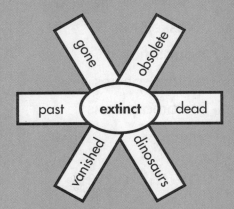

Make a Word Wheel!

Choose a vocabulary word and write it in the center of the Word Wheel graphic organizer. Write synonyms or related words on the wheel spokes.

---

a characteristic that increases an organism's ability to survive and reproduce in its environment

Write an example.

....

....

....

característica que aumenta la capacidad de un organismo de sobrevivir y reproducirse en su medio ambiente

---

....

....

....

....

....

....

....

---

a species that has no more members of its kind alive

Write an example.

....

....

....

....

especie de la que ya no queda vivo ningún miembro

....

....

....

....

....

....

Study Guide

REVIEW THE BIG ? How do plants and animals grow and change?

Lesson 1

What are some physical structures in living things?

- Sometimes the structures of organisms can be similar even though the organisms are different.
- Structures can be different even if they do similar jobs.

Lesson 2

How do adaptations help plants?

- Plants have adaptations to survive in different environments.
- Physical characteristics, such as leaf shape, help plants survive.
- Life cycle variations help plants survive.

Lesson 3

How do adaptations help animals?

- Physical and behavioral adaptations help animals survive.
- A species may become extinct if it cannot adapt to changes.
- Some behavioral characteristics are learned, and others are inherited.

Lesson 4

What are the life cycles of some animals?

- Metamorphosis is the process of an animal changing form during its life cycle.
- The stages of a frog's metamorphosis are egg, tadpole, and adult.

SavvasRealize.com

Lesson 1

What are some physical structures in living things?

1. **Vocabulary** A(n) _____ is a hard skeleton on the outside of some animals that gives structure and protection.
   A. internal skeleton
   B. exoskeleton
   C. vascular tissue
   D. system

2. **Compare** How are fish gills similar to plant stomata?

....

....

Lesson 2

How do adaptations help plants?

3. **Infer** The apricot tree produces fruit for two to three months out of the year. What can you tell about the climate where apricot trees grow?

....

....

....

Lesson 3

How do adaptations help animals?

4. **Predict** An individual animal may respond to a sudden storm by
   A. developing waterproof feathers.
   B. developing fins.
   C. hiding under a tree.
   D. building a nest.

5. **Justify** Are all behavioral adaptations learned? Explain.

....

....

....

6. Name one physical characteristic of the elephant in the picture below. List three purposes you think it might serve.

....

....

....

Lesson 4

What are the life cycles of some animals?

7. Identify Which stage in a frog's metamorphosis does the picture show?

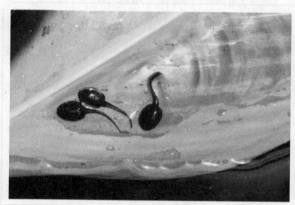

8. ◉ **Compare and Contrast** How are the stages of complete and incomplete metamorphosis alike and different?

Insects develop through metamorphosis. Some insects, such as butterflies, grow in four stages: egg, larva, pupa, and adult. Other insects, such as dragonflies, grow in three stages: egg, nymph, and adult.

....

....

....

9. APPLY THE BIG ? **How do plants and animals grow and change?**

A moth is growing inside this cocoon. How does a moth grow and change from egg to adult?

....

....

....

....

....

....

....

....

Benchmark Practice

Read each question and choose the best answer.

1 **Which of the following is a behavioral adaptation?**

A the strong wings of a hummingbird
B the way bees work together
C the green, slimy skin of a frog
D the long beak of a hummingbird

2 **What is an example of an organism adapting to a seasonal change?**

A Canada geese migrating south for the winter
B the snowshoe hare changing its fur color from white to brown in spring
C a chipmunk hibernating until spring
D all of the above

3 **Which of the following is an example of a structural adaptation of the animal shown below?**

A It builds burrows.
B It has spines.
C It hunts at night.
D It lives alone.

4 **What are the stages in the metamorphosis of a frog?**

A egg, larva, adult
B egg, tadpole, adult
C egg, larva, pupa, adult
D egg, tadpole, pupa, adult

5 **Choose an animal and describe its appearance and behavior. In your description, distinguish between traits that this animal inherited and those that the animal learned.**

....

....

....

....

....

....

....

....

Charles Darwin

Charles Darwin was born in England in 1809. As a boy, Charles wanted to become a naturalist and study animals, plants, and rocks. When he was 22 years old, he was invited on a long expedition on a ship called the *Beagle*. The *Beagle* took five years to travel around the world, stopping in places such as the Galápagos Islands.

Darwin worked hard collecting animals and plants and trying to understand why there were so many kinds. Twenty years after his trip, Darwin published his most famous work, *On the Origin of Species by Means of Natural Selection*. In this book, he proposed that species can change and adapt to their changing environments over a long time.

Since Darwin's time, many fossil and genetic discoveries have supported his theory. Today, biologists use this theory to answer questions such as how species are related and how germs become resistant to antibiotics.

These finches have different beaks for eating different kinds of food.

UNLOCK THE BIG ?

We know that climate can change over millions of years. How might Darwin's theory help explain the white fur of polar bears?

How can a PREDATOR also be PREY?

Ecosystems

△ **Try It!** What is in a local ecosystem?

△ **STEM Activity** Let It Self-Water!

Lesson 1 How do plants get and use energy?

Lesson 2 How do organisms interact in ecosystems?

Lesson 3 How do ecosystems change?

Lesson 4 How do humans impact ecosystems?

△ **Investigate It!** What heats up air?

Life Science

△ **Apply It!** How can salt affect the hatching of brine shrimp eggs?

Chapter 4

The little blue heron, the frog, and the plants all live in the same swamp. Many different living things interact with one another in this ecosystem.

△ **Predict** If the little blue heron left this swamp, what would happen to the frogs there?

....

....

 How do living things interact with their environments?

What is in a local ecosystem?

An ecosystem has living and nonliving parts.
Even the area around your school is an ecosystem.

☐ **1.** Choose an area at your school. Make an Ecosystem Map.

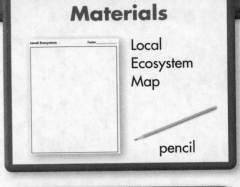

Materials

Local Ecosystem Map

pencil

Inquiry Skill   You use what you observe to **infer**.

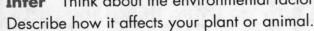

☐ **2.** Choose an environmental factor. Circle the factor you will study.

| sunlight | temperature | sound level | air movement |
| moisture | leaf litter | plant cover | human activity |

☐ **3.** Make a + on your map to show 3 areas where the environmental factor is high. Make a – to show 3 areas where the environmental factor is low.

☐ **4. Observe** and describe a plant or animal you observe in one area.

Local Ecosystem Observations

Draw	Describe

Explain Your Results

5. **Infer**   Think about the environmental factor you chose. Describe how it affects your plant or animal.

_____

_____

Main Idea and Details

- The **main idea** is the most important idea in a reading selection.
- Supporting **details** tell more about the main idea.

Wetlands

A wetland is partly covered with water or is flooded at least part of the year. There are many kinds of wetlands, including swamps, marshes, and bogs. A swamp has many trees and bushes. Plants such as water lilies, vines, and cypress trees grow in some swamps. Animals such as alligators, turtles, frogs, and insects may live there too.

Another kind of wetland is a marsh, which is grassy with no trees. Muskrats and wading birds often live in this kind of wetland. Bogs are another kind of wetland. Bogs contain peat, a material formed by decomposing plants that floats on the water. Evergreen trees, shrubs, and moss are some plants that grow in bogs. Moose, deer, and lynx are some animals that live near bogs.

muskrat in wetlands

Practice It!

Complete the graphic organizer below to show the main idea and details in the example paragraph.

Main Idea

Detail   **Detail**   **Detail**

Let It Self-Water!

Many people struggle with the problem of keeping houseplants watered when they are away on vacation. A family going on a five-day vacation has asked you to design a device that will automatically water an indoor plant.

Identify the Problem

☐ **1.** What problem will your self-watering system help solve? _____

_____

_____

☐ **2.** Why is there a need to solve this problem? _____

_____

_____

Do Research

Go to the materials station(s). Pick up each material one at a time.

☐ **3. Examine** the peat moss. Pick it up and hold it. Squeeze it over the bowl. What do you observe? _____

_____

☐ **4.** Look at the paper towels. **Describe** how they are interacting with water.

_____

_____

Leave the materials where they are.

☐ **5.** What are your design constraints? _____

_____

_____

Develop Possible Solutions

☐ **6. Describe** two ways that you could combine some of the materials to solve the problem.

_____

_____

Choose One Solution

☐ **7. Draw and describe** your device and how you will build it.

_____

_____

_____

☐ **8. List** the materials you will need.

_____

_____

_____

Design and Construct a Prototype

Gather your materials as well as a potted plant, a metric ruler, and water. **Build** your device.

☐ **9. Record** the details of your prototype. ✎ _____

_____

_____

_____

Test the Prototype

Test your self-watering system by setting it up as if you were leaving on a five-day vacation.

☐ **10. Observe** your plant and its soil every day for five days. **Record** the condition of the soil as well as the degree of wilting in the plant using these ratings:

Condition of soil: dry, medium, moist

Condition of plant: no wilting, moderate wilting, high degree of wilting

	Device 1 Soil Condition	Device 1 Plant Condition	Redesigned Device 2 Soil Condition	Redesigned Device 2 Plant Condition
Day 1				
Day 2				
Day 3				
Day 4				
Day 5				

Communicate Results

☑ **11.** After five days, **analyze your data** and summarize how well your system worked. Rate your self-watering system on a scale of 1-3 where: 1 — your device did not work at all, 2 — your device worked moderately well, 3 — your device worked very well. Share your summary and ratings with your classmates.

_____

_____

_____

_____

_____

Evaluate and Redesign

☑ **12.** What changes could you make to your design to make your device work better?

_____

_____

_____

_____

_____

☑ **13. Redesign** your system and run another test. **Compare your new results** with your initial test. Have your results improved? Explain._____

_____

_____

_____

_____

How do plants get and use energy?

How do you think plants get the energy they need to live?

my PLANET DIARY

DISCOVERY

What comes to mind when you think of corn? You might think of corn on the cob, popcorn, or cornbread. However, corn is not just food. Scientists have discovered that it can also be used to produce a liquid fuel called ethanol. Ethanol is a type of biofuel. Biofuels are fuels made from living things. Other plants used to make biofuel are soy and sugarcane. Biofuels are more environmentally friendly than other fuels such as gasoline. Because gasoline-powered vehicles produce air pollution, using biofuels instead might help preserve Earth's environment.

How do you think biofuels might affect your life?

....

....

....

I will know how plants use the energy from the sun.

Words to Know

photosynthesis
cellular respiration

Plants and Energy

What is your favorite type of green salad? You might like the one made of spinach. Perhaps you choose iceberg lettuce or crispy romaine lettuce. Spinach, iceberg lettuce, and romaine lettuce are all types of leaves. A leaf is a major plant part. Unlike animals, plants make their own food. Most of the food that a plant makes is made in the plant's leaves.

When you eat spinach or lettuce leaves, your body is getting energy from the plant. Your body cells need this energy to carry out its many functions. The energy you get comes from the energy stored in leaves. Where did the leaf get this energy? It came from the sun in the form of sunlight. The sun is Earth's primary energy source. The plant used the sunlight's energy to make food that the plant uses to grow. This form of energy passes on to you when you eat the leaves.

cabbage

1. **Identify** Where does the stored energy in these cabbage leaves come from?

....

2. **Explain** How does a plant get its food?

....

....

Cells and Tissues in Leaves

Leaves are organs made of cells and tissues. The cells of each kind of tissue are similar and do specific jobs. The outside layer of cells on the top and bottom of a leaf make up the *epidermis tissue.* The cells in epidermis tissue are flat and help protect the plant. Most leaves also have tiny openings called pores in the epidermis tissue. These pores can open and close. This action allows water vapor, carbon dioxide, and oxygen to enter and exit the leaf.

The cells under the top layer of epidermis are tall, thin, and tightly packed. This layer of tissue is the palisade tissue. Food is made in the cells of the palisade tissue. The cells above the lower layer of epidermis tissue have spaces that air can pass through. Therefore, this part of the inner tissue is called *spongy tissue.*

Very thin, long cells that form hollow tubes make up *veins.* Veins carry food and water through the plant to all the other plant parts. The diagram shows the three tissues that make up a leaf.

3. Infer The lines in this leaf are its vessels. What part of your body can best be compared to a plant's vessels?

Do the math!

Analyze Data

Water evaporates from the leaves of plants during the day. The graph shows how much water a certain plant loses during a day.

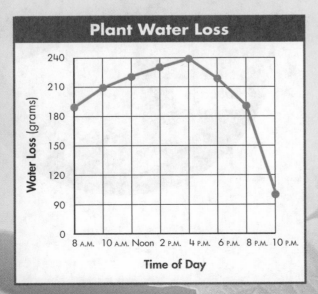

1 During what part of the day did the plant lose the most water? the least water?

2 What might explain the pattern of water loss shown?

4. Identify Look at the cross-section of a leaf. Fill in each blank with the correct leaf tissue.

A cross-section of a leaf

The outside layer of flat cells make up the

....

....

Food is made in the cells of the

....

....

The cells in ....

.... have

spaces between them that air can pass through.

....

contain very thin, long cells that form hollow tubes.

Photosynthesis

Most plants make food in their leaves. Leaves and other plant parts are green because their cells contain chlorophyll. Chlorophyll is stored in the chloroplasts of plant cells. It is a green substance that traps energy from the sun. The sun's energy is transformed into chemical energy in the food that plants make.

Photosynthesis is the process that plants use to make sugar for food. During photosynthesis, plants use the energy from sunlight, carbon dioxide from the air, and water absorbed by plant roots to make sugar. Oxygen is also released. The sun's energy is transformed and then stored in the sugar. The process can be summarized in this equation:

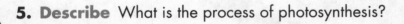

$$\text{carbon dioxide} + \text{water} \xrightarrow[\text{chlorophyll}]{\text{light energy}} \text{sugar} + \text{oxygen}$$

The equation shows that plants release oxygen during photosynthesis. Most organisms, including animals, could not live without the oxygen and sugar that plants make.

chloroplasts

5. **Describe** What is the process of photosynthesis?

....

....

....

6. **Fill in the blank** Look at the illustration of the chloroplast. Fill in each blank of the captions with the correct word or words.

7. CHALLENGE How do trees that lose their leaves in the fall survive all winter?

....

....

Sunlight

Chlorophyll in the chloroplasts absorbs sunlight. This is the source of energy used to make sugar

from ....

and ....

Carbon Dioxide

Carbon dioxide from the air enters the chloroplast. It enters the plant through the small holes in the bottom of the leaves.

Water

Water enters the chloroplast. Most often it is the water absorbed from the soil by the roots.

When the chloroplast absorbs more sunlight, more .... can be made.

During photosynthesis,

....

is released. The plant releases some of this oxygen through holes in the bottom of the leaves.

The large drawing is a chloroplast. The structures that look like stacked plates contain chlorophyll. The small inset is an image of these plates from a microscope.

Respiration

Plant cells need energy to do their work and grow. They use the food they make to get this energy. The process by which cells break down sugar to release energy is called **cellular respiration.**

During cellular respiration, sugar starts to be broken down through a series of chemical reactions. This process happens mostly in the mitochondria. Mitochondria are present in every cell and are the cell's power producers. The process makes carbon dioxide and water and releases energy. The process of cellular respiration can be summarized by this equation:

sugar + oxygen = energy + carbon dioxide + water

8. **Identify** Label the diagram to show the materials needed for and the products of cellular respiration.

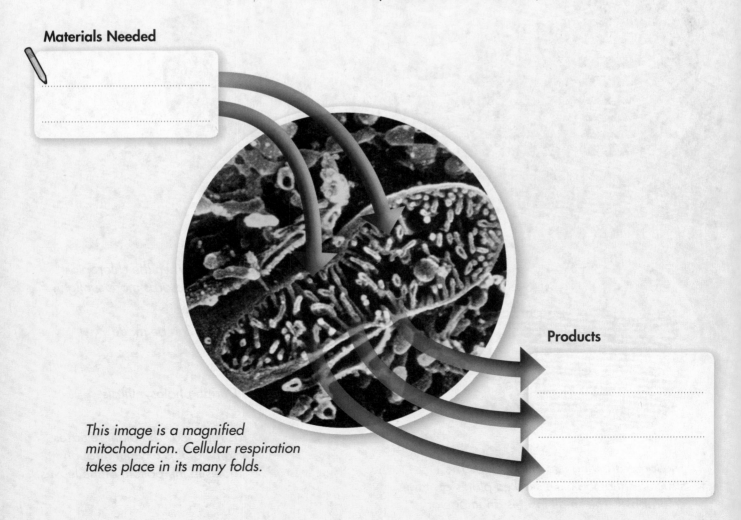

Materials Needed

Products

This image is a magnified mitochondrion. Cellular respiration takes place in its many folds.

Plants can make more sugar than they need. This extra sugar is changed into other kinds of sugars and starches that are stored in the plant. When plants need energy, they can break down the stored food to release its energy.

9. ⊙ **Compare and Contrast** Complete the chart to compare the processes of photosynthesis and respiration.

Questions	Photosynthesis	Respiration
What is used?		
What is produced?		

Got it?

10. **Identify** What is Earth's primary energy source?

....

11. **Describe** What are the processes of photosynthesis and cellular respiration in plants?

....

....

....

◻ **Stop!** I need help with ....

❚❚ **Wait!** I have a question about ....

▶ **Go!** Now I know ....

Lesson 2

How do organisms interact in ecosystems?

Envision It!

Tell how these organisms might interact in this ecosystem.

Inquiry | **Explore It!**

What do some molds need to grow?

Be careful! Wear gloves. Wash your hands when finished.

Materials

moldy strawberry

plastic cup with water

2 plastic bags

dropper   latex-free gloves

hand lens

foil square

bread slice (without preservatives)

☐ **1.** Rub some mold from a strawberry onto a piece of bread and onto a piece of foil.

☐ **2.** Put the bread in a bag. Put the foil in the other bag. Place 10 drops of water onto the 2 places you rubbed the mold.

☐ **3.** Place the sealed bags in a warm, dark place for 4 days.

☐ **4.** **Communicate** What did you **observe** in each bag?

....

....

Explain Your Results

5. **Draw a Conclusion** Why did the mold grow only in one bag?

....

....

....

I will know the different ways that organisms interact in an ecosystem.

Words to Know

predator	consumer
prey	decomposer
producer	food chain
	food web

Interactions in Ecosystems

Ecosystems are made up of living and nonliving things. The living things in ecosystems interact with each other in a variety of ways. Some organisms help one another meet their needs. Some organisms may eat other organisms and get energy or nutrients from them. Some organisms compete with one another for space or food.

In some ecosystems, birds may flock near larger animals. The animals may disturb insects in high grasses. As the insects fly or jump away, the birds are able to catch them for food. The birds are helped by this relationship, but the larger animal is not affected.

Some animals in an ecosystem must hunt other organisms to fill their energy needs. In this type of interaction, only one organism is helped. An animal that hunts and eats another animal is called a **predator.** Any animal that is hunted by others for food is called **prey.** The predator gets energy from the prey when the predator eats the prey.

1. **Classify** Use the picture below to classify the animals as predator or prey. Explain their roles.

....

....

....

....

....

....

These plants make their own food. They are producers.

The moose eats the plants. Moose are herbivores.

Bears are omnivores. They eat plants and animals.

Energy Roles in Ecosystems

Perhaps the most common interaction in an ecosystem occurs when organisms get energy. All organisms need energy to live. How an organism gets its energy determines its energy role. An organism's energy role makes up part of its niche in an ecosystem. Each organism in an ecosystem fills the energy role of producer, consumer, or decomposer.

Producers

Plants and some other organisms are producers. **Producers** make their own food for energy. Most producers use energy from the sun to make food. Some producers use chemicals from their environment for energy. Producers either use the energy to grow or store it for later. The food they make is often a source of energy for other organisms.

Consumers

Many organisms depend on producers to get energy. **Consumers** are organisms that cannot make their own food. They get energy from producers or other consumers. All animals and some microorganisms are consumers.

There are several kinds of consumers. They are classified by what they eat. Herbivores, such as moose, eat only plants. Carnivores eat only other animals. One example of a carnivore is a lion. Omnivores eat both plants and animals. Black bears are omnivores.

Some carnivores feed on dead animals. These consumers are called *scavengers*. Vultures and hyenas are two examples of scavengers.

2. **Give an Example** Write two examples of consumers. Tell whether they are herbivores, omnivores, carnivores, or scavengers.

....

....

....

....

Decomposers

Producers and consumers take in nutrients from the environment as they use energy and grow. Organisms also take in gases and water from the environment. They release waste matter (gases, liquids, or solids) back into the environment. **Decomposers** are organisms that get their energy by breaking down wastes and dead organisms. During this process, decomposers return materials to an ecosystem. In turn, other organisms reuse these materials for their own needs. Most decomposers are too small to see without a microscope.

3. **Classify** Read the caption to the right about the organisms shown. Use the key to label the organisms.

> **Key**
> **C** = consumer   **P** = producer   **D** = decomposer

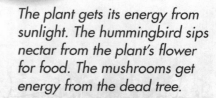

The plant gets its energy from sunlight. The hummingbird sips nectar from the plant's flower for food. The mushrooms get energy from the dead tree.

These decomposers are too small to be seen without a microscope. They are breaking down the dead leaf.

Lightning Lab

You in the Food Chain
Think about a fresh food you ate or drank yesterday, such as an apple or a glass of milk. Make a food chain to show the path of energy from sunlight to you.

Food Chains

Energy passes through an ecosystem when food is eaten. This energy often begins as the sunlight that plants use to make food. The energy can take many different paths in an ecosystem. This movement of energy through an ecosystem can be shown in food chains. A **food chain** is a series of steps by which energy moves from one type of living thing to another. The shortest food chains involve only a plant and a decomposer. Other food chains involve a carnivore or an omnivore too. Arrows on a food chain show the path in which energy moves.

4. Fill in the Blanks Write a word that best describes each part of the Prairie Food Chain diagram below.

Prairie Food Chain

Grass is an example of a

....

Deer eat grass. They are

....

Coyotes eat deer. They are

....

5. ◉ **Sequence** Water oak trees are a source of food for termites. Black bears often look in rotting logs for insects such as termites to eat. Make a food chain for these organisms.

Food Webs

Relationships among organisms in an ecosystem can be complicated. There are many food chains in an ecosystem, but a food chain can only describe one way energy flows in an ecosystem. To see how these food chains are all connected in an ecosystem, you can use a food web. A **food web** is a diagram that combines many food chains into one picture. Like a food chain, a food web uses arrows to show the energy relationships among organisms.

6. ◉ **Main Idea and Details** <u>Underline</u> the main idea in the paragraph about food chains. (Circle) the supporting details.

7. (Circle) Use different-colored crayons to show two food chains in this food web.

This food web shows the complex flow of energy in a salt marsh ecosystem.

Roles in Ecosystems

Every organism in an ecosystem has a niche, or role in that ecosystem. A niche includes the type of food the organism takes in, how it gets its food, and which other species use the organism as food. An organism may compete for the things it needs. Plants may compete for sunlight, soil, or water. Animals may compete for territory, water, light, food, or mates. For example, male black bears will compete with each other for territory and mates. Rabbits, mice, and other animals of a desert community compete with one another for plants to eat. An animal that cannot compete may die or be forced to move away.

8. **Infer** Kudzu is a vine that quickly grows and covers other plants. What is one resource for which kudzu competes with other plants?

....

kudzu

Do the math!

Read a Graph

The graph shows how the population sizes of a hunter, such as an owl, and the animal it hunts might change over time. Use the graph to answer these questions.

1. Which is a reasonable estimate for the difference between the greatest and the least number of hunters?

   A. 5   **B.** 16   **C.** 22   **D.** 40

2. What happens after the hunter's population becomes greater than the hunted animal's population?

   A. This never happens.

   B. The hunter's population decreases to zero.

   C. The hunter's population decreases.

   D. The hunted animal's population increases.

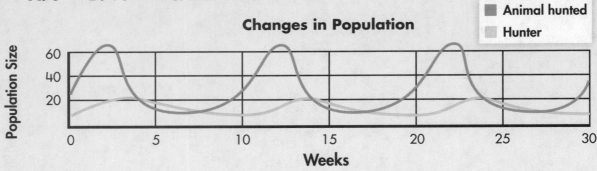

Changes in Population

Legend: ■ Animal hunted ■ Hunter

Symbiosis

A long-term relationship between two different organisms is called symbiosis. One organism is always helped. The other organism might be harmed, helped, or not affected. A *parasite* is an organism that lives on or inside of another organism. Parasites take nutrients away from the organisms where they live, which harms organisms.

In other relationships, both organisms are helped. For example, the cleaner shrimp eats parasites from the eel's mouth. The shrimp gets food and the eel keeps its teeth clean and free of parasites.

9. CHALLENGE Think about the interaction between bees and apple trees. How is this an example of symbiosis?

....

....

moray eel with cleaner shrimp

Got it?

10. Compare and Contrast How are food chains and food webs alike and different?

....

....

11. **Describe** What are the roles of producers, consumers, and decomposers in a food chain?

....

....

Stop! I need help with ....

Wait! I have a question about ....

Go! Now I know ....

How do ecosystems change?

Envision It!

Tell what benefit this fallen tree might have for other organisms in the forest.

MY PLANET DIARY

The first sign the fisherman saw was smoke rising from the ocean along the southern coast of Iceland. Was it a ship on fire? No, it was Surtsey, a volcanic island, being born on November 15, 1963.

At first, Surtsey was bare. But soon, life began to colonize the new land. Insects arrived early. Mosses, lichens, and then more complex plants established themselves. Birds nested on the island, and migrating birds stopped there. Seals basked on its shores. The island is now a nature reserve and has been named a World Heritage site.

Surtsey covers an area of about 3 square kilometers.

How might plants have arrived on Surtsey?

....

....

I will know how
environments change
and that some animals
and plants survive those
changes.

Words to Know

environment
competition

Environmental Changes

All organisms live in particular environments where
their needs are met. An **environment** is all of the
conditions surrounding an organism. Environments may
be hot or cold and on land or in water.

Environments change naturally as resources change.
For example, a population of millipedes lives in an
environment with dead plant matter. As the population
grows, it needs more food, water, and living space. As
these resources decrease, each millipede will have less
food, water, and space. Some millipedes will die or move
away. More resources will be available for the remaining
millipedes. The population will grow, and the cycle will
start again. Organisms must change to take advantage
of new opportunities and protect themselves from new
dangers in a changed environment.

1. **Explain** Puddles like this may be home to frogs, fish,
worms, or shrimp. Which of these animals might be able
to survive after the puddle is dry? Why?

....

....

*This puddle has been drying up for some time,
and the mud around it is cracking as it dries.*

2. ⊙ **Cause and Effect**
Use the graphic organizer
to list one cause and one
effect from the text.

Cause

....

....

Effect

....

....

....

Very slowly, the orange lichens growing on this rock are helping break down the rock to form new soil.

At-Home Lab

Long Ago
Work with an adult. Find out what your region was like 10 years ago. What was it like 100 years ago? What was it like 1,000 years ago? Discuss how your region has changed.

Slow Changes

Sometimes environments change very slowly. For example, the climate in a region may become drier and drier over thousands of years. This has happened in the Sahara, which has had both wet and dry periods in the past.

Seasons change slowly every year. This gives animals time to grow winter fur. Plants have time to grow new leaves for the summer.

The continents also change their position over millions of years. For example, Antarctica used to be much closer to the equator, and much warmer.

Rocks are slowly broken down by the weather and by plants and animals. They become part of the soil.

Fast Changes

Hurricanes, floods, and fires, along with volcanic eruptions and earthquakes, are natural events that can quickly change the environment. A hurricane's strong winds can rip up trees and flatten plants. Heavy rains and huge waves can flood a coastal community. When lightning strikes a tree, it can start a forest fire that burns almost everything in its path.

These rapid changes may force species to leave the area because the resources they need are no longer available.

3. **Underline** two examples of slow environmental changes. **Circle** two examples of fast changes.

4. **Give an Example** What is another type of fast environmental change?

A volcano can quickly destroy or bury many organisms, but it can also cover the soil with nutrients that other organisms can use.

Changes Caused by Organisms

Organisms themselves may alter their environment as they feed, grow, and build their homes. For example, locusts are insects that travel in large groups called swarms. The members of these large swarms can quickly eat all the plants in large fields and destroy farm crops. After locusts pass through, an area that was green and full of plants will look dead and bare.

Plants also cause changes. In fact, plants affect the quality of the air for the entire planet. They absorb carbon dioxide from the air and release oxygen back into the atmosphere.

A swarm of locusts can be many kilometers long and eat tons of plant matter.

5. Suggest What kind of animal might benefit from a locust swarm?

....

....

Changes Caused by Humans

Humans are one of the most important causes of environmental change. We change the land to plant crops, build dams to get energy, fish to get food, and clear forests to get construction materials. We change the environment when we build buildings and roads, and when we burn fuel.

There are many ways in which we can reduce the impact of human activity on the environment. For example, tunnels have been built in some places with busy traffic so that animals can cross from one side of the road to the other without getting hit by cars.

6. Classify Look at the picture of a farm on this page. What parts of this environment probably were not there before people arrived?

....

Farming often requires flat land with no trees or rocks.

Adapting to Changes

Changes that are harmful for some organisms may be beneficial for others. A forest fire destroys trees and bushes that help protect the soil from being washed away by rainwater. In addition, a forest fire adds smoke and carbon dioxide to the atmosphere and destroys the habitats of many animals. However, a forest fire may also help organisms in a forest. A forest fire clears away dead and dying plant matter, making room for new plants to grow. It also returns nutrients to the soil in the form of ashes.

In any environment, resources are limited. The struggle of organisms for the same limited resources is called **competition.** Organisms are more likely to survive if they are adapted to compete for resources.

7. **Explain** How can competition affect a group of organisms in an environment?

....

....

8. **Fill in the Blank** Look at this forest scene. Write the missing words in the captions that are incomplete.

Birds and other fast animals can easily escape the flames.

Some seeds only start to grow when there is smoke.

The growing parts of grasses are underground. They can quickly grow back after a fire. This helps them in the .... for nutrients.

Some plants store food in tuber roots. The food is used to regrow burned stems and leaves.

Some trees, such as the Table Mountain pine, have sealed cones that only open with the heat of a fire.

The thick bark of the sequoia tree protects it from the fire. This bark is an adaptation that helps the tree survive in its _____.

9. **Infer** Some trees lose their lower branches before there is a fire. How might this help the tree survive during a fire?

_____
_____
_____
_____
_____

Slow animals, such as the mole, can survive a fire if they live underground.

Resurrection plants can survive very dry seasons because they can dry up without dying. The plant below is the same plant as above, only one day after being watered.

Survival

In any species of plant or animal there are differences between individuals. A plant that has deeper roots than other plants may be able to reach deeper into the soil to get water. An animal that runs a little faster than others of its kind has a better chance of surviving an attack by a predator. Even a small advantage can help a plant or animal survive. Only the individuals that survive will be able to reproduce and pass along their beneficial characteristics to their offspring.

10. Infer How do you think the environment of a resurrection plant might change over time?

....

....

Do the math!

Subtracting Fractions

When subtracting fractions from a whole, use equivalent fractions.

Example

A forest fire destroys $\frac{1}{3}$ of a forest. If another $\frac{1}{4}$ of the forest area burns, what fraction of the forest is left unburned?

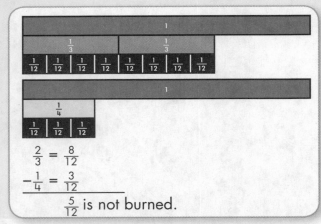

$$\frac{2}{3} = \frac{8}{12}$$
$$-\frac{1}{4} = \frac{3}{12}$$
$$\frac{5}{12} \text{ is not burned.}$$

1 One year, $\frac{1}{2}$ of a sea turtle population could not find nest space on a beach. The next year, another $\frac{1}{3}$ of the population relocated. What fraction of the turtle population is left?

Work area

The wood frog can survive the winter because its body can be frozen without killing the frog.

11. **CHALLENGE** What do you think might help the wood frog stay alive when it is frozen?

....

....

....

Got it?

12. Decide Do you think plants and animals can adapt more easily to slow changes or fast changes? Explain.

....

....

13. **UNLOCK THE BIG ?** Think about what you learned in this lesson. Give an example of how a change in the environment can affect the way living things interact.

....

....

⬜ **Stop!** I need help with ....

⏸ **Wait!** I have a question about ....

▶ **Go!** Now I know ....

How do humans impact ecosystems?

Envision It!

Tell how you think this factory might affect the environment.

Inquiry Explore It!

Which materials break down fastest in soil?

Materials

water

4 plastic straws

plastic cup

newspaper

soil

4 plastic bags

facial tissue

foam square

plastic wrap

☐ **1.** Put a cup of soil into each of 4 plastic bags. Add water to dampen the soil.

☐ **2.** Place a piece of tissue into one bag. Insert a straw at one edge and seal. Repeat with the plastic wrap, newspaper, and foam.

☐ **3.** Label each bag. Place bags in a warm, dark place for 1 week.

Be careful! Wear gloves. Wash your hands when finished.

Explain Your Results

4. Record how each material changed after 1 week.

....

....

5. Infer Why is it important to recycle materials? Explain how one of these materials can be recycled.

....

....

I will know how people can affect the environment and change ecosystems.

Words to Know

pollution
conservation

People Change Ecosystems

Organisms interact and can change their environments. Unlike most other organisms, people can change large parts of the environment. Changing the environment can upset the balance in ecosystems. People may cause pollution. People also change their environments by bringing new plants or animals into an ecosystem. They may also hunt and fish too much.

Pollution

Any substance that damages the environment is called **pollution.** Pollution can affect the air, water, and land. Cars and factories put gases that cause harm into the air. Chemicals that people use may end up in rivers and in the ocean. People also make trash. Some of it is dumped in landfills and then covered with soil. If the trash does not break down, it can cause pollution.

1. **Infer** Describe how chemicals dumped in a river might affect the organisms living in it.

....

....

2. **Hypothesize** What are three other items that should not be placed in trash and dumped in landfills?

....

....

....

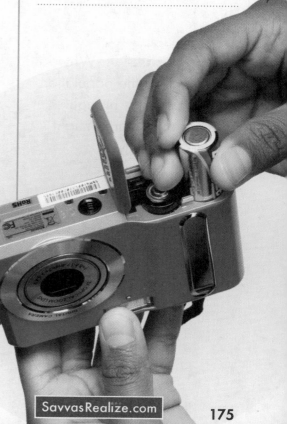

Batteries contain metals that can harm the environment if the batteries are not disposed of properly.

3. Infer Describe how these zebra mussels might affect the clam they are growing on.

....

....

....

....

4. Hypothesize Why do you think the population of a species brought into a new area might grow quickly?

....

....

....

....

....

Nonnative Species

People may bring new plants and animals into ecosystems. New species often harm some populations in ecosystems. A nonnative species is a plant or animal that does not grow naturally in an ecosystem.

Zebra mussels are animals that people accidentally brought to the United States around 1988. They entered the Great Lakes attached to a ship that traveled from Russia. Once here, they spread throughout the lakes and then moved into rivers. They ate the food and took the space that other species needed. These events changed some ecosystems permanently.

Zebra-mussel populations grow quickly. These animals can cover almost any surface.

The garlic-mustard plant grew only in Europe and parts of Asia many years ago. People brought the plant to the United States to use as food and medicine. Since animals did not eat the plant, it spread quickly. Less space was left for other plants to grow. As a result, some animals had less to eat.

Garlic-mustard plants can spread over a forest floor.

Regulation and Conservation

Too much hunting or fishing can also harm the environment. Regulation puts limits on how many animals a person can hunt and fish. Regulation is one way governments practice conservation. **Conservation** is an attempt to preserve or protect an environment from harmful changes. Towns, cities, states, and the government put aside large areas for conservation. People can go to these areas to enjoy nature.

5. [CHALLENGE] Describe how fishing licenses might help regulate overfishing.

FISHING LICENSE REQUIRED

Got it?

6. **Summarize** What are the ways that people can protect the environment?

7. **Describe** What is the consequence of bringing a nonnative species into an ecosystem?

■ **Stop!** I need help with

❚❚ **Wait!** I have a question about

▶ **Go!** Now I know

What heats up air?

Living things interact with the environment. Carbon dioxide is a gas given off by organisms into the environment. In this activity, you will use fizzy antacid tablets to make carbon dioxide and to find out how it affects the atmosphere.

Follow a Procedure

☐ **1.** Label one Bag A. Label the other Bag B. Tape a thermometer inside each bag. Make sure to tape the thermometer so you can read the numbers.

☐ **2.** Add 50 ml of water to Bag A. Remove as much of the air as possible from the bag. Add 4 fizzy antacid tablets and seal the bag.

☐ **3.** The fizzy antacid in Bag A will help inflate the bag. When Bag A is done inflating, seal up Bag B with only air inside it. Make sure both bags have similar volumes.

☐ **4.** **Record** the temperature in each bag. Place them in sunlight. Check and record the temperature every 10 minutes.

Materials

water

2 resealable plastic bags

clock

graduated cylinder

masking tape

4 fizzy antacid tablets

Inquiry Skill You can **draw conclusions** based on what you learn in an experiment.

Temperature in the Bags		
Time (minutes)	**Bag A** (temperature)	**Bag B** (temperature)
0		
10		
20		
30		
40		
50		
60		

5. Plot your data on the graph. Use one color for Bag A. Use another color for Bag B.

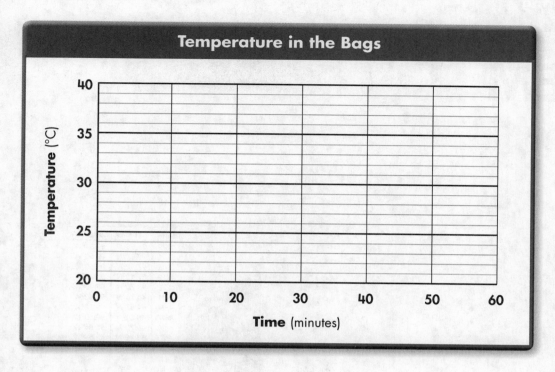

Temperature in the Bags

Temperature (°C) vs. Time (minutes)

Analyze and Conclude

6. Interpret Data Look at the two lines of your graph. How are they the same? How are they different?

....

....

....

7. UNLOCK THE BIG ? **Draw Conclusions** What does your model show you about how carbon dioxide from living things might affect the atmosphere?

....

....

....

....

....

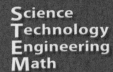

STEM

Tracking Migrations

Each year, spring signals change for many living things. These signals include longer days and warmer temperatures. During spring, many species migrate. They migrate from their winter homes in the warmer southern areas to areas farther north.

The sandhill crane is one species of migrating birds. Scientists use NASA satellites to track different sandhill crane populations. They combine this information with data about plant growth along the migratory path. The green in the image shows areas where food is available. This information shows the health of the species, the route they take, and how long migration lasts. Scientists use this information to learn about sandhill cranes. This information may help scientists protect the sandhill cranes from extinction.

Date	Latitude	Longitude
1/29	24.98°N	99.34°W
2/01	32.67°N	99.56°W
2/06	37.52°N	98.55°W
2/19	37.18°N	98.48°W
2/22	40.73°N	98.45°W
4/01	40.76°N	98.40°W
4/04	44.57°N	99.12°W
4/07	48.28°N	99.89°W
4/20	49.72°N	95.86°W
4/23	53.72°N	83.64°W
4/29	53.83°N	82.71°W

In April, sandhill cranes migrate from their southern feeding grounds to their northern breeding grounds.

Solve Look at the map and table showing the migration of a group of sandhill cranes. How far in degrees of latitude did this group of sandhill cranes travel? Show your work.

Vocabulary Smart Cards

photosynthesis
cellular respiration
predator
prey
producer
consumer
decomposer
food chain
food web
environment
competition
pollution
conservation

Play a Game!

Cut out the Vocabulary Smart Cards.

Work with a partner. Choose a Vocabulary Smart Card. Do not show the word to your partner.

Say clues to help your partner guess what your word is.

Have your partner repeat with another Vocabulary Smart Card.

prey

presa

photosynthesis

fotosíntesis

producer

productor

cellular respiration

respiración celular

consumer

consumidor

predator

predador

Interactive Vocabulary

the process in which plants make a sugar called glucose

Use a dictionary. What is the verb form of this word?

....

....

....

proceso en el que las plantas producen un azúcar llamado glucosa

---

any animal that is hunted by others for food

Write an example of this word.

....

....

cualquier animal que es cazado por otros para alimentación

---

the process by which cells break down sugar to release energy

Write a sentence using this word.

....

....

proceso mediante el cual las células descomponen el azúcar y liberan energía

---

organism that makes its own food for energy

Draw an example.

organismo que hace su propio alimento para obtener energía

---

a consumer that hunts and eats another animal

Write a sentence using the plural form of this word.

....

....

....

consumidor que atrapa a otro animal y se lo come

---

organism that cannot make its own food

Use this term in a sentence.

....

....

....

organismo que no puede hacer su propio alimento

---

water

oxygen

cellular respiration

sugar

carbon dioxide

energy

Make a Word Magnet!

Choose a vocabulary word and write it in the Word Magnet. Write words that are related to it on the lines.

conservation

conservación

environment

medio ambiente

decomposer

descomponedor

competition

competencia

food chain

cadena alimentaria

pollution

contaminación

food web

red alimentaria

organism that gets its energy by breaking down wastes and dead organisms

Draw an example.

organismo que obtiene su energía descomponiendo desechos y organismos muertos

---

all of the conditions surrounding an organism

Write a sentence using this word.

todas las condiciones que rodean a un ser vivo

---

an attempt to preserve or protect an environment from harmful changes

Write a sentence using the verb form of this word.

intento de conservar o de proteger el medio ambiente de cambios dañinos

---

a series of steps by which energy moves from one type of living thing to another

Draw an example.

serie de pasos mediante los cuales la energía pasa de un ser vivo a otro

---

the struggle among organisms for the same limited resources

Use a dictionary. Find another definition for this word.

lucha entre organismos por los mismos recursos limitados

---

a diagram that combines many food chains into one picture

Use this term in a sentence.

diagrama que combina varias cadenas alimentarias en una sola imagen

---

any substance that damages the environment

Draw an example.

cualquier sustancia que le hace daño al medio ambiente

Study Guide

REVIEW THE BIG ? How do living things interact with their environments?

Life Science

Lesson 1

How do plants get and use energy?

- Plants perform photosynthesis in leaves by using carbon dioxide, water, and sunlight to make oxygen and sugar for food.
- During cellular respiration, plants break down sugar to get energy.

Lesson 2

How do organisms interact in ecosystems?

- Food chains and food webs show the movement of energy.
- Organisms interact in ecosystems through competition, symbiosis, and predator-and-prey relationships.

Lesson 3

How do ecosystems change?

- Environments can change slowly over time or very quickly.
- Natural processes, animals, and people can change environments.
- Organisms must adapt or move to survive an environmental change.

Lesson 4

How do humans impact ecosystems?

- People may cause pollution that affects the air, water, and land.
- People may bring new species into an ecosystem that harm it.
- Too much hunting and fishing can negatively affect the environment.

SavvasRealize.com

Lesson 1

How do plants get and use energy?

1. **Describe** What is the role of chlorophyll in photosynthesis?

....

....

....

2. **Support** Use what you know about photosynthesis to support the conclusion that the sun is Earth's primary energy source.

....

....

....

Lesson 2

How do organisms interact in ecosystems?

3. ◎ **Main Idea and Details** **Underline** the main idea and (circle) the details in the following paragraph.

An organism may compete for the things it needs. Plants may compete for sunlight, soil, or water. Animals may compete for territory, water, light, food, or mates.

Lesson 3

How do ecosystems change?

4. **Vocabulary** When organisms share limited resources, there is
   A. an extra resource.
   B. competition.
   C. extinction.
   D. mutation.

5. **Analyze** How can a forest fire have both beneficial and harmful changes?

....

....

....

6. **Write About It** Describe an organism that has an adaptation that allows it to survive.

....

....

....

Do the
math!

7. In a forest, $\frac{1}{4}$ of birds' nests are blown away by high winds and $\frac{2}{5}$ are destroyed by a flood. What fraction of the birds' nests are left?

....

Lesson 4

How do humans impact ecosystems?

8. **Explain** Why must pollution be regulated?

....

....

9. **Predict** How might hunting too many rabbits affect the balance of an ecosystem?

....

....

....

....

10. **Apply** Purple loosestrife is a plant that people brought from Europe. It grows thickly in wetlands. How might this plant harm the wetlands ecosystem?

....

....

11. **APPLY THE BIG ?** **How do living things interact with their environments?**

Describe an ecosystem near you. Discuss how the living things interact. Use the terms *food chain, producer,* and *consumer.*

....

....

....

....

....

....

....

....

....

....

....

....

....

....

....

Read each question and choose the best answer.

1 Which of the following is an environmental change caused by humans?

A farm
B lichen on rocks
C heavy rain
D beaver dam

2 Which can be described as the reverse of photosynthesis?

A mitochondria
B chlorophyll
C metamorphosis
D cellular respiration

3 A nonnative plant in an ecosystem spreads quickly. This will most directly affect the native plants by

A leaving them less space.
B giving them more food.
C helping them grow.
D leaving them more sun.

4 In one ecosystem, snakes eat birds, plants make fruit, and birds eat fruit. Which is the correct food chain?

A snake → plant → bird
B bird → plant → snake
C plant → bird → snake
D snake → bird → plant

5 What is the role of this organism in a food chain?

A It breaks down wastes and dead organisms.
B It uses the sun's energy to make food.
C It eats other organisms.
D It cannot make its own food.

6 What are some benefits of a natural forest fire in an environment?

....

....

....

Create a Compost Pile

Go Green!

Food waste and yard clippings make up 24 percent of solid waste in the United States. You can help reduce this waste by putting food waste such as apple cores, stale bread, and eggshells into a compost pile.

A compost pile is a mixture of food scraps, wood products, yard trimmings, soil, and worms. The worms, which are decomposers, eat the food scraps and break them down into "worm castings," or rich, fertile soil.

Composting can be simple and fun. It can be done indoors or outdoors. To make a compost pile, start with a wood, plastic, or brick bin. Fill it with shredded cardboard or clean paper. Add water and soil. Then add some worms. Bury food scraps, tea bags, dry leaves, and grass under the paper. Avoid composting meat and dairy products. Keep the compost pile moist and turn it over every week or so. The worms and natural processes will do the rest. Soon you will have nutrient-rich soil that can be used to fertilize a garden. So the next time you finish an apple, don't put it in the trash. Compost it!

APPLY THE BIG ?

How do worms interact with a compost pile?

Materials

masking tape

5 clear plastic cups

plastic spoon

hand lens

pouring container with water

measuring cup

noniodized salt

flat toothpick

brine shrimp eggs

Inquiry Skill

You **control variables** when you make sure the conditions you are not testing remain the same. Controlling variables helps you make sure your experiment is a fair test.

How can salt affect the hatching of brine shrimp eggs?

Brine shrimp are tiny animals that live in salt water. They are in the same group of animals as crabs and lobsters.

Ask a question.

How does the amount of salt in the water affect how many brine shrimp eggs hatch?

State a hypothesis.

1. Write a **hypothesis** by circling one choice and finishing the sentence.

If brine shrimp are put in water with different amounts of salt, then the most eggs will hatch in the cup with (*a*) *no salt,* (*b*) *a low salt level,* (*c*) *a medium salt level,* (*d*) *a high salt level,* or (*e*) *a very high salt level* because

....

Identify and control variables.

2. When you conduct an **experiment,** you must change only one variable. The **variable** you change is the **independent variable.** What will you change?

....

3. The **dependent variable** is the variable you observe or measure in an experiment. What will you observe?

....

....

....

4. Controlled variables are the factors you must keep the same to have a fair test. List 3 of these factors.

....

Design your test.

5. Draw how you will set up your test.

6. List your steps in the order you will do them.

Do your test.

☐ **7.** Follow the steps you wrote.

☐ **8.** Make sure to **record** your results in the table.

Collect and record your data.

☐ **9.** Fill in the chart.

Interpret your data.

☐ 10. Analyze your data. Think about the level of salt. Think how many brine shrimp were moving after 4 days.

In which level of salt did you observe the most brine shrimp moving after 4 days?

....

....

....

State your conclusion.

11. Communicate your conclusion.
Compare your **hypothesis** with your results.
Compare your results with those of other groups.

....

....

....

....

....

....

Performance-Based Assessment

Soil Survival

Find a large clump of dry soil. If it is not dry, let it dry for a few days. Put it in a jar and add enough water to moisten it. Close the jar to keep the moisture in. After a few days, look at the soil closely.

• Are there any signs of life?

• Are there plants germinating?

• Are there small worms or insects?

Record your observations.

Animals Keeping Warm

Animals have body coverings that keep them warm in cold weather. Write a hypothesis and plan a test to see what kinds of materials best protect against cold. Wrap jars of warm water with different materials. Record how fast the water cools.

Science and Engineering Practices

1. Ask a question or define a problem.

2. Develop and use models.

3. Plan and carry out investigations.

4. Analyze and interpret data.

5. Use math and computational thinking.

6. Construct explanations or design solutions.

7. Engage in argument from evidence.

8. Obtain, evaluate, and communicate information.

Local Resources

Conduct research on how people in your local community impact the environment. Choose an issue, such as the development of land, overuse of water resources, littering and other pollution, invasive species, or conservation efforts. Consider these questions in your research:

- What are the different points of view on the issue?

- What are some possible solutions?

- How will each solution impact organisms and other resources?

- Are people using science information to make the best decisions?

- What are people doing about this issue?

- What can you do?

Write about your findings and share them with the class.

Create a Food Web Model

Choose an ecosystem, and research a food web within that ecosystem. Then create a model of the food web that includes each of the different organisms in the food web. Label the organisms.

- Which organisms are producers?

- Which are consumers?

- Which are decomposers?

You might choose to use drawings, photographs, or 3-D objects to make your model. Display your model and explain how it shows the movement of matter and energy through the ecosystem.

WHERE
did these drops
come
from?

The Water Cycle and Weather

 Try It! How can water move in the water cycle?

STEM Activity Filter It Out!

Lesson 1 What is the water cycle?

Lesson 2 What are the spheres of Earth?

Lesson 3 What is weather?

Lesson 4 How do clouds and precipitation form?

Lesson 5 What is climate?

Lesson 6 What are erosion and deposition?

Investigate It! Where is the hurricane going?

It has not rained, but after spending the night resting, this fly was covered with droplets in the morning.

 Predict Where do you think this water came from?

....

....

....

THE BIG ? How does water move through the environment?

How can water move in the water cycle?

☐ **1.** Put an ice cube in the cup.

☐ **2.** Place the cup into the bag. Seal the bag.

☐ **3.** Tape the bag to a sunny window.
Predict what will happen.

☐ **4.** **Observe** the bag. **Record** what happens.

ice cube

plastic cup

resealable
plastic bag

tape

Predictions and Observations of Changes Over Time		
Time	**Prediction**	**Observations**
After 2 hours		
After 2 days		
After 3 days		

Inquiry Skill
You can **communicate** by using drawings and labels.

Explain Your Results

5. **UNLOCK THE BIG ?** **Communicate** using a diagram of your **model.** Use arrows to show how water moved from the ice cube through the bag. Label the arrows *melting*, *evaporation*, and *condensation*.

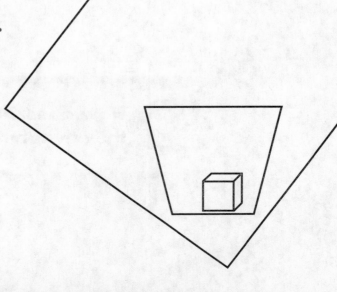

Draw Conclusions

- A good reader can put together facts to build a new idea, or a conclusion.
- Learning to **draw conclusions** can help you evaluate what you read and observe.

Fulgurite

Lightning strikes the ground about 25 million times per year in the United States alone! When lightning hits ground covered in sand, fulgurites can form. A fulgurite is a glassy formation of sand that has been melted by the heat of lightning. They are commonly found on the shores of the Atlantic Ocean and Lake Michigan.

Practice It!

Use the graphic organizer. List facts from the example paragraph and draw a conclusion.

Fact

Fact

Conclusion

fulgurite

Filter It Out!

Before water reaches the faucet at your home or school, it probably goes through an extensive cleaning process. Every city has a water purification system that removes most bacteria, viruses, metals, chemical toxins, sediments, and other impurities from the water. This makes the water safe for drinking. Your school's student council has nominated you to design a multi-layered water filtration system that will remove sediments from water.

Identify the Problem

☑ **1.** What problem will your water filter help solve? _____

_____

_____

☑ **2.** Why is there a need to solve this problem?

_____

_____

Do Research

☑ **3.** What is the source of your drinking water? _____

☑ **4.** What do you think is in the water from that source that needs to be removed in order to make it safe to drink? _____

_____

Go to the materials station(s). Pick up each material one at a time. Think about how it may or may not be useful in your design. Leave the materials where they are.

☑ **5.** What are your design constraints? _____

_____

_____

Develop Possible Solutions

☐ **6. Describe** two ways you could use some of the materials to build a water filter.

_____

_____

_____

_____

Choose One Solution

☐ **7. Draw** your water filter. **Label** all the parts. **Explain** how you will build the filter.

_____

_____

_____

☐ **8. List** the materials that you will need. _____

_____

_____

_____

Design and Construct a Prototype

Gather your materials plus a funnel, one cup of dirt, two one-liter plastic bottles, four clear plastic cups, and a beaker.

- If you need to make "dirty" water, use the funnel to pour about one cup of dirt into one of the bottles. Then, fill the rest of the bottle with water. Shake the bottle so that the dirt is suspended in the water. Pour some of the water from the bottle into one of the clear plastic cups. This is your control water.

- If you are using unpurified water from an outside source, skip the step above. Pour some of the unpurified water into one of the clear plastic cups. This will be your control.

Use the second 1-liter bottle to build your water filter. You will hold the filter over the beaker for the test.

☐ **9. Draw and label** your prototype.

Test the Prototype

Test your water filter. Place the filter above the beaker and pour the dirty water through the filter. Empty the filtered water from the beaker into a clear plastic cup. Repeat this process two more times. **Compare** the filtered water to your control water.

Communicate Results

☐ **10.** How well did your filter work? Rate your filter on a scale of 1 to 3 with 1 — poor results, 2 — good results, and 3 — great results. **Explain** why you give your filter this rating.

_____

_____

_____

Evaluate and Redesign

☐ **11.** What changes could you make to your design to make it work better?

_____

_____

_____

☐ **12.** **Make** your changes and **draw** your revised prototype.

☐ **13.** How well did your revised prototype work? Explain. _____

_____

_____

_____

What is the water cycle?

Envision It!

Why do you think it is possible to see the lion's breath?

my PLANET DiARY

Connections

One liter of sea water contains around 35 g of salt.

There's nothing like a tall glass of cool water on a hot day. Much of our planet is covered in water, but the water in the ocean is salt water. People in all parts of the world need fresh water to drink and to grow crops.

Geographically, there are places that do not have much fresh water, such as the Middle East. However, people can use water from the sea after the salt has been removed from it. Desalination removes salt from seawater to get fresh water. Seawater can be distilled. This involves boiling seawater to make water vapor, which condenses into fresh water and leaves the salt behind. Desalination takes a lot of energy and is expensive, but costs are decreasing as technology improves.

What do you think might happen to the salt that comes out of seawater during desalination?

....

....

....

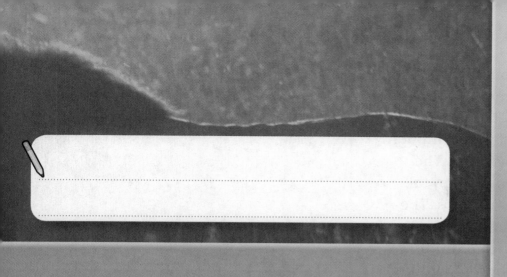

Words to Know

water cycle   condensation
evaporation   precipitation

Water in the Air

Look around you. Can you see any water? Even if you do not see it, water surrounds you all the time. This water is not in a liquid form as in rivers or a solid form as in glaciers. This water is an invisible gas called water vapor. Air always has some water vapor in it, even in the driest deserts. This water vapor was liquid water at some time in the past. A water particle from a plant, a tropical river, or the Arctic Ocean could become water vapor, and eventually it could return to Earth's surface in the form of rain.

Water vapor makes up a small percentage of the gases in the air. Particles of water vapor, like particles of other gases, are constantly moving.

1. ◉ **Sequence** Use the graphic organizer to sequence the events described above.

First

Next

Finally

2. **Synthesize** Moisture has frozen on this man's beard. Where might the moisture have come from?

The Water Cycle

Water is always moving on, through, and above Earth as it changes from one form to another in the water cycle. The **water cycle** is the repeated movement of water through the environment in different forms. The water cycle is continuous, but we can talk about the different processes as steps. The steps of the water cycle include evaporation, condensation, precipitation, and runoff. These steps can be affected by temperature, pressure, wind, and the elevation of the land. A diagram of the water cycle is shown here.

Evaporation is the changing of a liquid, such as water, to a gas. Water evaporates from the ocean or other water bodies into the atmosphere. Water vapor is water in the form of a gas in the air. In **condensation**, a gas, such as water vapor, turns into liquid. Clouds form when water vapor condenses into water droplets and ice crystals. In **precipitation,** the water falls from clouds as rain, snow, sleet, or hail. The water cycle can follow different paths. For example, condensation forms clouds, but it can also form dew.

Sublimation and frost formation are other possible paths in the water cycle. Sublimation is ice changing into water vapor without first melting. Water vapor can turn into ice without first becoming liquid water. The ice crystals that form on surfaces are called frost.

3. **Fill in the Blank** In the diagram to the right, complete the sentences to finish the labels.

4. [CHALLENGE] Look at the diagram below. Where do you think the water cycle begins?

....

....

....

....

Some water vapor rises and .... to form clouds. Some water vapor turns into frost or dew. Frost and dew often form in the morning and evaporate soon after sunrise.

Water .... from the ocean, lakes, and puddles.

5. Apply How might pesticides and fertilizers on land become a problem in an ocean ecosystem?

....

....

Very slowly, snow and ice turn into water vapor by sublimation.

Raindrops and snowflakes fall to Earth. Most .... falls on the ocean.

Some rain or melted snow soaks into the ground and becomes groundwater.

Runoff is water that flows off the land into streams, rivers, lakes, and the ocean.

Groundwater slowly moves into rivers, lakes, and the ocean.

Water condenses as it loses energy.

Water evaporates as it absorbs energy from the sun.

Frozen water .... (absorbs/loses) energy from the sun as it melts.

At-Home Lab

Watering Can
Fill a can with ice and water. Add a drop of food coloring to the can and stir until the color is even. Observe. When droplets form on the outside of the can, wipe them with a white paper towel. What are the droplets and where did they come from? How do you know?

Energy in the Water Cycle

The sun has a major effect on the water cycle. The energy of sunlight causes most evaporation, sublimation, and melting. Energy is needed to evaporate the water and to move the water vapor by winds. This energy originally comes from the sun.

When water vapor condenses into liquid water, it releases energy and cools. This energy warms the air or water in the immediate area.

6. ◎ **Main Idea and Details** Circle the main idea and **underline** two details in the first paragraph above.

7. **Determine** Read and complete the captions in the diagram above. Circle the part of the diagram that shows water vapor turning into liquid water.

Estimating Area

One way to estimate the area of a shape is to use a grid that divides the shape into square units. On the map below, each square unit represents 1 square kilometer. The lake completely covers six squares. Eight squares are about half covered, making 4 more whole squares. A good estimate for the area of the lake is 10 square kilometers.

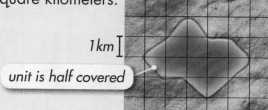

1km

unit is half covered

On the map below, each square unit represents one square kilometer. Estimate the area of the lake below.

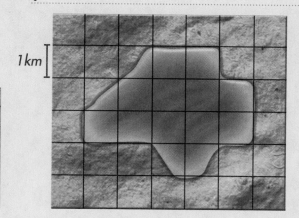

1km

Got it?

8. **Infer** There is usually more water vapor in the air in summer than in winter. What could be a reason?

....

....

9. **UNLOCK THE BIG ?** Think about what you learned in this lesson. How does water move through the environment?

....

....

▢ **Stop!** I need help with ....

⏸ **Wait!** I have a question about ....

▶ **Go!** Now I know ....

Lesson 2

What are the spheres of Earth?

Tell which spheres of Earth helps this person to windsurf.

MY PLANET DiARY

FunFact

A glacier is a large mass of ice and snow moving on land. Its huge mass pushes down the land under it. When glaciers melt, the land that was under them rises slowly, like the way some seat cushions come back into shape after you stand up. This process is happening in parts of Alaska and in other parts of the world. Because the land is rising, some areas that were once underwater are now dry land.

What impact might the rising land have on the state of Alaska?

....

....

....

Alaska, 1941

Alaska, 2004

Words to Know

atmosphere   lithosphere
hydrosphere   biosphere

Earth as a System

Earth is a system. A system is a group of parts that work together. Earth's system is made up of parts called spheres. Four major spheres of Earth's system are air, water, land, and all living things. These spheres interact because parts of them move into each other. For example, air always contains dirt particles and evaporated water. The dirt falls into oceans, rivers, and lakes. The water falls on the land as rain or snow. Events also happen that result in spheres interacting. When a volcano erupts, materials from the land move into the air as gas and ash. The ash can fall into water. The way the air, water, and land interact makes it possible for organisms to live on Earth.

1. ◎ **Sequence** Complete the graphic organizer below. **Write** what happens when a volcano erupts.

First

A volcano erupts.

Next

Last

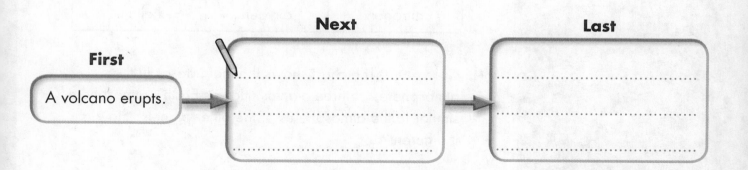

Atmosphere

The mixture of water vapor and other gases, as well as particles of matter such as dust that surrounds Earth's surface is called the **atmosphere.** Nitrogen and oxygen are the main gases in the atmosphere. It also contains a small amount of carbon dioxide. Most of the atmosphere is close to the surface of Earth. Thunder, lightning, wind, and rain occur here. As you go higher and higher, there is less and less gas, and the air pressure decreases.

The atmosphere is essential for life on Earth. No other planet in the solar system contains the same mixture of gases that organisms need to live. The atmosphere also holds in heat from the sun, making Earth warm enough to support life. The atmosphere helps protect living things from being damaged by too much sunlight.

2. **Identify** What does the atmosphere contain?

....

....

3. **Generalize** What are the components of the atmosphere that help organisms live on Earth?

....

Gases in Planets' Atmospheres		
Venus	**Earth**	**Jupiter**
carbon dioxide nitrogen	nitrogen oxygen	hydrogen helium

4. **Compare** The chart shows the main gases in the atmospheres of three planets. How is Earth's atmosphere similar to the atmospheres of the other planets? How is it different?

....

....

Hydrosphere

All the waters of Earth make up the **hydrosphere.** The hydrosphere covers a little less than $\frac{3}{4}$ of Earth's surface. Most of the hydrosphere is ocean water. The Pacific Ocean is the largest and deepest part of the ocean, followed by the Atlantic Ocean, the Indian Ocean, the Southern Ocean, and the Arctic Ocean. The oceans are connected.

The hydrosphere also contains fresh water. Most lakes, rivers, streams, and glaciers are fresh water. So is groundwater. Groundwater is rain or melted snow that soaks into the ground. Fresh water is not evenly spread over Earth. Some places have more fresh water than others.

5. Predict Describe what Earth would be like if the hydrosphere covered only 25 percent of its surface.

....

....

Lightning Lab

Bodies of Water Near You
Look at a local map. List the bodies of water close to where you live. Do they help you travel, provide drinking water, or give you a beautiful place to visit? Tell how they are changing.

Do the math!

Read a Circle Graph

Water covers most of Earth's surface. Only a very small percentage of that water is drinkable.

Earth's Water

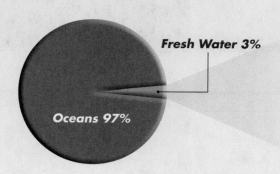

Fresh Water 3%

Oceans 97%

Fresh Water

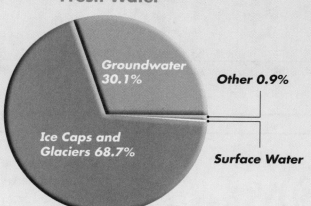

Groundwater 30.1%

Other 0.9%

Ice Caps and Glaciers 68.7%

Surface Water

1 Compute What percentage of Earth's fresh water is surface water?

2 CHALLENGE What water might be included in the label *Other*?

The Lithosphere

The solid, rocky outer layer of Earth is the **lithosphere.** The lithosphere contains rocks, soils, and minerals. It covers the entire surface of Earth and is made up of the continents, islands, and the ocean floors. The surface of the lithosphere varies from flat plains to hills and valleys to mountaintops. The distance from Earth's surface to its center is about 6,400 kilometers. Scientists have drilled holes into Earth as deep as 12 kilometers. The drills have brought up samples of rock. Using rock samples and other methods, scientists have inferred that the lithosphere averages about 100 kilometers thick. This measurement is about as far as you can travel in a car on the highway in one hour. Compared to the radius of Earth, the lithosphere is very thin!

6. Calculate What is the distance from the bottom of the Mariana Trench to the summit of Mount Everest? Express your answer in meters and in kilometers.

7. Exemplify If you use a hard-boiled egg as a model for Earth, which part of the egg would represent the lithosphere?

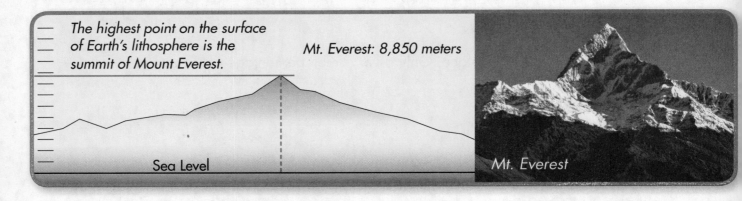

The highest point on the surface of Earth's lithosphere is the summit of Mount Everest.

Mt. Everest: 8,850 meters

Sea Level

Mt. Everest

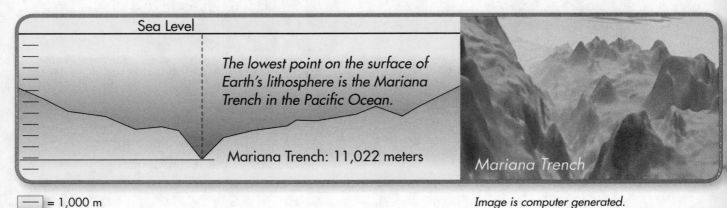

Sea Level

The lowest point on the surface of Earth's lithosphere is the Mariana Trench in the Pacific Ocean.

Mariana Trench: 11,022 meters

Mariana Trench

⊐ = 1,000 m

Image is computer generated.

Biosphere

Living things can be found almost everywhere on Earth. The part of Earth in which living things are found is the **biosphere.** The biosphere extends from about 10 kilometers above Earth's surface to about 10 kilometers below the surface of the ocean. Although living things may live in different parts of the biosphere, they all share resources such as water, air, and light.

8. **Identify** What parts of Earth allow organisms to live in areas like the one shown?

....

....

Got it?

9. **Identify** What makes up the hydrosphere?

....

....

10. **Explain** How does life on Earth depend on the atmosphere?

....

....

....

■ **Stop!** I need help with ....

❚❚ **Wait!** I have a question about ....

▶ **Go!** Now I know ....

Lesson 3
What is weather?

Envision It!

This map shows different weather conditions in a particular region. **Circle** the areas where you might find clear skies.

Inquiry ## Explore It!

How accurate are weather forecasts?

☐ **1.** Look at the current 5-day weather forecast. **Record** the forecasted high temperatures.

☐ **2.** Check the weather report each day for the next 5 days. Record the actual high for the previous day.

☐ **3.** Compare the forecasted data with the actual data.

Explain Your Results

4. What was the largest difference between the forecast and actual temperatures?

....

5. Draw a Conclusion Do you see a pattern in the accuracy of the forecasts? Explain.

....

....

....

Materials

local 5-day weather forecast

Weather Report Predictions			
Day	Forecast High (°C)	Actual High (°C)	Difference Between Forecast and Actual (°C)
1			
2			
3			
4			
5			

I will know the factors that determine weather.

Words to Know

weather
barometric pressure
humidity
circulation

Weather

You probably know that a thermometer can be used to measure air temperature. But it takes more than a temperature reading to describe the weather. **Weather** is the state of the atmosphere, including its temperature, wind speed and direction, air pressure, moisture, amount of rain or snow, and other factors.

Scientists called meteorologists study and predict weather. Meteorologists collect data from many tools to tell about the weather today and to predict future weather. Almost all of the data they use are collected automatically at weather observation stations. Knowing and predicting the weather is very important for planning all sorts of activities, including farming, fishing, and outdoor concerts.

1. ◉ **Draw Conclusions** Use the graphic organizer below to draw a conclusion from the text above.

2. **Suggest** Where might be a good place to set up this measuring tool? Explain.

....

....

....

....

....

....

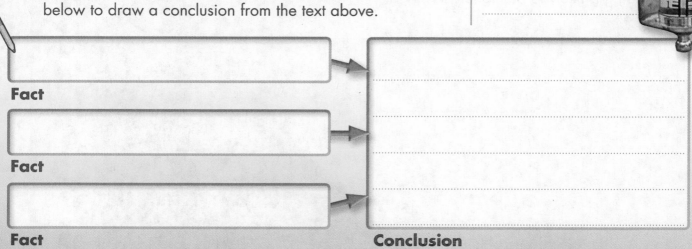

Fact	
Fact	
Fact	Conclusion

Barometric Pressure

When you look up on a clear day, you see a high, blue sky. You are really looking through 9,600 km (about 6,000 mi) of air. The blanket of air that surrounds Earth is its atmosphere. Like other matter, air has mass and takes up space.

Air is made up of a mixture of invisible gases. Over $\frac{3}{4}$ of Earth's atmosphere is nitrogen. Most of the rest is oxygen, but small amounts of carbon dioxide gas are also present. The part of the atmosphere closest to Earth's surface contains water vapor. The amount of water vapor depends on time and place. For example, air over the ocean or a forest has more water vapor than air over a desert.

Gravity pulls the mass of air in the atmosphere toward Earth's surface. The pushing force of the atmosphere is called **barometric pressure.** Air pushes with equal force in all directions. Many kilograms of gas are pressing down on your school building. They do not crush it because the air inside the building exerts pressure too. Air pushing down is balanced by air pushing up and sideways. Air pressure decreases as you go higher in the atmosphere.

3. CHALLENGE Suppose you take two readings from a barometer. One reading is taken at the top of a tall building and the other at ground level. Which reading is likely to be higher? Why?

....

....

....

....

A barometer is an instrument that shows air pressure.

Air particles are represented here by small, blue spheres. As you move upward through the atmosphere, air particles are farther apart. This means that higher in the atmosphere, the pressure is lower.

- 12 km
- 11 km
- 10 km
- 9 km
- 8 km
- 7 km
- 6 km
- 5 km
- 4 km
- 3 km
- 2 km
- 1 km
- 0 km

Temperature

Air temperature also affects weather. As the sun warms Earth's surface, air that is in contact with the surface becomes warmer. As the air particles move farther apart, the air pushes down with less pressure. The warm air rises, causing an area of low pressure to form, and air from areas with higher pressure rushes in. If the air near Earth's surface cools, the particles in the air become more closely packed. This denser, cooler air pushes down with more pressure. An area of high pressure forms. Air from this area flows into lower-pressure areas. The temperature of the air also affects the type of precipitation—rain, snow, or sleet.

4. Predict What would happen if the air outside the hot air balloon were as hot as the air inside?

....

....

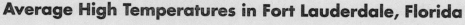
Do the math!

Line Graphs

Look at the graph of average monthly high temperatures for Fort Lauderdale, Florida.

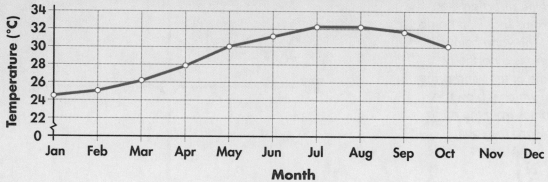

Average High Temperatures in Fort Lauderdale, Florida

① In November, the average high temperature was about 27°C. In December, it was about 25°C. Plot the missing data points and complete the graph above.

② Between which two months did Fort Lauderdale have the greatest decrease in average temperature? About how many degrees did the temperature decrease?

....

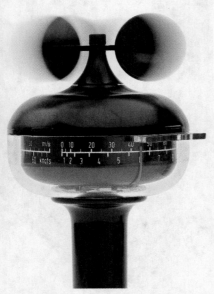

Meteorologists measure wind speed using an instrument called an anemometer.

Wind direction can be observed with a weather vane. The arrow points toward the direction the wind comes from. That is, it points into the wind. The vane below shows that there is a northerly wind. The name of the wind is the direction from which it blows. A north wind comes from the north and moves toward the south.

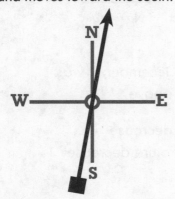

Winds

Wind is air movement caused by differences in pressure. In general, air moves from areas of high pressure to areas of low pressure. Think about a balloon. When you let air out of a balloon, air rushes from inside the balloon where pressure is higher to where pressure is lower outside the balloon. You can feel wind.

Wind speed and direction affect weather. Local weather can be affected by special winds called jet streams. A jet stream is a narrow band of high-speed wind. A polar jet stream blows from west to east high in the atmosphere over North America. The jet stream affects day-to-day weather and seasons. In the winter, the jet stream can bring cold air from the north to states as far south as Kentucky. In the summer, the jet stream brings warmer air north into Canada.

Winds interact with landforms like mountain ranges, which in turn affects local weather. Mountains force the air to rise upwards and cool. Clouds form in the cooler air and release precipitation. This causes wet weather on the side of the mountain facing the wind. As air passes over to the opposite side of the mountain, it sinks and absorbs moisture. This causes the weather patterns to be drier in that area.

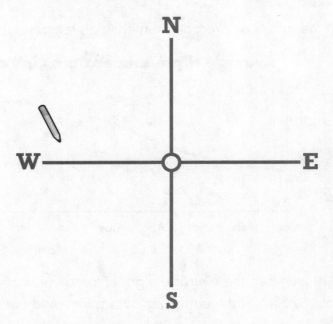

5. **Draw** On the blank weather vane diagram above, draw an arrow to represent a southeasterly wind.

Water in the Atmosphere

Three other factors for determining weather are humidity, clouds, and precipitation. **Humidity** is the amount of water vapor in the air. The particles of water vapor are too small to be visible, but when conditions are right, they can come together to form small water droplets and ice crystals. These droplets and crystals are bigger than water vapor particles and can reflect light from the sun. At this point, we can see the water as a cloud. If the droplets or crystals get large enough, they can fall to the ground as precipitation, such as rain or snow.

6. **Summarize** What do the factors humidity, clouds, and precipitation have in common? List two things.

....

....

7. **Describe** Write two or more sentences that tell what is going on in the picture below. Use the words *humidity*, *clouds*, and *precipitation*.

....

....

....

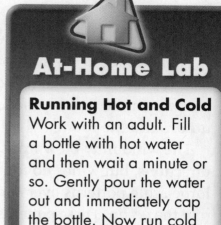

At-Home Lab

Running Hot and Cold
Work with an adult. Fill a bottle with hot water and then wait a minute or so. Gently pour the water out and immediately cap the bottle. Now run cold water over the bottle. What happens? Can you reverse this process?

Meteorologists use an instrument called a hygrometer to measure humidity. Zoos use hygrometers to monitor the air for animals that need high humidity.

Circulation

Have you ever used an electric fan to cool a room in the summer? You can also use a fan to make a heater more efficient in the winter. The fan moves air around the room.

The wind may blow from different directions, but winds do follow some large-scale patterns over continents and the ocean. These patterns are determined by differences in temperature and pressure in different parts of the atmosphere. The large-scale movement of air is called circulation. **Circulation** is the movement of air that redistributes heat on Earth.

For example, the trade winds are a persistent pattern of winds that blow near the equator. The warmest parts of our planet are near the equator. The air above this region becomes warm and rises, creating a low pressure zone. High in the atmosphere, this warm air travels away from the equator, cools down, and sinks. It then blows back toward the equator along the surface, causing the trade winds.

In summer, a ceiling fan should blow the air downward. This makes sweat evaporate faster and people feel cooler.

8. **Demonstrate** Below is an example of a route from Europe to the Americas. Draw arrows on the route showing the direction a ship might take to save the most fuel. Explain your answer.

....

....

....

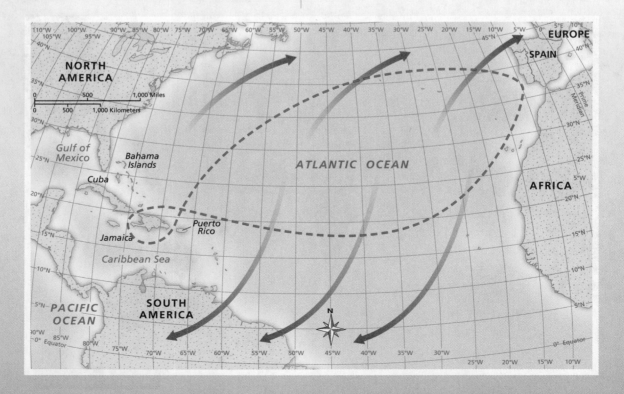

222

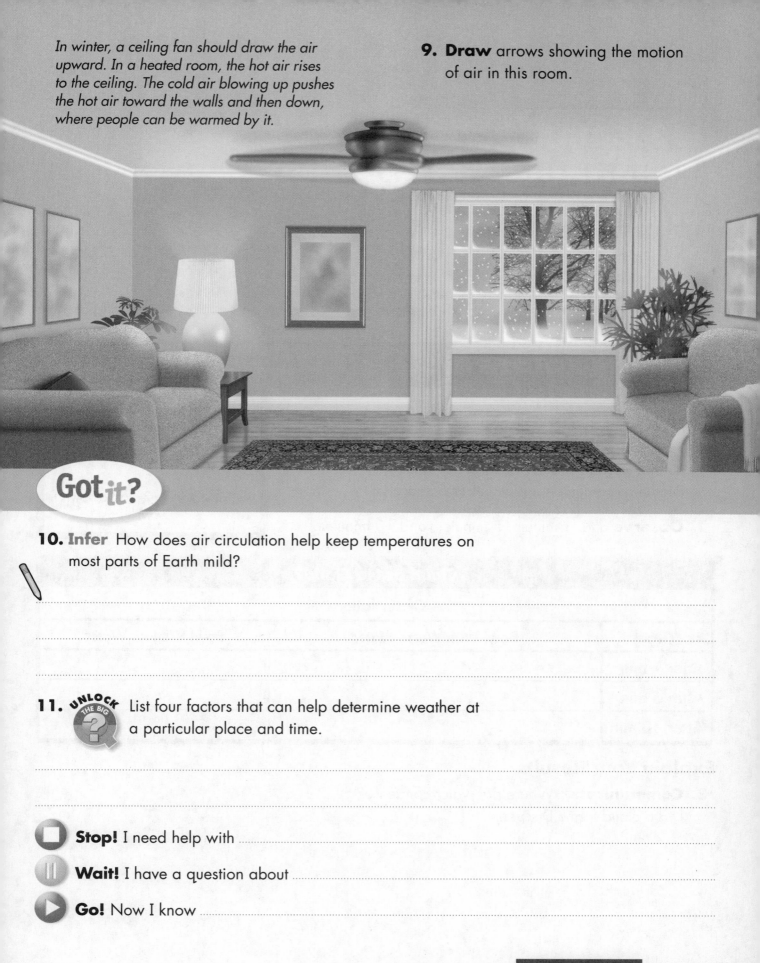

In winter, a ceiling fan should draw the air upward. In a heated room, the hot air rises to the ceiling. The cold air blowing up pushes the hot air toward the walls and then down, where people can be warmed by it.

9. Draw arrows showing the motion of air in this room.

Got it?

10. Infer How does air circulation help keep temperatures on most parts of Earth mild?

....

....

....

11. UNLOCK THE BIG **?** List four factors that can help determine weather at a particular place and time.

....

....

⬜ **Stop!** I need help with ....

⏸ **Wait!** I have a question about ....

▶ **Go!** Now I know ....

Lesson 4

How do clouds and precipitation form?

Envision It!

A typical snowflake has six points. **Shade** in the spaces that contain six-pointed snowflakes.

Inquiry **Explore It!**

Materials

ice cubes

warm water

2 plastic bowls with lids

Does a cloud form?

☐ **1.** Fill one bowl about $\frac{1}{3}$ full with warm water. Put nothing in the other bowl. Close both lids. Put the same number of ice cubes on each lid.

☐ **2. Observe** after 1 minute, 5 minutes, and 10 minutes.

Cloud or No Cloud?		
Observations		
Time	Bowl With Warm Water	Bowl Without Water
After 1 min		
After 5 min		
After 10 min		

Explain Your Results

3. Communicate   Where did water condense? Did a cloud form? Discuss.

....

....

....

I will know that there are different types of precipitation and each is connected with other weather conditions.

Words to Know

sleet
hail

Water in the Air

Have you ever watched a cloud get larger? Have you tried to see shapes in the clouds? Clouds come in many shapes and sizes. Remember that clouds form when water vapor changes into tiny water droplets or ice crystals.

Whether a cloud is made of water droplets or ice crystals depends partly on air temperature. The temperature of air high in the clouds is often much lower than the temperature of the air close to the ground. Even on summer days, many clouds are made of ice crystals.

The ice crystals and water droplets in clouds can join together to make larger particles. The particles can get so large that the gravitational force due to the mass of the particles can cause them to fall out of the cloud. This is how precipitation forms.

1. **Identify** What are clouds made of? **Underline** a statement or statements to support your answer.

   ....

2. **Write About It** Use what you know about water on Earth. Tell why clouds are important.

   ....

   ....

Heavy rain storms can happen when there is a large amount of water in the air.

Precipitation

You may be surprised to learn that most rain in the United States starts as snow. The temperature of the air high above the ground is often below 0°C. Clouds of ice crystals form in the cold air. The ice crystals grow larger until they start to fall as snowflakes. As they fall, the crystals sometimes stick to other crystals and become larger snowflakes. If the temperature of all the air between the cloud and the ground is less than 0°C, the ice crystals will fall to the ground as snowflakes.

The ice crystals from a cloud may change as they fall through different layers of air. If the ice crystals fall into air that is warmer than 0°C, they will melt and fall as rain. If the air near the ground is very cold, the rain sometimes freezes before it hits the ground. The frozen raindrops are **sleet.**

Hail Formation

Sometimes, strong winds can blow upward through a thunderstorm cloud. These winds blow raindrops back up into the freezing air at the top of the cloud. This creates a small piece of ice. As the ice is blown through the cloud many times, many layers of water freeze on it. Finally, it gets too heavy for the winds to carry it back up. This frozen precipitation that forms in layers is called **hail.** The hailstone falls to the ground. Most hailstones are about the size of a pea. Some can get bigger than a baseball.

examples of large hailstones

3. ◉ **Draw Conclusions**
Suppose you know the air temperature from the ground all the way to a cloud is cold enough for water to freeze. The cloud forms precipitation. What conclusion could you draw about the type of precipitation that falls? **Underline** the facts that helped you draw your conclusion.

....

....

4. Summarize What causes layers to form in hail?

....

....

....

....

....

....

Rain, Sleet, and Snow Formation

Rain	Sleet	Snow

Most clouds are made of ice crystals and water droplets.

Ice crystals melt as they fall through a thin layer of warm air high above the ground.

Ice crystals melt as they fall through warmer air. They fall to the ground as liquid drops.

If raindrops fall for a longer time through cold air, they freeze and fall to the ground as frozen drops called sleet.

If air between the clouds and the ground has a temperature below 0°C, ice crystals fall as snow. They reach the ground as frozen crystals.

5. **Give an Example** Three types of precipitation are rain, sleet, and snow. Do you know two other types? List them here.

....

....

....

6. **Compare** Look at the chart. (Circle) one way rain and sleet are alike. **Underline** one way sleet and snow are alike.

At-Home Lab

Rainmaker
Spray the inside of a pot lid with water. Keep spraying until droplets form. Use a toothpick to push the smaller drops together to form larger drops. Continue until the droplets run in a stream.

7. Identify Look outside. Do you see any clouds? If so, (circle) the names of the cloud or clouds on this page.

Types of Clouds

When you look at clouds in the sky, you may notice they can look different from day to day. Different cloud types form depending on the type of weather present. Clouds that form at different heights in the atmosphere have different names. Here are five common types of clouds.

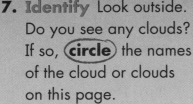

Cirrus

High-level clouds form more than 6 km above the ground. This region overlaps the region for midaltitude clouds. Cirrus clouds are high-altitude clouds that are often thin, wispy, and white.

Cumulonimbus

Clouds that grow vertically have rising air inside them. The bases of these clouds may be as low as 1 km above the ground. The rising air may push the tops of these clouds higher than 12 km. Vertical clouds can cause thunderstorms.

Altocumulus

The bases of mid-level clouds are between 2 km and 7 km above the ground. Altocumulus clouds are midlevel clouds that look like small, puffy balls. The bottoms of the clouds can look dark because sunlight may not reach them.

Stratus

Low-level clouds are often seen less than 2 km above the ground. Stratus clouds are low-level clouds that cover the whole sky. They look dark because little sunlight gets through the layer of clouds.

Fog

Fog is a cloud at ground level. As air near the ground cools, water vapor condenses into tiny droplets and forms a cloud at or near the ground. As more droplets form and get larger, the fog appears thicker.

Sometimes many types of clouds may appear at the same time. Combinations of clouds can help determine the weather at a given place and time.

Clouds interacting with landforms can also determine the weather. Water from large bodies of water like oceans evaporates and condenses to form clouds. Tall landforms, such as mountains, push the clouds up higher into the atmosphere where it is cooler. Clouds can hold less moisture at lower temperatures. As the clouds rise, they release their moisture as precipitation. This often causes wet weather patterns high in the mountains.

8. **Classify** Using the information on the left, label the types of clouds in this picture.

8 km

7 km

6 km

5 km

4 km

3 km

2 km

1 km

0 km

Got it?

9. ◉ **Sequence** Write the steps taken from water vapor to sleet.

....

....

....

10. **UNLOCK THE BIG ?** How are clouds and weather related?

....

....

....

Stop! I need help with ....

Wait! I have a question about ....

Go! Now I know ....

Lesson 5

What is climate?

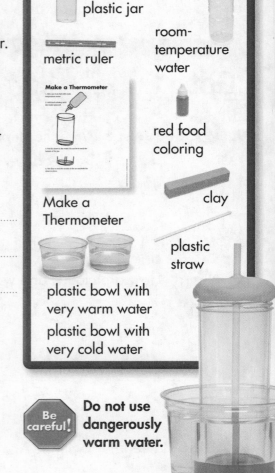

Envision It!

What do you think the climate is like here? **Tell** how the house is protected against some features of the climate.

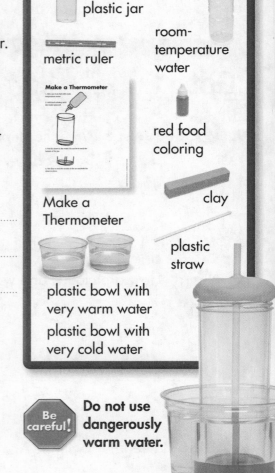

Inquiry **Explore It!**

How does a thermometer work?

☐ **1.** Use the Make a Thermometer sheet. Make a thermometer. Will it work like a regular thermometer? Discuss.

☐ **2.** Place your thermometer in warm water. **Observe.**

☐ **3.** **Predict** what will happen if you place your thermometer in cold water. Tell how you made your prediction. Test your prediction.

....

....

....

Explain Your Results

4. **Communicate** Explain how you think your thermometer might work.

....

....

....

....

Materials

plastic jar

metric ruler

room-temperature water

Make a Thermometer

red food coloring

clay

plastic straw

plastic bowl with very warm water

plastic bowl with very cold water

Be careful! Do not use dangerously warm water.

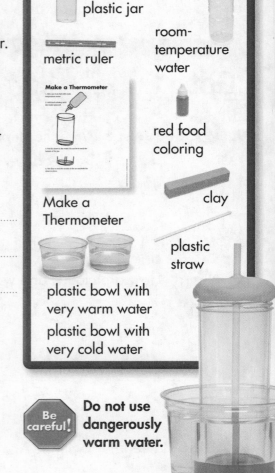

I will know that different climate zones have specific characteristics.

Words to Know

climate
latitude
elevation

Average Weather

The words *weather* and *climate* do not have the same definitions. Weather is made up of all the conditions in one place at a single moment. Weather changes very often. **Climate** describes the weather conditions over a long time, at least thirty years. Climate includes things such as the average amount of precipitation, the average temperature, and how much the temperature changes during the year. Climates do not change as much as the daily weather does.

Giant sequoia trees grow naturally in a small area of California, in the western Sierra Nevada. The climate of this area is generally humid, with mostly dry summers and snowy winters. Some giant sequoias have been alive for thousands of years.

1. **Infer** How do you know this is a good climate for giant sequoias?

   ....

   ....

   ....

Sequoias are able to live for thousands of years because the climate remains nearly steady where they grow.

Factors That Affect Climate

Different areas of the world have different climates. Some factors that affect climate include latitude, elevation, and closeness to large bodies of water.

Latitude

One factor that affects the climate of a place is its latitude. **Latitude** is a measure of how far a place is from the equator. Latitude is measured in degrees, starting at 0° at the equator. Energy from the sun hits Earth's surface more directly at the equator. An area nearer to the equator is usually hotter than places farther away.

There are three major zones of climate according to latitude. The tropical zone extends from 23.5° south to 23.5° north latitude and contains the equator itself. Here, the sun's energy hits most directly all year. The tropical zone is usually warm.

You may know that places like the North and South Poles are generally quite cold. The polar zones receive energy from the sun less directly than the tropical zone. The polar zone extends from 66.5° to 90° north and from 66.5° to 90° south.

In between the polar and tropical zones are the temperate zones. Most of the United States is in a temperate zone. Here, energy from the sun is more direct during the summer, causing the temperature to be higher. The sun's energy is less direct in the winter, which causes winters to be colder.

2. **Support** Why are the polar regions usually cold? **Underline** one statement that supports your answer.

66.5° N

23.5° N

Equator (0°)

23.5° S

66.5° S

3. Describe Write two words to describe each climate zone.

polar zone

temperate zone

tropical zone

temperate zone

polar zone

4. Justify Deciduous trees have leaves that fall off during some seasons. Might you find deciduous trees in the tropical zone? Why?

Climate Zones

Find your city or town on a relief map. Note its latitude. Note nearby features such as lakes or mountains. Look for another city on the map that is at about the same latitude. Would you expect this city to have a similar climate to yours? Explain.

Bodies of Water

The ocean can affect a climate by slowing the rise and fall of air temperature. Remember that bodies of water become warm and cool more slowly than land. Because of this, the temperature of the air near water does not change as quickly as air inland. In the winter, large beaches often do not get as cold as areas just a few miles inland. In the summer, the air over beaches is often cooler than air over areas inland.

Ocean currents can make a climate warmer or cooler. The Gulf Stream and the North Atlantic Drift are large currents that carry warm water northward. The water warms the winds above it. These winds make northern Europe's climate much warmer than it would be otherwise. A change in these currents could change the climate of Europe. On the other hand, cold currents that flow from Alaska to California make that coastal climate cooler.

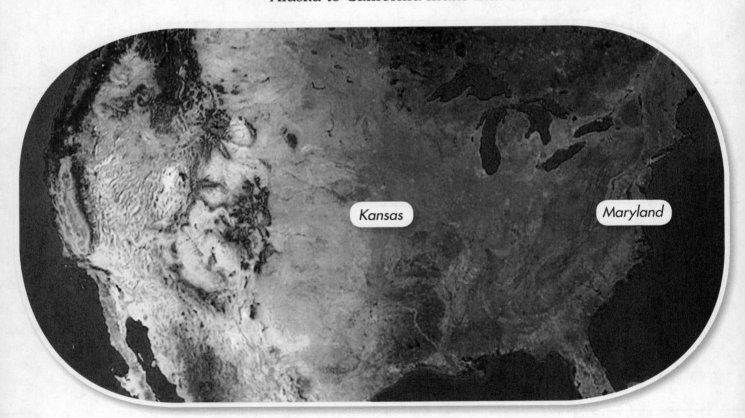

Kansas

Maryland

5. **Infer** Think of the effect of the ocean. Would Kansas be warmer or colder than Maryland in the winter? Explain.

Elevation

Mountain ranges may have different climates than areas around them. Higher land is cooler because in the lower part of the atmosphere temperature decreases with increased elevation. **Elevation** is the height above sea level.

Areas on opposite sides of a mountain range can have very different climates. This happens because the air does not have much moisture in it by the time it reaches the other side.

Plaza Huincul, Argentina, average yearly precipitation: 132 mm

This image shows the southern portion of South America.

Valdivia, Chile, average yearly precipitation: 2,593 mm

6. Show Draw an arrow to show how wind flows between the cities shown on the map. Explain your answer.

Got it?

7. ◉ **Draw Conclusions** You take a bus trip along the Florida coast, from Miami north to Jacksonville. What temperature change would you expect? Explain.

8. **UNLOCK THE BIG ?** Name three factors that can influence climate.

 Stop! I need help with

 Wait! I have a question about

 Go! Now I know

Lesson 6

What are erosion and deposition?

Tell what you think caused this arch to form.

Inquiry Explore It!

How does melting ice cause erosion?

☑ **1.** Put 1 cup of sand on each container.
Make a model of 2 landforms.
Make a hill on one container.
Make a flat plain on the other container.

☑ **2.** Place 1 ice cube in the middle of each pile of sand.
Observe.

Explain Your Results

3. Which landform **model** eroded more?

....

....

4. Draw a Conclusion   How does the shape of the
land affect erosion?

....

....

....

Materials

2 containers

2 plastic cups
with sand

2 ice cubes

UNLOCK THE BIG ?

I will know how erosion and deposition can change Earth's surface.

Words to Know

erosion

deposition

Erosion and Deposition

Materials such as rock particles on Earth move. Water, wind, and ice can carry particles from one place to another place. The movement of materials away from a place is called **erosion.** Gravity is the main force causing erosion. In a landslide, gravity quickly pulls rocks and soil downhill. Landslides often occur during earthquakes and after heavy rains. Landslides are more likely to happen on steep slopes with no trees.

Materials moved by erosion end up in other places. **Deposition** is the process of laying down materials, such as rocks and soil. These sediments can be deposited in different places by wind or flowing water. This process may happen quickly, or it may take a long time.

1. **Infer** How might trees on steep slopes help prevent landslides?

....

....

....

2. Conclude What conclusion can you draw about the speed of moving water on flatter land and its ability to cause erosion?

....

....

....

....

3. ◉ **Cause and Effect** Reread the paragraph on rain. **Underline** the effect of rainwater flowing over bare farm fields.

As the brownish water of the Mississippi River flows along, it can carry sediment thousands of miles to the Gulf of Mexico.

Water Erosion and Deposition

Moving water causes much of the erosion that shapes Earth's surface. Water can also deposit materials in other places to create new landforms. Rivers, rain, waves, ocean currents, and glaciers are all forms of moving water.

Rivers

Gravity causes rivers to flow. As rivers flow downhill, they pick up and carry sediments, such as rock, soil, and sand. The sediments can erode the riverbeds by grinding against the riverbeds again and again. The faster a river flows, the more sediments it can carry and the heavier those sediments can be. Rivers also erode the land around them. A fast-flowing river can form V-shaped valleys. Slow rivers form looping bends, which erode the sides of the valley and make it wider. The deposited material from rivers forms areas called deltas.

Rain

Rain can loosen sediments from the soil and carry them away. Rain can cause flooding in low, flat areas. Flooding damages soil, roads, and buildings. Rainwater flowing over bare farm fields on slopes can erode tons of soil and deposit it downhill. To prevent soil erosion, farmers plow furrows perpendicular to the field's slope. The furrows catch rainwater, keeping the rain from carrying soil away.

Waves

Waves cause erosion along coastlines. As waves hit against rocks, the rocks can break. Sand and gravel in the waves act like sandpaper, weathering the rocks over time. Waves that erode one shoreline may drop sand somewhere else to form other beaches. Storms, tides, and currents can erode beaches. Grasses and plants can help hold soil in place to prevent beach erosion.

Glaciers

Water frozen in glaciers can cause erosion. Gravity pulls glaciers down along a valley. As this movement happens, glaciers grind rocks beneath them into sediments. The glaciers deposit sediments downhill. Over a long time, the action of glaciers wears away the bottom of a valley, which becomes U-shaped.

4. **Infer** Why might it have taken many years for a glacier to form this U-shaped valley?

....

....

....

....

....

Do the math!

Calculate Rates

Because of water erosion, a sandy coast can erode about 5 meters every 5 years.

1 Suppose that the coast continues to erode at the same rate. How much will the coast erode in 50 years? Show your work.

2 Suppose that during each severe storm the coast erodes an additional 4 meters. If there were 15 severe storms in one year, how much did the coast erode because of the storms?

Wind Erosion and Deposition

Wind erosion is caused by wind blowing dust, soil, or sand from one place to another. When sand and dust blow against a rock, tiny bits of the rock might break off. These bits are immediately blown away. Wind erosion also changes sand dunes and fields.

Sand Dunes

Sand dunes are large, loose deposits of sand. The size and shape of a sand dune depend on the speed and direction that the winds are blowing, the amount of sand available, and the number of plants that live in the area. The stronger the wind, the farther sand particles can move. Winds that move in a steady direction can move a dune. This kind of wind will consistently pick up sand from one side and deposit it on the other side. This process causes the entire dune to move slowly in the same direction the wind moves.

5. **CHALLENGE** Why is wind erosion more likely to happen in dry areas than moist areas?

....

....

6. **Hypothesize** How could sand dunes be held in place to keep them from drifting onto a road?

....

....

....

Fields

Wind erosion can be a serious problem on farms. Bare, plowed fields can become very dry. Winds can blow topsoil off the fields. This topsoil is the best kind of soil for growing crops. It cannot be quickly replaced. Farmers often plant rows of tall trees along the edges of fields to prevent wind erosion of topsoil. The trees prevent some of the wind from blowing on the field. Some farmers are able to grow their crops with less plowing. In this way, the soil stays in larger clumps that do not get blown away.

7. Explain How is wind erosion being prevented in the photo?

....

....

....

Got it?

8. Identify What is one cause of erosion? How can it be prevented?

....

....

....

9. UNLOCK THE BIG ? How does deposition change Earth's surface?

....

....

🔲 **Stop!** I need help with ....

⏸ **Wait!** I have a question about ....

▶ **Go!** Now I know ....

Where is the hurricane going?

Weather forecasters record where a hurricane was and where it is. They find the direction it was going. They look at other things too. Then they predict its path. They warn people in the path that a hurricane might be coming.

Follow a Procedure

☐ **1.** Look at the Storm Map.
Find where the hurricane was on Day 1 and Day 2. Think about its direction. **Predict** where it will go. What places would you warn that a hurricane might come? Record your first prediction in the Prediction Chart.

Materials

Storm Map

Inquiry Skill To help **predict** where a hurricane might go, you make inferences based on what you already know (where the hurricane has been and where it is currently).

Day	Latitude	Longitude
1	22°N	62°W
2	24°N	65°W
	Your teacher will give you the rest of the information as you work through the activity	
3		
4		
5		

Map Scale 1 cm = 160 km

Prediction Chart

	Prediction What places would you warn that a hurricane might be approaching?	**Accuracy** How accurate was your prediction?
1st prediction (from Step 1)		
2nd prediction (from Step 2)		

☑ **2.** Your teacher will tell you the hurricane's location on Day 3.
Mark this position on the Storm Map.
Predict where the hurricane will go next.
What places would you warn? Record your second prediction.

☑ **3.** Your teacher will tell you the hurricane's locations on Day 4 and Day 5.
Mark these locations on the Storm Map.
Complete the Prediction Chart.

Analyze and Conclude

4. Communicate How did you **predict** where the hurricane might go?

....

....

5. How might people be affected by an accurate prediction? How might they be affected by one that is not accurate?

....

....

....

....

....

Predicting Tsunamis

Engineers use math and technology to warn people of tsunamis, or large waves of water that affect coastlines. One system they have developed consists of technology, such as buoys, sensors, satellites, and computers. The system is called Deep-ocean Assessment and Reporting of Tsunamis (DART®). Each DART station has a buoy on the surface. There is a pressure sensor anchored on the ocean floor. A radio system sends information between the sensor and buoy. The buoy then sends information to a satellite, which sends information to computers for analysis.

The United States government has 32 stations located throughout the Pacific Ocean. Each station has internal detection software. This software converts pressure and temperature data from the sensor to predict and measure tsunamis. The DART system is one example of how science, technology, engineering, and math can work together.

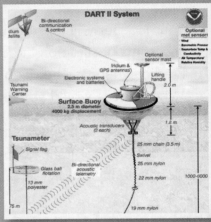

This illustration shows how the DART system uses information to detect tsunamis.

A DART station warns people of tsunamis. DART calculates the height and speed of a tsunami. This early warning can help save lives and property from damage.

Infer How do you think engineers warned people about possible tsunamis before DART?

....

....

....

Vocabulary Smart Cards

water cycle
evaporation
condensation
precipitation
atmosphere
hydrosphere
lithosphere
biosphere
weather
barometric pressure
humidity
circulation
sleet
hail
climate
latitude
elevation
erosion
deposition

Play a Game!

Cut out the Vocabulary Smart Cards.

Work with a partner. One person puts the cards picture-side up. The other person puts the cards picture-side down.

Take turns matching each word with its definition.

precipitation

precipitación

water cycle

ciclo del agua

atmosphere

hidrosfera

evaporation

evaporación

hydrosphere

hidrosfera

condensation

condensación

repeated movement of water through the environment in different forms

Draw a picture that represents the term.

movimiento repetido del agua en formas distintas a través del medio ambiente

---

water that falls from clouds as rain, snow, sleet, or hail

Use a dictionary. Find another definition for this word.

....

....

....

agua que cae de las nubes en forma de lluvia, nieve, aguanieve o granizo

---

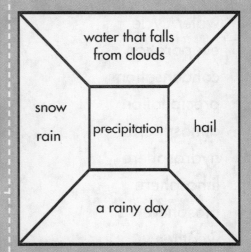

water that falls from clouds

snow

rain

precipitation

hail

a rainy day

Make a Word Frame!

Choose a vocabulary term and write it in the center of the frame. Write details about the vocabulary term.

---

the changing of a liquid to a gas

Write a sentence using verb form of this word.

....

....

....

cambio de líquido a gas

---

the mixture of water vapor and other gases, as well as particles of matter that surrounds Earth's surface

Write a sentence using this word.

....

mezcla de vapor de agua y otros gases, así como partículas de materia que rodean la superficie de la Tierra

---

the process in which a gas turns into a liquid

Write a sentence using this word.

....

....

....

....

proceso en el que un gas se convierte en líquido

---

all the waters of Earth

Write a sentence using this word.

....

....

....

....

toda el agua de la Tierra

sleet	barometric pressure	lithosphere

aguanieve	presión atmosférica	litosfera

hail	humidity	biosphere

granizo	humedad	biosfera

climate	circulation	weather
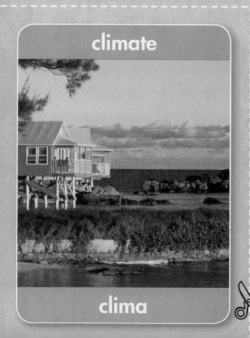		
clima	circulación	tiempo atmosférico

the solid, rocky layer of Earth What is the prefix of this word? .... capa rocosa y sólida de la Tierra	**the pushing force of the atmosphere** Use a dictionary. Find another term for this phrase. .... fuerza que ejerce la atmósfera	**frozen raindrops** Write a sentence using this word. .... gotas de lluvia congeladas
the part of Earth in which all living things are found What is the prefix of this word? .... la parte de la Tierra donde están todos los seres vivos	**the amount of water vapor in the air** Write a sentence using the verb form of this word. .... cantidad de vapor de agua en el aire	**frozen precipitation that forms in layers** Write a sentence using this word. .... precipitación congelada que se forma en capas
the state of the atmosphere Write three examples. .... estado de la atmósfera	**movement of air that redistributes heat on Earth** Write a sentence using the verb form for this word. .... movimiento del aire que redistribuye el calor en la Tierra	**the average of weather conditions over a long time** Write another definition for this word. .... promedio de las condiciones del tiempo durante un período largo

deposition

sedimentación

latitude

latitud

elevation

elevación

erosion

erosión

a measure of how far a place is from the equator

Write another definition for this word.

....

....

....

medida de la distancia entre un objeto y el ecuador

---

process of laying down materials, such as rocks and soil

Draw an example.

proceso por el cual materiales como rocas y partículas de suelo se asientan

---

....

....

....

....

---

height above sea level

What is the suffix of this word?

....

....

....

....

altura sobre el nivel del mar

....

....

....

....

....

....

....

....

....

....

---

the movement of materials away from a place

Write a sentence using the verb form of this word.

....

....

....

movimiento de materiales que se alejan de un lugar

....

....

....

....

....

....

....

....

....

Study Guide

REVIEW THE BIG ? How does water move through the environment?

Earth Science

Lesson 1

What is the water cycle?

- Water can be a solid, liquid, or gas and can change state.
- Evaporation, condensation, precipitation, and runoff are parts of the water cycle.

Lesson 2

What are the spheres of Earth?

- Earth is a system made up of four spheres: atmosphere, hydrosphere, lithosphere, and biosphere.
- Earth's spheres interact when spheres overlap.

Lesson 3

What is weather?

- Air temperature, pressure, humidity, wind speed and direction, and precipitation determine the weather in a given place and time.
- Air circulates throughout the planet in predictable patterns.

Lesson 4

How do clouds and precipitation form?

- Precipitation is made up of particles of water that fall from clouds.
- Some forms of precipitation are rain, snow, sleet, and hail.
- Different clouds form from different types of weather.

Lesson 5

What is climate?

- Climate is the average weather conditions over a long period of time.
- Climate is affected by latitude, elevation, and distance from water.
- The climate in a region may change over time.

Lesson 6

What are erosion and deposition?

- Wind, water, ice, changes in temperature, and chemical changes can weather, or break down, rock.
- Erosion moves rock away. Deposition places rock in other areas.

SavvasRealize.com

Chapter Review

Lesson 1

What is the water cycle?

1. The particles of water vapor
   A. are always moving.
   B. are as small as a drop.
   C. form a liquid.

2. A certain cloud contains 220 water droplets per cubic centimeter. If 1 cubic meter = 1,000,000 cubic centimeters, how many drops are in one cubic meter of the cloud?

Lesson 2

What are the spheres of Earth?

3. **Vocabulary** The _____ contains a mixture of gases, water vapor, and particles of matter.
   A. atmosphere
   B. hydrosphere
   C. lithosphere
   D. biosphere

4. Rivers, swamps, and lakes make up Earth's fresh surface water. Rivers make up 2%. Swamps make up 11%. How much of Earth's fresh surface water is lakes?

Lesson 3

What is weather?

5. **Vocabulary** The state of the atmosphere at a given time and place is called _____.
   A. climate
   B. weather
   C. circulation
   D. altitude

6. **Write About It** How does a difference in barometric pressures cause wind?

7. **List** Write three factors that determine the weather shown below.

Lesson 4

How do clouds and precipitation form?

8. ⊙ **Draw Conclusions** Read the paragraph and fill in the graphic organizer.

> Hail forms when falling ice crystals get blown up through a thunderstorm cloud by a strong wind. After they begin to fall again, the upward wind blows them up through the cloud again. Hail happens during thunderstorms.

Fact	**Fact**

Conclusion

Lesson 5

What is climate?

9. **Identify** *Tropical*, *temperate*, and *polar* describe climate zones due to
A. latitude.
B. rainfall amount.
C. temperature.

Lesson 6

What are erosion and deposition?

10. **Explain** How can water cause the loss of soil from bare farm fields on slopes? How can this erosion be prevented?

....

....

....

....

11. **ANSWER THE BIG ?** **How does water move through the environment?**

Describe the movement of water near where you live. Is there a large body of water, such as the ocean? Does it rain a lot? Does the water come from wells in the ground?

....

....

Benchmark Practice

Read each question and choose the best answer.

1 In the water cycle on Earth, water is in which form?

- **A** solid
- **B** liquid
- **C** gas
- **D** all of the above

2 The hydrosphere covers about how much of Earth's surface?

- **A** $\frac{4}{5}$
- **B** $\frac{1}{2}$
- **C** $\frac{3}{4}$
- **D** $\frac{2}{3}$

3 An area's latitude helps determine its

- **A** climate zones.
- **B** elevation.
- **C** precipitation.
- **D** time zone.

4 Which of the following land features affects weather?

- **A** mountains
- **B** swamps
- **C** deserts
- **D** all of the above

5 Precipitation includes

- **A** rain, snow, and air.
- **B** rain, wind, and snow.
- **C** snow, sleet, and hail.
- **D** all of the above

6 How does the water cycle affect the salinity of the ocean?

....

....

....

....

....

....

....

Science in Your Backyard

Keep a Weather Journal

The date is July 4, 1776. The business at hand is the Declaration of Independence. The weather this day in Philadelphia is mild—in the mid-70s. How do we know? We know because a young Thomas Jefferson kept a weather journal.

You can keep a weather journal too. Start by looking at the sky each day. Is the sun shining brightly? Is the sky cloudy or hazy? Make a note. Record the high and low temperatures for the day. Now add more detail. This might include the wind speed and direction and the relative humidity. Note rainfall or snowfall amounts. Use your own observations whenever you can. You can also watch the weather reports or check online for information. Organize your findings in a chart.

If you like, add a sentence or two about how the weather affected you or your plans each day.

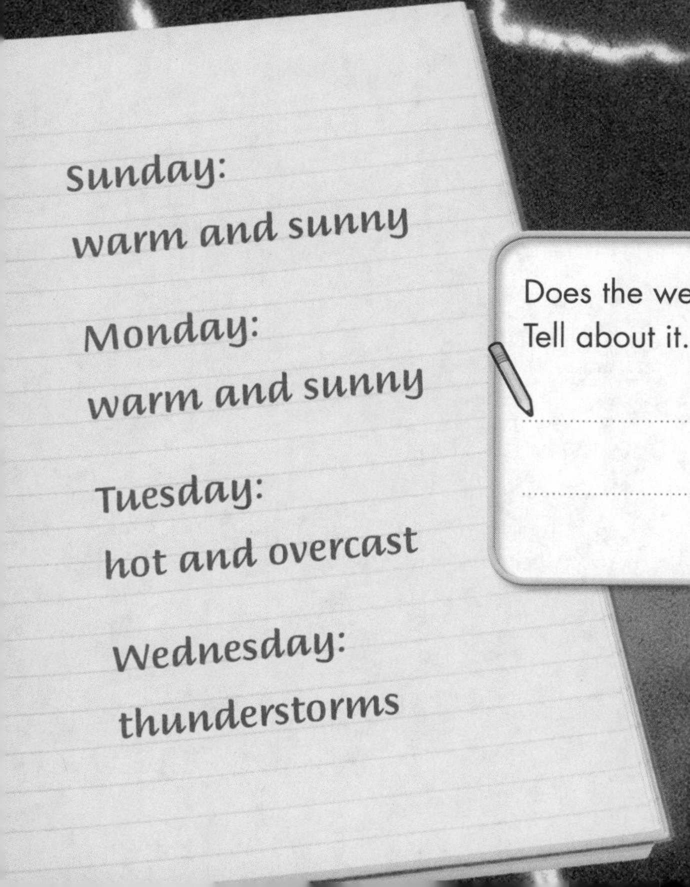

Sunday:
warm and sunny
Monday:
warm and sunny
Tuesday:
hot and overcast
Wednesday:
thunderstorms

Does the weather change quickly where you live? Tell about it.

....

....

What is happening in the SKY?

Earth and Space

 Try It! What does a spiral galaxy look like from different angles?

STEM Activity Breathe Deeply!

Lesson 1 How does Earth move?

Lesson 2 What is a star?

Lesson 3 What are the inner planets?

Lesson 4 What are the outer planets?

Lesson 5 What are asteroids, meteors, comets, and moons?

Investigate It! How can spinning affect a planet's shape?

Earth Science

Apply It! How does the speed of a meteorite affect the crater it makes?

You may have seen the moon when it looks like a crescent, a shape that looks like a circle with a bite taken out of it. This happens when we can see only part of the moon's sunlit side. The sun usually looks like a full circle, but sometimes the sun can look like a crescent too.

Predict When do you think the sun might look like a crescent?

....

....

 How do objects move in space?

What does a spiral galaxy look like from different angles?

☐ **1.** Use cups to make this spiral galaxy.

These cups represent a spiral galaxy. The sun is a star near the edge of the Milky Way, a spiral galaxy.

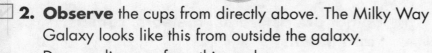

Materials

25 cups

☐ **2. Observe** the cups from directly above. The Milky Way Galaxy looks like this from outside the galaxy. Draw a diagram from this angle.

☐ **3.** Kneel to observe the cups at eye level from the edge. The Milky Way Galaxy looks like this from Earth, which is near the edge of the galaxy. Draw a diagram from this angle.

Inquiry Skill
You can use a physical **model** to help see things from different angles.

Explain Your Results

4. UNLOCK THE BIG **?** Describe the differences in **observations** from different angles.

....

....

....

5. How is your **model** like a spiral galaxy? How is it different?

....

....

....

Drawings of Spiral Galaxy Model

Viewed from Above

Viewed from the Edge

◎ Compare and Contrast

- When you **compare** things, you tell how they are alike.
- When you **contrast** things, you tell how they are different.

Deciding About Distance

Mercury takes 88 days to travel around the sun. Neptune takes about 164.5 years. Each planet travels in its own path and is a different distance from the sun. Mercury is closer to the sun, so its path is shorter. Neptune is farther from the sun, so its path is longer.

Practice It!

Use the graphic organizer to show how Mercury and Neptune are alike and how they are different.

The sizes and distances in this diagram are not true to scale. Also, the planets rarely line up.

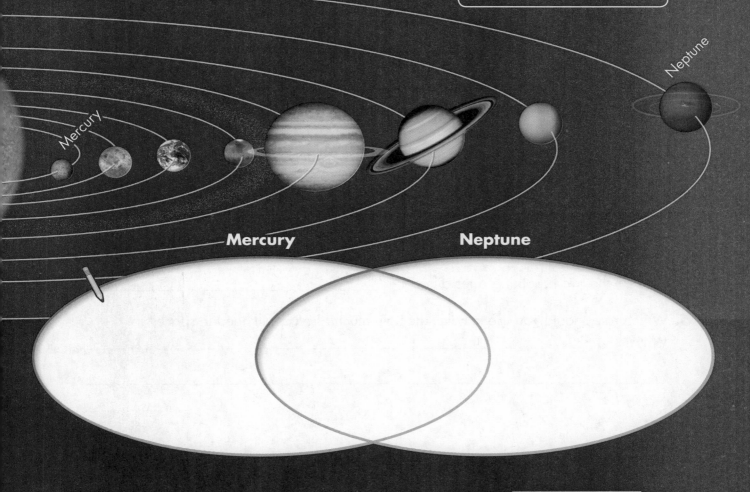

Mercury

Neptune

Breathe Deeply!

With the right equipment, people can travel deep under the ocean's surface or high above Earth's atmosphere into space. Neither of these places has the air that people need to breathe. To make such a trip, people must take air with them. You can calculate how much air you need for a trip into space by finding how much air you inhale and exhale over a given period of time. You can do this using a spirometer. A spirometer captures the air that a person exhales in one breath and measures its volume.

As an astronaut, you will design a spirometer to measure your lung capacity. Then you will calculate how much air you would need to transport with you on a two-day journey into space.

Identify the Problem

☑ **1.** What is your task? _____

_____

Do Research

☑ **2.** While you are sitting still and breathing normally, count how many times you breathe in and out. Use a clock with a second hand or a digital seconds display to time yourself for one minute.

How many breaths did you take in one minute while at rest? _____

☑ **3.** Now, get up and walk around the room. Again count the number of breaths you take per minute.

How many breaths did you take in one minute while active? _____

☑ **4.** How do the two breathing rates differ? _____

☑ **5.** Which rate should you use to calculate how much air you will need in space? Why? _____

_____

6. Using the breathing rate you have chosen, **calculate** approximately how many breaths you take in an hour, in a day, and in two days. Show your work.

1 hr = 60 minutes

1 day = 24 hours

Breaths per hour: _____

Breaths per day: _____

Breaths per two days: _____

To determine the amount of air you will need, you will multiply the rate of your breathing by the volume of air that your lungs hold in one breath. First you must capture the air you exhale in one breath and measure its volume. You will **build** a spirometer that captures the air that you exhale in one breath and measures its volume.

Go to the materials station(s). Pick up each material one at a time. Think about how it may or may not be useful in your design. Leave the materials where they are.

7. What are your design constraints? _____

_____

Develop Possible Solutions

8. List two different ways you could use the materials provided to build a spirometer to contain the air that you exhale and measure its volume. _____

_____

_____

_____

_____

Choose One Solution

☐ **9. Describe** the spirometer you will build. Include an explanation of how the device will contain your exhaled breath and whether it will measure the volume of your breath (your lung capacity) directly or by displacement.

_____

_____

_____

☐ **10. List** the materials that you will need. _____

_____

_____

Design and Construct a Prototype

Gather your materials. **Build** your spirometer.

☐ **11. Record** the design details of your prototype. **Describe** the dimensions of the finished device and the measurements of the materials that you used. _____

_____

_____

_____

Test the Prototype

To test your prototype, inhale normally then exhale normally into the tubing connected to your spirometer. Be sure not to forcefully exhale. This is called your "tidal volume." Do three trials and **record** your measurements in milliliters (mL). **Calculate** the average of your three trials in mL.

	TIDAL VOLUME (mL)
Trial 1	
Trial 2	
Trial 3	
Average of three trials	

12. Then using the conversion of 1 Liter = 1000 ml, **convert** your average tidal volume into liters. Show your work:

Tidal volume in liters = _____ .

13. Use this average tidal volume in liters to **calculate** the total volume of air you would need for your two-day trip into space. Show your work:

Volume of air needed for two days in space (liters) = ____ _____ .

Communicate Results

14. Did your spirometer enable you to measure the volume of air you breathe in one breath? Explain. _____

_____

15. Rate how well your spirometer worked using the scale below. Then, **explain** why you gave the spirometer that rating.

0 — did not work

1 — worked but not very well

2 — worked well

My spirometer prototype rating: _____

Explanation: _____

_____

Evaluate and Redesign

16. **Explain** how you would change your design to make it better. _____

_____

_____

How does Earth move?

The sun is rising in the eastern sky. Describe the path you think the sun will take across the sky during the day.

Inquiry Explore It!

How does sunlight strike Earth's surface?

☐ **1.** Hold a flashlight about 15 cm directly above a piece of cardboard. Turn the flashlight on.

☐ **2. Observe** the light on the cardboard. Trace the shape the light makes.

☐ **3.** Repeat Step 1 slowly tilting the flashlight to the side. Repeat Step 2.

Explain Your Results

4. How did the light change?

....

....

5. Infer What determines how concentrated the sunlight is that strikes Earth's surface?

....

....

Materials

flashlight

white cardboard

marker

I will know how Earth rotates and revolves. I will know why the sun, the moon, and stars appear to move across the sky.

Words to Know

axis   orbit
rotation   revolution

Earth and the Sun

Think about a time thousands of years ago, before telescopes had been invented and before astronauts had ever traveled into space. If you look at the daytime sky, the sun rises in the east and sets in the west. People naturally thought the sun was moving around Earth.

We now know that the sun is the center of our solar system. Earth and the other planets move around the sun. Earth spins, causing the sun and other objects, such as other stars, to appear to move across the sky.

1. ◉ **Compare and Contrast** Use the graphic organizer below to list what is alike about and different between the way people used to think about Earth and the sun and what we know now.

Before telescopes and space exploration, some people thought Earth was the center of the universe.

Then   **Now**

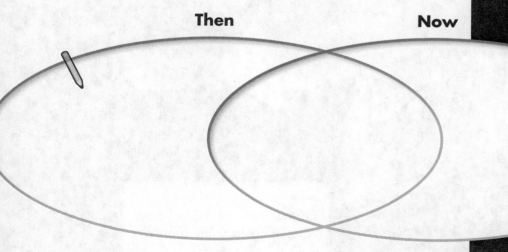

Earth's Rotation

Earth and the other planets of the solar system rotate, or spin, much like a top spins. They each rotate around an imaginary line called an **axis.** The northern end of Earth's axis is the North Pole. The southern end of Earth's axis is the South Pole. One whole spin of an object on its axis is called a **rotation.** One full rotation is what we call a *day*.

Earth rotates around its imaginary axis from west to east. As Earth spins, the sun, moon, stars, and planets only seem to rise in the east and set in the west. When you watch the sun set, remember that it is you who are moving. You are riding on the rotating Earth.

2. Explain Why does the sun appear to move from east to west across the sky?

....

....

3. Fill in the Blank In the illustration below, fill in the missing words in the labels.

Earth completes one

....

in about 24 hours.

Earth's ....
is an imaginary line around
which Earth rotates.

Earth's Revolution

Earth also moves in an orbit. An **orbit** is the path an object takes as it revolves around a star, planet, or moon. Earth's orbit is elliptical—it has an oval shape. The moon's orbit around Earth is also elliptical. One full orbit of an object around another object is called a **revolution.** Earth's revolution around the sun lasts for just a few hours longer than 365 days. This period may sound familiar to you. It is one year. The moon's revolution around Earth takes 27.3 days, or about a month.

Just as gravity keeps you on Earth, gravity keeps Earth in its orbit around the sun. Because the sun is so massive, its gravity pulls all the planets toward it. This pull keeps the planets from moving in straight lines into space.

Lightning Lab

Day and Night
Shine a flashlight on a globe one meter away. Darken the room. Which parts of the globe have light shining on them? Which are in shadow? Have a partner slowly turn the globe. Explain what you see.

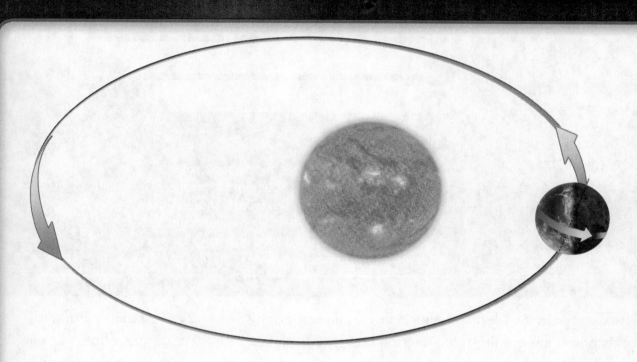

4. **Infer** Draw a representation of the moon's orbit in the diagram above.

5. ◎ **Compare and Contrast** How are the orbits of Earth and the moon alike? How are they different?

....

....

Seasons

Earth always tilts the same way during its revolution around the sun. Earth's tilt affects how much sunlight parts of Earth receive. The amount of sunlight an area receives affects its climate and seasons. Seasons change as Earth's axis tilts either toward or away from the sun at different times during its revolution. When the North Pole is tilted away from the sun, sunlight is less concentrated in the Northern Hemisphere. Temperatures drop, and winter sets in. At the same time, the South Pole is tilted toward the sun. The Southern Hemisphere receives concentrated sunlight and has the warm temperatures of summer.

axis

In this diagram, look at how the sun's rays strike Earth. During the Southern Hemisphere summer, the Sun's rays strike Earth more directly south of the equator. The rays are concentrated, not spread out. Concentrated energy gives this region warm summer weather.

equator

6. [CHALLENGE] In the Northern Hemisphere summer, Earth's axis points toward the sun. Describe how you think the axis looks in the spring.

....
....
....
....
....
....

7. **Calculate** Earth's distance from the sun in January is about 147,000,000 km. In July its distance from the sun is about 152,100,000 km. About how much closer is Earth to the sun in January than in July?

The number of daylight hours also changes as the seasons change. On the first day of its summer, a hemisphere has more hours of daylight than at any other time of the year. The least number of daylight hours occurs on the first day of winter. Twice a year the hours of day and night are equal. At this time, Earth's axis points neither toward nor away from the sun.

8. Identify In the diagram, label each part of Earth's orbit with the Northern Hemisphere season that it represents.

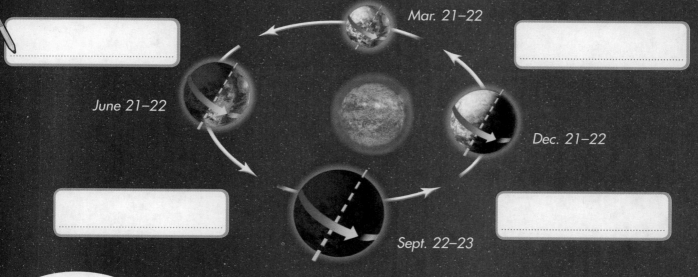

Mar. 21–22

June 21–22

Dec. 21–22

Sept. 22–23

Got it?

9. Describe What is a rotation? What is a revolution?

....

....

....

10. Explain In what direction do stars, the moon, and the sun seem to move across the sky? Why?

....

....

....

Stop! I need help with ....

Wait! I have a question about ....

Go! Now I know ....

What is a star?

Envision It!

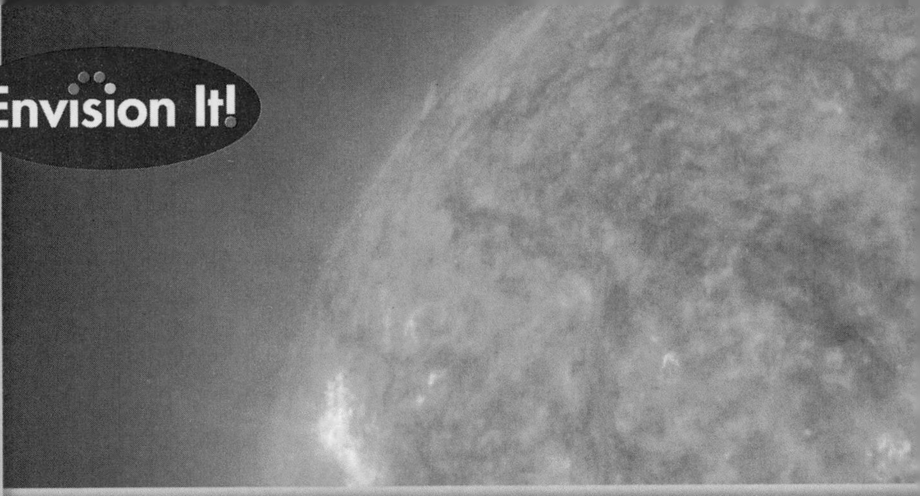

Discuss whether or not you think the sun has a hard surface like Earth.

MY PLANET DIARY

//// **MISCONCEPTION** ////

What happens to the stars during the day? You might think they disappear, but they do not. The stars are always in the sky during the day just as they are at night. However, the sun's light is so much brighter than the faint light coming from the stars that the stars cannot be seen. On a dark clear night, without the aid of a telescope, you might see over a thousand stars in the sky.

Do all stars look the same? Explain.

....

....

....

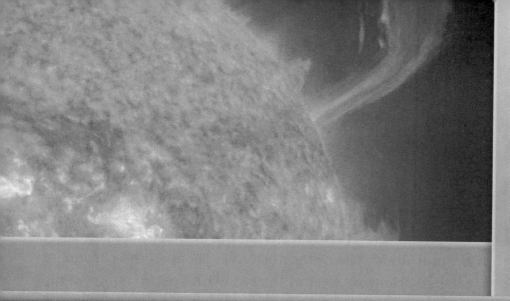

I will know the physical characteristics of the sun. I will know why the star Polaris is important.

Words to Know

solar flare   constellation

Stars

Stars are gigantic balls of very hot gases that give off radiation. The sun is a medium-sized star. Stars known as giants may be eight to 100 times as large as the sun. Supergiants are even larger. They may be up to 300 times as large as the sun. A star at the end of its life can collapse and become very small—only about the size of Earth.

Even though the sun is only a medium-sized star, it is the largest object in our solar system. Scientists have been able to calculate the sun's mass from the speeds of the planets and the shapes of their orbits around the sun. The sun's mass is nearly two million trillion trillion kilograms — you can write that as a two followed by 30 zeros! The sun has almost 100 percent of the mass in the solar system. The sun is huge when compared to Earth. In fact, the sun has more than one million times the volume of Earth. If you think of the sun as a gumball machine, it would take over one million Earth gumballs to fill the sun gumball machine!

1. **Summarize** Compare the size of the sun to the size of other stars. Compare its size to Earth.

....

....

....

....

2. **Recognize** How can scientists determine the mass of the sun?

....

....

....

....

....

sun

Earth

Lightning Lab

Measuring Shadows
Have a partner measure your shadow at different times during the day. Write down what you find. Describe how your shadow changes as the sun moves.

4. **Apply** Why might space agencies not want to send astronauts into space during solar flares?

....

....

....

....

Characteristics of the Sun

The sun is a fiery ball of hot gases and has no hard surfaces. It gives off enormous amounts of light and heat. The outer part of the sun is about 5,500°C. The inner core could be as hot as 15,000,000°C.

The Sun's Atmosphere

Like Earth, the sun has an atmosphere. The innermost layer is called the photosphere. It gives off the light energy you see. The layer above the photosphere is the chromosphere. The outermost layer is called the corona.

When scientists look at the sun with special equipment, they see dark spots, called sunspots, moving on the face of the sun. Sunspots are part of the photosphere. They may be the size of Earth or larger. They look dark because they are not as hot as the rest of the photosphere. The number of sunspots increases and decreases in cycles of about eleven years.

Solar Eruptions

Two types of eruptions that take place on the sun are prominences and solar flares. A prominence looks like a ribbon of glowing gases that leaps out of the chromosphere into the corona. Prominences may appear and then disappear in a few days or months.

A **solar flare** is an explosive eruption of waves and particles into space. Solar flares are similar to volcanoes here on Earth. A solar flare causes a bright spot in the chromosphere that may last for minutes or hours. Along with extra-bright light, solar flares also give off other forms of energy. This energy is powerful enough to interrupt radio and satellite communication on Earth.

3. **Identify** What are the physical characteristics of the sun?

....

....

....

....

Solar flares give off more light than other parts of the sun. They emit radio waves, visible light, X rays, plasma, and other radiation.

Core

6. **Explain** Why is Polaris called the North Star?

_____

_____

_____

7. **Infer** How might constellations help scientists study the sky?

_____

_____

_____

_____

Constellations

In the past, people looked up at the night sky and "connected the dots" formed by the stars. They saw patterns that reminded them of bears, dogs, and even a sea monster! Today, scientists divide the night sky into eighty eight constellations. A **constellation** is a group of stars that forms a pattern. Many constellation names are the names of the star patterns that people used long ago.

The star pattern called the Little Dipper contains a star called Polaris. Polaris, or the North Star, is a very hot and very large yellow-white star. It is almost 2,500 times brighter than the sun. It does not look larger than the sun because it is much farther away. Polaris is an important star in navigation. Because it is almost directly above the North Pole, Polaris doesn't seem to move as Earth rotates. If you can find Polaris in the sky, you can tell which direction is north. Early explorers used Polaris as a guide to direct them in their travels. If they located Polaris, then they could determine in which direction they were headed.

Little Dipper

Polaris

Big Dipper

Stars on the Move

Stars are not always in the same place in the sky. They move in predictable ways. Suppose you looked at the sky early one evening and found the Big Dipper. When you looked two hours later, the Big Dipper seemed to have moved toward the west. Actually, the Big Dipper did not move, but you moved. The spinning of Earth makes the stars appear to move from east to west across the sky.

8. **Infer** This time-lapse photo shows how stars seem to move as Earth rotates. Why are the stars in a circular pattern?

....

....

....

Stars appear to spin around Polaris in this time-lapse photo.

Got it?

9. **Summarize** If other stars are brighter and larger than the sun, why does the sun appear so large?

....

....

10. **Describe** What is the significance of Polaris, the North Star?

....

....

....

⬜ **Stop!** I need help with ....

⏸ **Wait!** I have a question about ....

▶ **Go!** Now I know ....

What are the inner planets?

What planet do you think this picture shows?

Inquiry Explore It!

How does distance affect orbiting time?

☐ **1.** Make 2 clay balls the size of golf balls.

☐ **2.** Push one ball onto the end of a meterstick. Push the other ball onto the end of a ruler.

☐ **3.** Hold up each stick. Set the empty ends on the floor.

☐ **4.** Let go of both sticks at the same time. **Observe** closely.

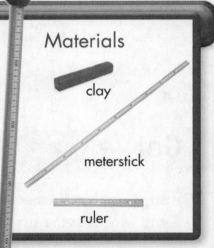

Materials

clay

meterstick

ruler

Explain Your Results

5. Which ball hit the ground first?

....

6. Infer How might a planet's distance from the sun affect the time it takes to make one orbit?

....

....

UNLOCK
THE BIG
?

I will know the inner and outer planets and Earth's position in the solar system. I will know how technology has helped people explore space.

Words to Know

planet   space probe
inner planet   moon

...nets

...here are eight known planets that revolve around ...un. A **planet** is a large, round object that revolves ...nd a star and has cleared the region around its ... The four closest planets to the sun are called **inner ...nets.** Inner planets have rocky surfaces. Mercury, ...s, Earth, and Mars are the inner planets.

...cause all the planets revolve around the sun and ...tars that we see in the sky are much further away, ...an see the planets change positions relative to the ... from one night to the next.

Even though some planets seem to shine, they do not give off their own light like stars do. A planet shines because light from a nearby star reflects off the planet's surface.

Locate The illustrations show what the night sky might ...ook like three weeks apart. **Circle** the object in the sky ...hat might be a planet.

November 4

November 25

Orbiting Objects

Every planet in the solar system revolves around the sun. The orbits of the planets have a slightly elliptical shape.

Objects in the solar system stay in their orbits because of gravity. Gravity is the force of attraction between objects. The force of the sun's gravity is large enough to keep planets around the sun. Without this force, the planets would not stay in their orbits.

2. **Infer** Planets have years of different lengths because of the lengths of their orbits. Draw an ✕ on the planet with the longest year.

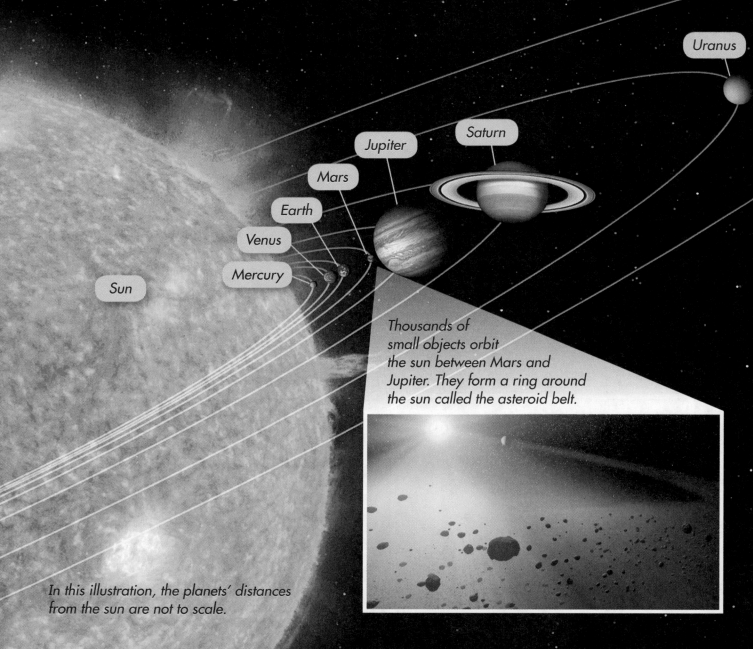

Uranus

Saturn

Jupiter

Mars

Earth

Venus

Mercury

Sun

Thousands of small objects orbit the sun between Mars and Jupiter. They form a ring around the sun called the asteroid belt.

In this illustration, the planets' distances from the sun are not to scale.

Mercury

Mercury is the closest planet to the sun. It is a small planet, slightly bigger than Earth's moon. Mercury is covered with thousands of low spots called craters. Craters are made when meteorites, or rocks that fall from space, crash into the surface.

The *Mariner 10* was the first spacecraft to visit Mercury. Scientists sent the *Mariner 10* space probe in 1973, and it reached the planet in 1974. A **space probe** is a spacecraft that gathers data without a crew. It carries cameras and other tools for studying different objects in space.

Mercury has almost no atmosphere. Because it is so close to the sun, Mercury is scorching hot during the day. Daytime temperatures are much higher than those in the hottest place on Earth. But with no atmosphere to hold in the heat, Mercury is very cold at night.

3. **Predict** How might Mercury be different if it had a thicker atmosphere?

Neptune

Without an atmosphere to protect it, Mercury is struck by many objects that leave craters on its surface.

Venus

Venus is the second planet from the sun. It is about the same size as Earth, but Venus rotates in the opposite direction. Like Mercury, Venus is very hot and dry. Unlike Mercury, Venus has an atmosphere made of thick, swirling clouds. There are strong winds and lightning.

The clouds of Venus are very hot and toxic. They reflect the sun's light very well. This makes Venus one of the brightest objects in Earth's night sky. The clouds also hide the surface of Venus, but scientists have mapped the surface in spite of the clouds. The image on the right was made using radar data from a space probe. The colors were added by computer for better viewing.

Venus with clouds

This image shows what Venus would look like without clouds.

4. **⦿ Cause and Effect** What makes Venus so bright?

Do the math!

Analyze a Bar Graph

How much does an astronaut weigh? That depends. Weight is the measure of the pull of gravity on an object. Different planets have different amounts of gravitational pull.

When an astronaut wears a complete space suit, he or she might weigh about 480 pounds on Earth! The astronaut would weigh less on Mars. The graph shows how much the astronaut would weigh on different planets.

1. The astronaut's weight on Venus would be about $\frac{9}{10}$ of his or her weight on Earth. How much would the astronaut weigh on Venus? Fill in the bar graph to show your answer.

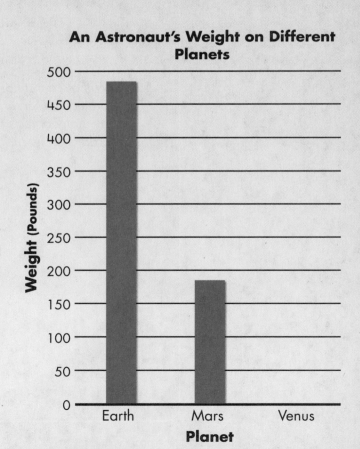

An Astronaut's Weight on Different Planets

Weight (Pounds)

Planet

Earth and the Moon

Earth, our home, is the third planet from the sun. It is also the solar system's largest rocky planet. Earth is the only planet that has liquid water on its surface. In fact, about $\frac{3}{4}$ of Earth's surface is covered with water.

Earth is wrapped in a layer of gas that is about 150 kilometers thick. This layer of gas, or atmosphere, makes life possible on Earth. It filters out some of the sun's harmful rays. It also contains nitrogen, oxygen, carbon dioxide, and water vapor. Plants and animals use these gases. Earth is the only planet in the solar system known to support life.

Earth has one large moon, which is about $\frac{1}{4}$ as wide as Earth. A **moon** is a natural object that revolves around a planet. Our moon has almost no atmosphere. It has many craters that formed when meteorites crashed into its surface. The moon is Earth's natural satellite. A satellite is an object that orbits another object in space. Gravity keeps the moon revolving around Earth, just as it keeps Earth revolving around the sun. As the moon revolves around Earth, there are observable patterns of movement. For example, the moon appears in different places in the sky at different times of the day, month, and year.

It takes the moon 27 days to revolve around Earth.

Earth spins, or rotates, once every 24 hours.

5. [CHALLENGE] The circles below represent Earth and the moon. Measure the diameter of the large circle, and multiply it by 30. That would be the correct distance from Earth to the moon at this scale. Draw the two circles in the space provided. Use the correct distance you found.

● = Earth   • = moon

Mars is the fourth planet from the sun. The soil that covers most of this rocky planet contains iron oxide. This is a reddish-brown material that makes up rust. This material is why Mars is sometimes called the "Red Planet." Mars has two very small and deeply-cratered moons.

The atmosphere of Mars does not have enough oxygen for plants or animals to live. Winds on Mars cause dust storms. These storms are sometimes large enough to cover the whole planet.

Mars has seasons. It also has polar ice caps that grow in the winter and shrink in the summer. Mars has a canyon that is nearly 10 times longer than the Grand Canyon in Arizona.

A Martian day is called a sol and lasts just 40 minutes longer than an Earth day. However, the day sky on Mars looks pink instead of blue!

Lightning Lab

Model Planets
Work in small groups. Make models of the inner planets to scale. The diameter of Mercury is 0.4 that of Earth. The diameter of Venus is 0.9 that of Earth. The diameter of Mars is 0.5 that of Earth.

6. **Infer** Mars is the coldest of the inner planets. What could be a reason?

....

....

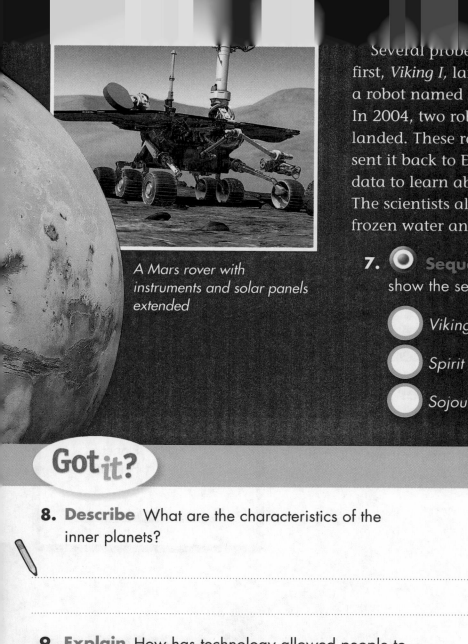

A Mars rover with instruments and solar panels extended

Several probes have landed on Mars. The first, *Viking I,* landed on Mars in 1976. In 1997, a robot named *Sojourner* explored part of Mars. In 2004, two robot rovers, *Spirit* and *Opportunity,* landed. These rovers gathered information and sent it back to Earth. Scientists have used the data to learn about the rocks and soil on Mars. The scientists also found evidence that Mars has frozen water and that it once had liquid water.

7. **Sequence** Number the sentences to show the sequence of events described above.

○ *Viking I* landed on Mars.

○ *Spirit* and *Opportunity* landed on Mars.

○ *Sojourner* explored parts of Mars.

Got it?

8. **Describe** What are the characteristics of the inner planets?

....

....

9. **Explain** How has technology allowed people to explore space?

....

....

....

◻ **Stop!** I need help with ....

❚❚ **Wait!** I have a question about ....

▶ **Go!** Now I know ....

What are the outer planets?

Envision It!

The surface of Jupiter changes every day. What do you think causes these changes?

Inquiry Explore It!

How are the sizes of the inner and outer planets different?

☐ 1. **Measure** the diameter of each paper planet.
Use your measurements and the chart to
identify and label the planets.
Cut out each planet.

☐ 2. Put the **models** of the
planets in order by size.
Compare the sizes of the
inner and outer planets.

Explain Your Results

3. After **observing** your models, compare the sizes of
the inner and outer planets.

....

....

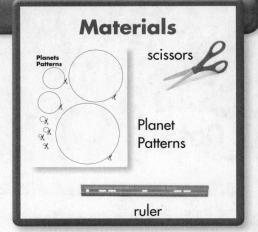

Materials

Planets Patterns

scissors

Planet Patterns

ruler

Comparing Planetary Diameters			
	Planet	Diameter of Planet (rounded to the nearest 100 km)	Diameter of Model* (mm)
Inner Planets	Mercury	4,900	5
	Venus	12,100	12
	Earth	12,800	13
	Mars	6,800	7
Outer Planets	Jupiter	143,000	143
	Saturn	120,500	121
	Uranus	51,000	51
	Neptune	49,500	50

*1mm = 1000km

I will know that the outer planets are Jupiter, Saturn, Uranus, and Neptune and that they have common characteristics.

Words to Know

outer planet

Gas Giants

There are still four more planets in our solar system beyond Mars—Jupiter, Saturn, Uranus, and Neptune. They are known as the **outer planets.**

The outer planets are much larger than the inner planets. They do not have clearly defined surfaces, like those of the inner planets. We only see the atmospheres of the outer planets. For these reasons these planets are often called gas giants. However, they have liquid inner layers and solid cores.

Each of the outer planets has rings of particles and many moons orbiting it.

1. ◉ **Compare and Contrast** Write some similarities and differences between the inner planets and the outer planets.

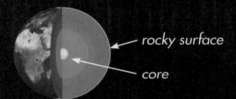

Inner planets have solid crusts.

rocky surface

core

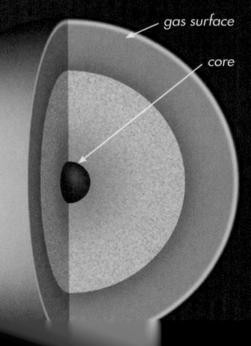

Outer planets do not have a solid crust.

gas surface

core

Jupiter

Jupiter, the fifth planet from the sun, is the largest planet in the solar system. It is a gas giant. Jupiter's atmosphere is mostly hydrogen and helium. The atmosphere of Jupiter shows many bands of color. The planet rotates much faster than Earth. In the time it takes Earth to complete one rotation, Jupiter completes more than two.

Jupiter has many moons. A moon is a natural object that orbits a planet. Some planets, especially the outer planets, have several moons. In 1610, Galileo was the first person to see the four largest moons of Jupiter through his telescope. They are shown to the right.

2. **Contrast** How are Jupiter and Earth different?

....

....

....

....

Ganymede

Io

Europa

Great Red Spot

Callisto

Saturn

The sixth planet from the sun is Saturn. Like Jupiter, Saturn has an atmosphere that contains mostly hydrogen and helium. Saturn is very large, but its density is low.

When Galileo looked at Saturn through his telescope, he saw what looked like a planet with handles! The "handles" were really the brilliant rings that orbit Saturn. The particles making up the rings vary in size from tiny grains to boulders, and they are made of ice, dust, and rock. The inner rings of Saturn revolve faster around the planet than the outer rings.

In 2009 a giant new ring was discovered. The ring is invisible, but its infrared glow was detected by the Spitzer Space Telescope. This ring is tilted relative to the other rings, and rotates in the opposite direction.

3. [CHALLENGE] Two rocks on the rings of Saturn start orbiting at points 1 and 2. After a while, the rock that started at point 1 has moved to point 3. Fill in the number that shows where rock 2 is likely to be, considering its speed.

Lightning Lab

Reading in the Dark
Make a night vision flashlight for reading star charts in the dark. Fold a sheet of red cellophane in half and then into quarters. Use a rubber band or tape to attach it to the end of a flashlight. Test the light. If necessary, add more layers to make the light as red as possible.

The small dot at the center of the ring is Saturn, which is hundreds of times smaller than the ring.

sun and the most distant planet you can see without a telescope. Uranus is a gas giant with an atmosphere of hydrogen, helium, and methane. The planet is so cold that the methane can condense into a liquid. Tiny drops of this liquid methane form a thin cloud that covers the planet, giving it a fuzzy, blue-green look.

Like other gas giants, Uranus has rings and many moons. Unlike the rings of Saturn, the rings of Uranus are dark and hard to see with Earth-based telescopes.

Uranus rotates on its side. No one knows why Uranus has this odd tilt. Scientists think a large object may have hit the planet when the solar system was still forming. This bump may have knocked Uranus onto its side.

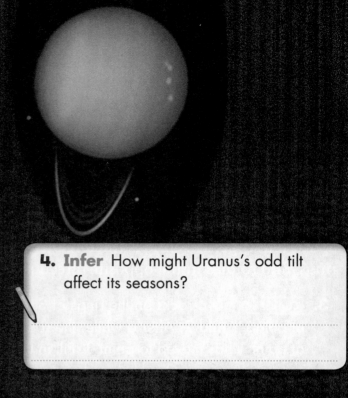

4. **Infer** How might Uranus's odd tilt affect its seasons?

....

....

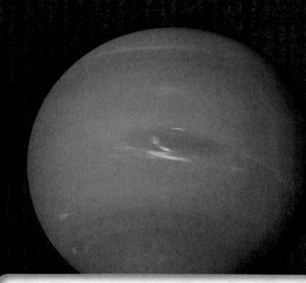

Neptune

Neptune is too far away to see without a telescope. It is the eighth planet from the sun. Astronomers discovered Neptune in 1846. It takes more than one hundred Earth years for Neptune to orbit the sun. Neptune is the smallest of the gas giants. Even so, if Neptune were hollow, it could hold about 60 Earths.

Neptune's atmosphere is like that of Uranus. Like Uranus, Neptune has a bluish color because of the methane in its atmosphere. Neptune also has storms and bands of clouds like Jupiter.

Neptune has at least 13 moons. The largest one is Triton, which may be the coldest object in the solar system.

5. **Compare** What is similar about the atmospheres of Uranus and Neptune?

....

....

Exploring the Giants

Several probes have been sent to explore the outer planets. They were launched from Florida. *Pioneer 10* and *Pioneer 11* were launched in the 1970s, followed by *Voyager 1* and *2*. The *Galileo* probe explored Jupiter in great detail, and the *Cassini* mission has sent back a huge amount of information on Saturn. A smaller probe, named *Huygens*, was launched from *Cassini* and was able to land on Saturn's largest moon, Titan.

6. **Write About It** What information might you like to have sent to you from a space probe?

....

....

7. **Group** Think of three terms to describe some characteristics of the inner planets and the outer planets. Use the terms to contrast the inner and outer planets.

....

....

8. **UNLOCK THE BIG ?** What are some common characteristics of all planets?

....

....

 Stop! I need help with ....

 Wait! I have a question about ....

▶ **Go!** Now I know ....

What are asteroids, meteors, comets, and moons?

Envision It!

Write an X on the rock that might have started out as an asteroid. Tell why you made that choice.

Inquiry Explore It!

How does a meteoroid fall through Earth's atmosphere?

☐ **1.** Lightly place a chunk of a fizzy antacid tablet into a bottle of water.

☐ **2.** Describe what you **observed.**

....

....

....

Explain Your Results

3. After completing this lesson, compare the process of a meteoroid entering Earth's atmosphere with what you **observed** in this **model.**

....

....

....

....

Materials

chunk of fizzy antacid tablet

2 L plastic bottle with water
(filled to the bottom of the neck)

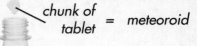

chunk of tablet = meteoroid

water = Earth's atmosphere

bottom of bottle = Earth's surface

I will know the difference
between moons, asteroids,
comets, meteoroids,
meteors, and meteorites.

Words to Know

asteroid   dwarf planet
comet

Asteroids

A rocky mass up to several hundred kilometers
wide that revolves around the sun is an **asteroid.** In
our solar system, most asteroids orbit in the region
between Mars and Jupiter called the asteroid belt.

Most asteroids have uneven shapes. Some have
smaller asteroids orbiting them. The smallest asteroids
are pebble-sized. Most asteroids complete a revolution
in three to six years.

Can Earth be hit by asteroids? It has happened, and
you can see the huge craters that have been the result.
Such collisions are very rare. Fortunately, Jupiter's
gravity holds most asteroids in the area beyond Mars.

1. **Explain** Why is the
   gravitational force of
   Jupiter important to Earth?

....

....

....

....

....

*Asteroid Ida has a smaller asteroid
orbiting around it. The smaller
asteroid is named Dactyl.*

Dactyl

Ida

Meteors

Have you ever seen a shooting star? Shooting stars look like bright lines of fast-moving light that form in the night sky. They last a very short time. Shooting stars are not really stars but meteors.

A meteor forms when a meteoroid hits Earth's atmosphere. A meteoroid is a small piece of rock moving in space. Meteoroids are boulder-sized or smaller. Most are the size of pebbles or grains of sand. When a meteoroid shoots through the air, it heats up quickly. It gets so hot that it glows as a streak of light. Very bright meteors are called fireballs.

Most meteors burn up before they hit Earth's surface. If a meteor does not burn up completely, it may fall to Earth. A piece of a meteor that lands on Earth is called a meteorite. Most meteorites are quite small. The biggest known meteorite is in Namibia, Africa, and weighs 60 tons.

2. **Calculate** The diameter of this crater may be 24 times larger than the diameter of the meteor that formed it. Measure the crater from point A to point B. Then, measure the circles and draw an ✗ on the circle that best represents the probable size of the meteor.

Meteor Crater, in Arizona, was formed by a meteorite impact.

Comet Lulin

Comets

A frozen mass of different types of ice and dust orbiting the sun is a **comet.** Rocky matter may be frozen in the ice. Comets come from areas of the solar system beyond Neptune. Most pass through the solar system in very stretched out and elliptical paths. Several comets a year may travel into the solar system and orbit the sun. You may not see them, though. Only the largest comets can be seen without a telescope.

At certain times each year, meteor showers take place. These occur when Earth passes through the orbit of a comet. A comet heats up and loses dust and rocky matter each time it orbits the sun. These loose pieces remain in the comet's orbit. When these pieces collide with Earth's atmosphere, they become meteors.

Discovering a comet is exciting. How can you discover one? Most comets today are found by people who use telescopes to photograph the sky each night. The photos may show a fuzzy object. Another clue is that stars stay in the same relative position with other stars, but comets do not. If an unknown object keeps changing position compared with stars over a few hours or days, it might be a comet. If you are the first person to discover a comet, it could be named after you.

3. Cause and **Effect** What causes a meteor shower?

Some objects in the solar system have been classified as dwarf planets. A **dwarf planet** is a large, round object that revolves around the sun but has not cleared the region around its orbit.

In 1930, Clyde Tombaugh discovered Pluto. Pluto has an icy solid surface. Astronomers thought for a long time that Pluto was the ninth planet—the only outer planet that is not a gas giant.

Today, astronomers do not consider Pluto a planet. Pluto is a dwarf planet. It is even smaller than Earth's moon. Pluto has an odd orbit. The other planets travel around the sun at the same angle, while Pluto's orbit is tilted. During parts of the orbit, it is closer to the sun than Neptune. This occurred from 1979 to 1999. The next time this will occur is in the year 2227.

Clyde Tombaugh with a telescope

4. Calculate In how many more years will Pluto be closer to the sun than Neptune?

_____

_____

The orbit of Pluto is not aligned with the orbits of the other planets.

Charon was the first moon of Pluto to be discovered. Since then, other moons have been found orbiting Pluto.

Moons

The solar system contains many moons. You may remember that a moon is a natural object that orbits a body bigger than itself. Like planets, moons often have a spherical shape. Earth and Mars are the only inner planets that have moons. The outer planets have many moons.

The moons in the solar system are very different from one another. Earth's moon has no atmosphere. Saturn's largest moon, Titan, has an atmosphere so thick that it lets little light pass through. Jupiter's moon Io has volcanoes on its surface that release sulfur. Sulfur gives Io a colorful appearance.

Moon craters like these form when a moon is struck by another object.

5. ◉ **Compare and Contrast** How are moons and asteroids alike? How are they different?

....

....

....

Got it?

6. **Explain** How can you tell the difference between a comet and a star?

....

....

7. **UNLOCK THE BIG ?** How are comets and asteroids alike and different?

....

....

⬛ **Stop!** I need help with ....

⏸ **Wait!** I have a question about ....

▶ **Go!** Now I know ....

Inquiry Investigate It!

How can spinning affect a planet's shape?

Follow a Procedure

☐ **1.** Cut 2 strips of construction paper, each 2 cm × 45 cm. Cross them at the center and staple them to make an X.

☐ **2.** Bring the 4 ends together and overlap them. Staple them to form a sphere.

Materials

construction paper

scissors

stapler

hole punch

pencil

ruler

Inquiry Skill Scientists **use a model** when the real object is hard to study.

☐ **3.** Punch a hole through the center of the overlapped ends.

☐ **4.** Push a dull pencil through the hole. Only about 5 cm of the pencil should go in.

about 5 cm

5. Hold the pencil between your palms. Move your hands back and forth to make your **model** spin.

6. What shape do you **observe** when it spins?

....

7. **Record** your observations.

Effect of Spinning on a Planet's Shape	
Shape When Not Spinning	**Shape When Spinning**
◯	

Analyze and Conclude

8. How did the sphere change shape when you spun it? Make an **inference** about what happened.

....

....

9. UNLOCK THE BIG ? How is your **model** similar to a spinning planet? How is it different?

....

....

....

....

Planet Hunting

You may think you need a telescope to view planets from your backyard. This is not necessarily true! Planets look like bright stars in the night sky. If you view the sky for several nights, the stars will appear to stay in the same place relative to the other stars, but a planet's position will change. This is how you can tell a planet from a star. Two of the planets that appear the brightest are Venus and Jupiter.

Ask an adult to help. Go outside at night to view the sky. The sky should be relatively clear, with few or no clouds. Do you see any planets? Record your observations. Repeat your sky watching on another night. What do your observations tell you about the objects you see?

....

....

....

....

Vocabulary Smart Cards

axis
rotation
orbit
revolution
solar flare
constellation
planet
inner planet
space probe
moon
outer planet
asteroid
comet
dwarf planet

Play a Game!

Work with a partner. Choose a Vocabulary Smart Card. Do not let your partner see your card.

Play Password. Try to get your partner to say the word or phrase by giving only one-word clues, one at a time. Take turns giving clues and guessing.

299

revolution

traslación

axis

eje

solar flare

fulguración solar

rotation

rotación

constellation

constelación

orbit
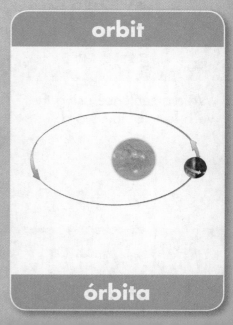
órbita

an imaginary line around which an object spins	one full orbit around the sun
Draw an example.	Write a sentence using this word.
	....
	....
	....
	....
línea imaginaria en torno a la cual gira un objeto	una órbita completa alrededor del Sol

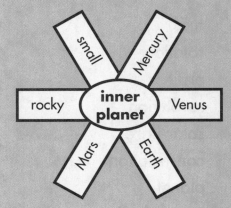

Make a Word Wheel!

Choose a vocabulary word and write it in the center of the Word Wheel graphic organizer. Write examples or related words on the wheel spokes.

one whole spin of an object on its axis	an explosive eruption of waves and particles into space
Write a sentence using this term.	Write one fact about this word.
....	....
....	....
....	....
....	
una vuelta completa de un objeto en torno a su eje	erupción explosiva de ondas y partículas emitidas hacia el espacio

the path an object takes as it revolves around a star, planet, or moon	a group of stars that forms a pattern
Write a sentence using the verb form of this word.	Write a fact about this word.
....	....
....	....
	....
	....
el camino que sigue un objeto al girar alrededor de una estrella, un planeta o una luna	grupo de estrellas que forma una figura

comet

cometa

moon

luna

planet

planeta

dwarf planet

planeta enano

outer planet

planeta exterior

inner planet

planeta interior

asteroid

asteroide

space probe

sonda espacial

a large, round object that revolves around a star and has cleared the region around its orbit

Write two related words.

....

....

cuerpo grande y redondo que orbita una estrella y que ha despejado la zona que rodea su órbita

---

a natural object that revolves around a planet

Draw an example.

satélite natural que orbita un planeta

---

a frozen mass of different types of ice and dust orbiting the sun

Draw an example.

masa helada de distintos tipos de hielo y polvo que orbita el Sol

---

any of the four closest planets to the sun

Write three examples.

....

....

....

cualquiera de los cuatro planetas más cercanos al Sol

---

any of the four planets in our solar system beyond Mars

Write a sentence using this term.

....

....

cualquiera de los cuatro planetas de nuestro sistema solar que quedan más allá de Marte

---

a large, round object that revolves around the sun but has not cleared the region around its orbit

Write one example.

....

....

cuerpo grande y redondo que orbita el Sol, pero que no ha despejado la zona que rodea su órbita

---

a spacecraft that gathers data without a crew

Write a sentence using this term.

....

....

....

nave espacial sin tripulantes que recoge datos

---

a rocky mass up to several hundred kilometers wide that revolves around the sun

Write one fact about this word.

....

....

....

masa rocosa de hasta varios cientos de kilómetros de ancho que gira alrededor del Sol

---

....

....

....

....

Lesson 1

How does Earth move?

- Earth rotates around an imaginary line called an axis.
- Earth revolves around the sun in an elliptical orbit. Earth's tilt and revolution cause seasonal differences in parts of Earth.

Lesson 2

What is a star?

- The sun is a medium-sized star.
- A constellation is a group of stars that forms a pattern.
- Stars appear to move across the sky because Earth rotates.

Lesson 3

What are the inner planets?

- Mercury, Venus, Earth, and Mars are the inner planets.
- The inner planets have solid surfaces and are relatively small.
- Objects in the solar system stay in their orbits because of gravity.

Lesson 4

What are the outer planets?

- Jupiter, Saturn, Uranus, and Neptune are the outer planets.
- The outer planets have gaseous surfaces and are relatively large.
- Space probes have been sent to study the outer planets.

Lesson 5

What are asteroids, meteors, comets, and moons?

- An asteroid is a rocky mass that revolves around the sun.
- A comet is a frozen mass that orbits the sun.
- A piece of a meteor that lands on Earth is called a meteorite.

Lesson 1

How does Earth move?

1. **Vocabulary** Earth's _____ takes 365 days.
   A. rotation
   B. revolution
   C. orbit
   D. axis

2. **Explain** The picture below shows how the moon moves in the sky. Why does the moon appear to move from east to west?

3. **Predict** What would happen to the seasons of the world if Earth's axis tilted in the opposite direction?

....

....

....

....

....

Lesson 2

What is a star?

4. **Vocabulary** What is a constellation?

....

....

....

5. **Identify** Which layer of the sun gives off the light energy we see?

....

....

6. ◎ **Compare and Contrast** Read the passage below and then answer the question.

> Prominences and solar flares are eruptions on the surface of the sun. A prominence looks like a ribbon of glowing gases that leaps into the corona. Prominences may appear for days or even months. Solar flares appear as bright spots on the chromosphere. They may last for minutes or hours.

What do prominences and solar flares have in common? How are they different?

....

....

....

Lesson 3

What are the inner planets?

7.  **Sequence** List the inner planets in order of distance from the sun.

....

....

....

....

....

....

Lesson 4

What are the outer planets?

Do the math!

8. Venus orbits the sun at an average distance of 108 million km. Uranus orbits the sun at an average distance of 2.8 billion km. How many times farther from the sun is Uranus than Venus?

....

....

....

Lesson 5

What are asteroids, meteors, comets, and moons?

9. **Summarize** Explain the difference between asteroids, meteors, comets, and moons.

....

....

....

....

....

....

10. **APPLY THE BIG ?** **How do objects move in space?**

Think about what you have learned about the solar system. Why would it be difficult for humans to travel to visit the planets that you have learned about? Name specific planets and moons in your answer.

....

....

....

....

Benchmark Practice

Read each question and choose the best answer.

1 Earth and the other planets closest to the sun are made mostly of

  A gas.

  B metal.

  C water.

  D rock.

2 What kind of technology has allowed people to explore the outer planets?

  A robot rover

  B space probe

  C space shuttle

  D robot

3 Which shows the inner planets correctly ordered from farthest to closest from the sun?

  A Mars, Earth, Venus, Mercury

  B Mars, Venus, Mercury, Earth

  C Venus, Mercury, Earth, Mars

  D Earth, Mercury, Mars, Venus

4 What type of object is abundant between the orbits of Mars and Jupiter?

  A planet

  B star

  C comet

  D asteroid

5 What kind of movement does this diagram show?

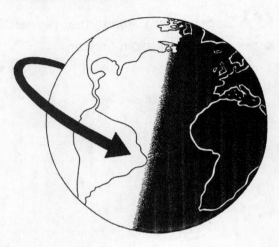

  A Earth' orbit

  B Earth's revolution

  C Earth's rotation

  D Earth's axis

6 Suppose you are an astronaut taking a trip to the moon. Write about what you see when you arrive. Include what you see on the surface of the moon and what you see in the sky.

....

....

....

....

....

Green Bank Observatory

Do you like learning more about the universe? The National Radio Astronomy Observatory in Green Bank, West Virginia, is just the place for young scientists like you to come and explore space.

Green Bank is located in the Allegheny Mountain Range. The telescope there, the Green Bank Telescope, is the world's largest fully movable radio telescope. A radio telescope works by receiving information in the form of radio waves. These waves come from all over the universe. The telescope at Green Bank can be turned so that it can get data from all angles.

APPLY THE BIG ?Q

How might a trip to the Green Bank Telescope help you know more about the solar system and other objects in space?

....

....

....

....

If you take a trip to Green Bank, you can take a guided tour of the telescope. You can also stop at the science center and view and interact with exhibits about space.

Materials

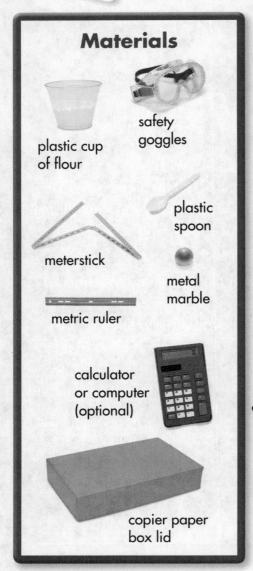

plastic cup of flour

safety goggles

meterstick

plastic spoon

metal marble

metric ruler

calculator or computer (optional)

copier paper box lid

Be careful! Wear safety goggles.

Inquiry Skill

When scientists conduct an experiment, they identify the **independent variable,** the **dependent variable,** and the **controlled variables.**

How does the speed of a meteorite affect the crater it makes?

In this **experiment** you will create a model to find out how a meteorite's speed affects the size of the impact crater.

Ask a question.

Will meteorites that move faster make a smaller or larger crater than meteorites that move more slowly?

State a hypothesis.

1. Write a **hypothesis** by circling one choice and finishing the sentence. If a meteorite is moving faster, then it will make a crater with a width that is
a) larger than
b) smaller than
c) about the same size as
a crater made by a slower-moving meteorite because

....

Identify and control variables.

2. The marble is a **model** of a meteorite. The flour is a model of the surface the meteorite hits. **Controlled variables** are things you must keep the same in an experiment if you want a fair test. What will you keep the same?

....

3. The **independent variable** is the variable you change in an experiment. What will you change in this experiment?

....

....

4. The **dependent variable** is the variable you **measure** in an experiment. What will you measure in this experiment?

....

Design your test.

5. Draw how you will set up your **model.**

6. List your steps in the order in which you will do them.

Do your test.

☐ **7.** Follow the steps you wrote.

☐ **8.** Select a tool to **measure** the width of the crater in millimeters. **Record** your results in a table.

☐ **9.** Scientists repeat their tests to improve their accuracy. Repeat your test if time allows.

Collect and record your data.

☐ **10.** Fill in the chart.

Interpret your data.

☐ **11.** Use your data to make a bar graph.

Work Like a Scientist
Scientists work with other scientists. They compare their methods and results. Talk with your classmates. Compare your methods and results.

☐ 12. Study your chart and graph. What patterns do you see in your data?

....

....

....

....

Technology Tools
Your teacher may want you to use a computer (with the right software) or a graphing calculator to help collect, organize, analyze, and present your data. These tools can help you make tables, charts, and graphs.

☐ 13. Infer Describe your results. What can you infer from your results?

....

....

....

....

....

....

State your conclusion.

14. Communicate your conclusion. Compare your **hypothesis** with your results. Share your results with others.

....

....

....

....

....

....

Crater Formation

The surfaces of Earth's moon and of the planet Mercury are covered with craters. Craters are bowl-shaped low spots that form when meteorites crash into the surface of a moon or planet.

Write a hypothesis about how the mass of a meteorite affects the size of the crater it makes. Then design and carry out an experiment to test your hypothesis.

Rain Gauge

A rain gauge is an instrument used to measure how much rain falls at a given place. Rain gauges may be of different sizes or shapes. What effect do you think changing the size of the opening of the rain gauge has on the amount of rain the gauge collects?

Write a hypothesis to answer the question. Then design and carry out an experiment to test your hypothesis.

Science and Engineering Practices

1. Ask a question or define a problem.
2. Develop and use models.
3. Plan and carry out investigations.
4. Analyze and interpret data.
5. Use math and computational thinking.
6. Construct explanations or design solutions.
7. Engage in argument from evidence.
8. Obtain, evaluate, and communicate information.

Model a Planet's Orbit

What is the shape of a planet's orbit? Position two pushpins near the center of a square of cardboard. The pins should be about 5 cm (2 in.) apart. Tie the ends of a piece of string together to form a loop. Place the loop around the pins. Place the point of a pencil against the inside of the loop and stretch the string tight. Move the pencil around inside the loop unit it is back at the starting point. What shape can you draw using only one pin?

Landforms and Weather

Remember that winds interact with landforms, such as mountain ranges, which can affect weather patterns in an area. A mountain range can force air to rise upwards and cool, forming clouds that release precipitation.

- Ask a question about how a mountain range influences weather patterns.

- Write a prediction to answer your question.

- Conduct research and record any data you find on the weather patterns in areas with mountain ranges.

- Draw a diagram to model how the mountain range influences winds and clouds in the atmosphere.

- Share your research and data with the class.

What is
she trying
to
DISCOVER?

The Nature of Science

Try It!   What questions do
scientists ask?

STEM Activity   Where's the Wind Going?

Lesson 1   What do scientists do?

Lesson 2   How do scientists investigate?

Lesson 3   How do scientists collect and
interpret data?

Lesson 4   How do scientists support their
conclusions?

Investigate It!   How does a banana slice
change over time?

Scientists use a variety of skills and tools to discover new things about the world around them.

Predict   How is this young scientist using tools to learn more about her world?

....

....

 What is science?

What questions do scientists ask?

Scientists ask questions about objects, organisms, and events. Good scientific questions can be answered by making observations and measurements.

Scientific or Not?

scissors

☐ **1.** Work in a group. Cut apart the questions.
Classify the questions into 2 piles.
Pile 1 Good Scientific Questions

Pile 2 Not Good Scientific Questions

☐ **2.** Discuss how you made each sorting decision.

Inquiry Skill
You **classify** when you sort things into groups.

Explain Your Results

3. Draw a Conclusion
Pick one question from Pile 1. Letter of question: _____
Explain why is it a good scientific question.

....

....

....

4. Pick one question from Pile 2. Letter of question: _____
Explain why it is not a good scientific question.

....

....

....

5. **UNLOCK THE BIG ?** Pick another question from Pile 2. Letter of question: _____
Rewrite it to make it into a good scientific question.
Then explain why it is a good scientific question.

....

....

Text Features

Text features, such as headings, highlighting, pictures, and captions, give you clues about what you will read.

heading   picture of a pencil

A **caption** tells specific information about a picture.

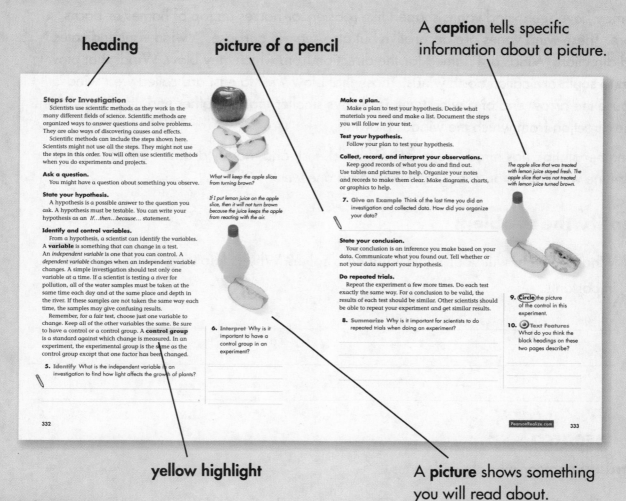

Steps for Investigation
Scientists use scientific methods as they work in the many different fields of science. Scientific methods are organized ways to answer questions and solve problems. They are also ways of discovering causes and effects.

Scientific methods can include the steps shown here. Scientists might not use all the steps. They might not use the steps in this order. You will often use scientific methods when you do experiments and projects.

Ask a question.
You might have a question about something you observe.

State your hypothesis.
A hypothesis is a possible answer to the question you ask. A hypothesis must be testable. You can write your hypothesis as an *If...then...because...* statement.

Identify and control variables.
From a hypothesis, a scientist can identify the variables. A **variable** is something that can change in a test. An *independent variable* is one that you can control. A *dependent variable* changes when an independent variable changes. A simple investigation should test only one variable at a time. If a scientist is testing a river for pollution, all of the water samples must be taken at the same time each day and at the same place and depth in the river. If these samples are not taken the same way each time, the samples may give confusing results.

Remember, for a fair test, choose just one variable to change. Keep all of the other variables the same. Be sure to have a control or a control group. A **control group** is a standard against which change is measured. In an experiment, the experimental group is the same as the control group except that one factor has been changed.

5. **Identify** What is the independent variable in an investigation to find how light affects the growth of plants?

What will keep the apple slices from turning brown?

If I put lemon juice on the apple slice, then it will not turn brown because the juice keeps the apple from reacting with the air.

6. **Interpret** Why is it important to have a control group in an experiment?

Make a plan.
Make a plan to test your hypothesis. Decide what materials you need and make a list. Document the steps you will follow in your test.

Test your hypothesis.
Follow your plan to test your hypothesis.

Collect, record, and interpret your observations.
Keep good records of what you do and find out. Use tables and pictures to help. Organize your notes and records to make them clear. Make diagrams, charts, or graphics to help.

7. **Give an Example** Think of the last time you did an investigation and collected data. How did you organize your data?

State your conclusion.
Your conclusion is an inference you make based on your data. Communicate what you found out. Tell whether or not your data support your hypothesis.

Do repeated trials.
Repeat the experiment a few more times. Do each test exactly the same way. For a conclusion to be valid, the results of each test should be similar. Other scientists should be able to repeat your experiment and get similar results.

8. **Summarize** Why is it important for scientists to do repeated trials when doing an experiment?

The apple slice that was treated with lemon juice stayed fresh. The apple slice that was not treated with lemon juice turned brown.

9. **Circle** the picture of the control in this experiment.

10. **Text Features** What do you think the black headings on these two pages describe?

332   333

PearsonRealize.com

yellow highlight   A **picture** shows something you will read about.

Practice It!

Read the text features in the chart below. Find the text features in the textbook pages shown above. Write a clue that each one gives you about the content.

Text Feature	Clue
picture of a pencil	
yellow highlight	
heading	

Where's the Wind Going?

You may have seen wind vanes shaped like roosters or horses on top of homes or barns before. These wind vanes are decorative but also serve a purpose. A wind vane indicates wind direction. Winds are named for the direction from which they blow. Winds that blow north to south are called north winds. Those that blow west to east are called west winds. Because the arrow end of a wind vane is always smaller than the other end, the arrow points in the direction from which the wind is blowing.

A weather station has hired you to design, build, test, and modify a wind vane and use it to determine wind direction changes in your area one week.

Identify the Problem

☐ **1.** What problem will your wind vane help solve? Why is knowing wind direction important?

_____

_____

_____

Do Research

Examine photographs of wind vanes.

☐ **2.** Which elements of a wind vane do you think are the most important to its function? Which are not? Explain._____

_____

_____

☐ **3.** The weight of a wind vane is evenly distributed between the ends. How is the surface area distributed? Why does the distribution of surface area matter?_____

_____

_____

4. What does it mean if a wind vane is pointing north? _____

_____

_____

Go to the materials station(s). **Examine** the materials, and think about how each one may or may not be useful for your wind vane. Leave the materials where they are.

5. What are your design constraints? _____

_____

_____

Develop Possible Solutions

6. Describe two ways in which you could use the materials to build a wind vane.

_____

_____

_____

Choose One Solution

7. Draw your design. **Label** all the parts. **Describe** how you will build your wind vane.

_____

_____

_____

8. How will you position your wind vane to give you an accurate reading?

_____

_____

_____

9. **List** the material(s) you will use for your wind vane. _____

_____

_____

Design and Construct a Prototype

Gather the materials you need to build your wind vane as well as a ruler. **Build** your prototype. **Measure** the length and height of your wind vane, as well as the dimensions of its head and tail.

10. **Record** the design details of your prototype. _____

_____

_____

_____

Test the Prototype

Test your prototype. Take your wind vane outside to an open area away from trees and other objects that might affect the flow of wind. Holding your wind vane well above the ground, position it so it will give you an accurate reading.

11. From what direction is the wind blowing today? _____

Communicate Results

12. **Compare your results** with your classmates. Did you have similar conclusions? Explain.

_____

_____

Evaluate and Redesign

☐ **13.** Use a scale of 1 to 3 to rate your wind vane where 1 — it did not turn at all, 2 — it turned but there were other problems, 3 — it worked well, and you were accurately able to determine wind direction. Explain your rating.

_____

_____

☐ **14.** What changes could you make to your wind vane to make it more accurate?

_____

_____

_____

☐ **15.** **Make** your changes and **record** the new design details. _____

_____

_____

☐ **16.** Use your modified wind vane to find the direction of the wind every day for the next seven days. **Record** your data below.

Date	Wind Direction	Weather Conditions: Temperature and Precipitation

Do you notice any correlation between wind direction changes and weather changes? Explain. _____

_____

What do scientists do?

Tell what you think this scientist is learning about the ocean.

mY pLaNeT DiaRY

Deep in the ocean lies a world that is almost completely unexplored by humans.

Animals, such as the giant tubeworm, live in extreme conditions 2,600 meters below the ocean's surface. That far below the surface there is extremely high pressure and not very much oxygen or light. Structures called hydrothermal vents are near volcanoes and release very hot water. The water temperature can be more than 400°C!

Giant tubeworms can grow to be up to 2.5 meters long and 10 centimeters wide. They do not have mouths. Instead, giant tubeworms absorb nutrients made by tiny bacteria that live inside of them!

giant tubeworms

Describe What might a scientist do to find out how giant tubeworms interact with their environment?

....

....

....

I will know how scientists use inquiry to learn about the world around them.

Words to Know

hypothesis
observation

Problems, Decisions, and New Ideas

How deep is the ocean? What creatures live in its depths? The world around us is filled with things that are still unknown. To better understand the world, scientists first define a problem and then try to find answers.

Scientific investigation begins with a testable question. Almost every part of your life has been improved in some way by science or by something science made possible. Science can help you get the information you need to make good decisions too. Should you snack on a banana or a soda? What can you do to avoid catching a cold? Scientists can help people answer questions, solve problems, and form new ideas through the use of scientific processes.

1. ⊙ **Text Features** Complete the chart to explain the text features on this page.

This instrument shows water temperature and depth. It is used in fishing.

2. **Predict** Tell what problem you think the tool above might help solve.

Text Feature	Clue
photograph	shows an example of a tool used to find depth
blue heading	

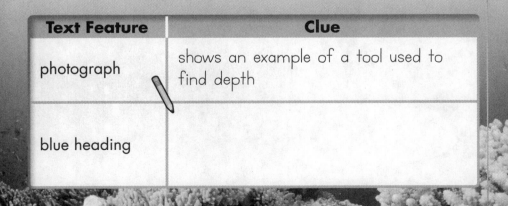

Scientific Research and Knowledge

After scientists define a problem, they begin their investigation with research. Scientists need to use a variety of appropriate reference materials to do research. The reference materials they use need to be sources of information that scientists have agreed upon. Scientists cannot draw valid conclusions from information that cannot be verified by other scientists. For example, a scientist researching ocean water cannot simply find information from a random Internet source and use it in an investigation. The source must be reliable, and the information must have been reviewed and verified by other scientists.

Examples of appropriate reference materials may include books and scientific journals. Scientists may use articles in the scientific journals to do their research. These articles are written by scientists and reviewed by other scientists before they are published. Many of these journals can be found in libraries and on the Internet. Sometimes, information even from reliable sources can change. New findings might cause scientists to rethink old ideas.

3. **Analyze** The scientists below found information on the Internet in a blog. Could they use this piece of information to answer a scientific problem they have defined?

....

....

....

....

....

....

Predict and Make Hypotheses

Scientists use a problem they have defined and research from appropriate sources to form a prediction, or a hypothesis. A **hypothesis** is a statement of what you think will happen during an investigation. It is often written in the form of an *if... then... because* statement. Scientists use experience and what they have found in their research to predict what they think will be a solution to the problem.

Look at the picture above. One example of a hypothesis that scientist might have made is, *If the level of water pollution increases, then the population of manatees will decrease because the plants they eat cannot live in highly polluted water.*

4. **Compose** You have read one possible hypothesis about manatees. Write an example of a different hypothesis the scientist could have formed.

....

....

....

....

Go Green

A Bright Invention
Through research and careful observation, scientists often find solutions to everyday problems. Think about your community. Define a pollution problem that affects it. What are some ideas you can think of to solve this problem? Share your ideas with others.

Make Observations

Scientists use many skills and processes to find answers to problems. One of these is making observations. An **observation** is something you find out about objects, events, or living things by using your senses. Scientists make observations very carefully. In this way, they can be sure that the information they gather is reliable. Scientists often use tools, such as thermometers, to extend their senses. Scientists are also good at organizing their observations. When scientists have collected their information, they analyze and evaluate it to draw conclusions. They also share their findings with other scientists, who can then see if their own results are similar.

For example, scientists may have observed that a group of sea turtles returns to the same beach every year to lay eggs. The scientists want to find out what causes the turtles to return and where they go between the yearly beach visits. Scientists used identification tags and radio transmitters to observe that a sea turtle might travel thousands of kilometers in one year and return to the same beach.

5. Analyze The scientist below is observing a sea turtle. What problem might the scientist define, and how might she find answers to the problem?

....

....

....

....

....

....

Draw Conclusions

Scientists use their observations to draw conclusions. When they draw a conclusion, they summarize what they have learned by analyzing their observations. For example, a scientist may observe that some populations of birds that eat certain fish are decreasing. The scientist may then observe that the fish have been dying. By testing the properties of soil samples from the riverbed, the scientist may be able to observe qualities of the soil, such as the presence of pollution. Using this observation, the scientist might conclude that pollution in the river is causing the living things there to be unhealthy and to die or move away.

These scientists are testing for pollution.

6. **Describe** Tell how scientific testing helps scientists draw conclusions.

Got it?

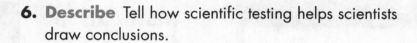

7. **Explain** What are four things that scientists do?

....

....

8. **Explain** How can people solve problems?

....

....

9. **Draw Conclusions** Why should you use a variety of sources when you do research for an investigation?

....

⬛ **Stop!** I need help with ....

⏸ **Wait!** I have a question about ....

▶ **Go!** Now I know ....

How do scientists investigate?

Envision It!

Tell how you think scientists use this wind tunnel to build better cars.

Inquiry Explore It!

Which method keeps bread freshest?

Materials

4 slices of bread

paper bag

waxed paper

plastic bag

paper plate

hand lens

☐ **1.** Put 2 slices of bread on a plate. **Observe** with a hand lens. **Record.** Cover 1 slice with waxed paper.

☐ **2.** Put another slice in a paper bag. Close the bag. Put another slice in a plastic bag. Seal the bag.

☐ **3.** Wait 5 days. Observe the slices. Record your observations on the chart.

Bread Observations				
	Waxed Paper	**Plastic Bag**	**Paper Bag**	**Uncovered Slice**
Day 5				

Explain Your Results

4. Interpret Data Compare the freshness of the bread slices after 5 days.

5. Infer How could you combine methods to keep bread fresh longer?

UNLOCK THE BIG ?

I will know how scientists investigate problems in many different ways.

Words to Know

experiment	control group
variable	procedures

Scientific Investigation

Scientific investigation usually begins with an observation. Someone observes that cars with a certain shape are more fuel efficient. Scientists then ask a question about the observation and collect data to answer their question. One important way to find reliable answers is to do an experiment. An **experiment** is the use of scientific methods to test your hypothesis. Remember that a hypothesis is a statement of what you think will happen in an investigation.

There is no single "scientific method" for finding answers. Biologists study living things with different methods than astronomers use to study the stars. For both types of scientists, however, it is important to observe, collect information, test ideas, make predictions, and share their findings with other scientists who can disagree with or confirm the findings.

However, it is not always possible to manipulate variables in a way that can answer scientific questions. Sometimes you have to design an investigation to test a hypothesis without doing a controlled experiment. In addition to controlled experiments, three types of investigations that scientists use are models, surveys, and sampling. These often help scientists test hypotheses.

1. **Predict** Write a possible hypothesis that this scientist is thinking about as he does his experiment.

....

....

....

....

....

Models

Scientists often use models to learn more about the world or to test designs and materials. Models are objects or ideas that represent other things. They show how something is constructed or how it works. Models are often used to study things that are very large, have many parts, or are difficult to observe directly.

The car model in the picture below is a computer-generated model. Testing a computer model of a car has some advantages over testing real cars. For example, it is easier to control parts of the experiment, such as driving conditions, in a computer model. Once a computer-generated model car has been tested virtually, a machine is used to carve the car out of clay. The physical model can be used to help scientists learn more about how an actual car will work.

Models are helpful tools. However, they are not the actual objects. Testing different models or the real car, for example, may give different results. Scientists may have to do more research and testing to find more information about the cars. Even so, models are valuable tools that help scientists understand the world around them.

2. **Give an Example** What is another advantage of using a computer-generated model of a car?

....

....

....

These models help scientists study cars.

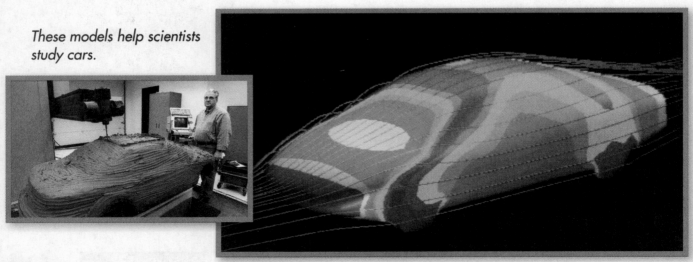

Surveys and Sampling

Scientists do investigations in many different fields of science. Sometimes the best way for a scientist to investigate is by using a survey. Surveys can be questionnaires that are given to a number of people whose answers are recorded and then analyzed. Sometimes people are interviewed in person or on the phone. For example, if a number of people became ill at a picnic, doctors would want to know what each person ate and drank. They would also want to know who got sick and who did not. The answers will help them find the source of the illness.

Scientists also use sampling to collect data. Scientists examine random individuals from a population. For example, doctors may examine a few people from the picnic and see how healthy they are. Doctors can then generalize their results to all the people at the picnic. This may also help the doctors find the source of the illness.

3. Evaluate Write one question that the doctor could be asking the patients in the picture below in his survey.

....

....

4. [CHALLENGE] How could a scientist use sampling to investigate the health of the deer population in a forest preserve?

....

....

....

....

....

....

....

....

Steps for Investigation

Scientists use scientific methods as they work in the many different fields of science. Scientific methods are organized ways to answer questions and solve problems. They are also ways of discovering causes and effects.

Scientific methods can include the steps shown here. Scientists might not use all the steps. They might not use the steps in this order. You will often use scientific methods when you do experiments and projects.

What will keep the apple slices from turning brown?

Ask a question.

You might have a question about something you observe.

State your hypothesis.

A hypothesis is a possible answer to the question you ask. A hypothesis must be testable. You can write your hypothesis as an *If…then…because…* statement.

If I put lemon juice on the apple slice, then it will not turn brown because the juice keeps the apple from reacting with the air.

Identify and control variables.

From a hypothesis, a scientist can identify the variables. A **variable** is something that can change in a test. An *independent variable* is one that you can control. A *dependent variable* changes when an independent variable changes. A simple investigation should test only one variable at a time. If a scientist is testing a river for pollution, all of the water samples must be taken at the same time each day and at the same place and depth in the river. If these samples are not taken the same way each time, the samples may give confusing results.

Remember, for a fair test, choose just one variable to change. Keep all of the other variables the same. Be sure to have a control or a control group. A **control group** is a standard against which change is measured. In an experiment, the experimental group is the same as the control group except that one factor has been changed.

6. Interpret Why is it important to have a control group in an experiment?

....

....

....

5. Identify What is the independent variable in an investigation to find how light affects the growth of plants?

....

....

Make a plan.

Make a plan to test your hypothesis. Decide what materials you need and make a list. Document the steps you will follow in your test.

Test your hypothesis.

Follow your plan to test your hypothesis.

Collect, record, and interpret your observations.

Keep good records of what you do and find out. Use tables and pictures to help. Organize your notes and records to make them clear. Make diagrams, charts, or graphics to help.

7. **Give an Example** Think of the last time you did an investigation and collected data. How did you organize your data?

State your conclusion.

Your conclusion is an inference you make based on your data. Communicate what you found out. Tell whether or not your data support your hypothesis.

Do repeated trials.

Repeat the experiment a few more times. Do each test exactly the same way. For a conclusion to be valid, the results of each test should be similar. Other scientists should be able to repeat your experiment and get similar results.

8. **Summarize** Why is it important for scientists to do repeated trials when doing an experiment?

The apple slice that was treated with lemon juice stayed fresh. The apple slice that was not treated with lemon juice turned brown.

9. Circle the picture of the control in this experiment.

10. ● **Text Features** What do you think the black headings on these two pages describe?

Document Procedures

Meaningful scientific results come from experiments that can be replicated. In order for a scientific experiment to be replicated, the procedures must be thoroughly explained, or documented. **Procedures** are step-by-step instructions for completing a task.

Procedures are important when experimenting but also when doing things such as making certain foods or playing games.

A recipe is a type of procedure.

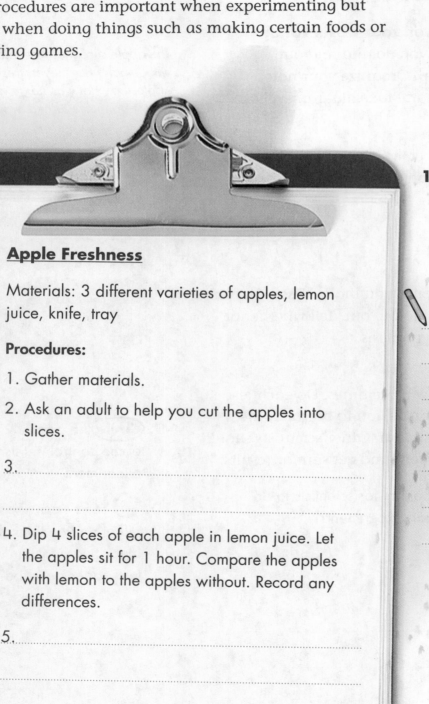

Apple Freshness

Materials: 3 different varieties of apples, lemon juice, knife, tray

Procedures:

1. Gather materials.

2. Ask an adult to help you cut the apples into slices.

3. ....

....

4. Dip 4 slices of each apple in lemon juice. Let the apples sit for 1 hour. Compare the apples with lemon to the apples without. Record any differences.

5. ....

....

....

11. CHALLENGE Read the procedure for apple freshness. Fill in the missing procedures. What might happen if one step was missing?

....

....

....

....

....

....

....

....

When you design an experiment, it is important to write your procedures so that someone who reads them can follow them and repeat your experiment. If you leave out details, your procedure may not be followed exactly. The experiment may then give unintended results. This means the original experiment was not repeated and the conclusion may be different.

12. **Evaluate** Look at the procedures for the Apple Freshness experiment again. What might you change about the procedures to make it easier for others to follow?

....

....

....

Got it?

13. **Explain** Why would a scientist use a model in an investigation? Write two reasons.

....

....

14. **Describe** What are some ways you can use to investigate different types of questions?

....

....

⬛ **Stop!** I need help with ....

⏸ **Wait!** I have a question about ....

▶ **Go!** Now I know ....

Lesson 3
How do scientists collect and interpret data?

Tell how scientists studying strong storms could help people stay safe.

Inquiry **Explore It!**

Why do scientists use thermometers?

☐ **1. Record** the air temperature of the room.

☐ **2.** Pour room-temperature water into Cup A. Pour warm water into Cup B. Pour slightly warm water into Cup C.

☐ **3.** Feel the water in each. Record *cool, warm,* or *neither.* **Measure** the temperatures in °C and °F. Record.

Comparing Temperatures			
	Temperature		
	Feels (warm, cool, neither)	**° C**	**° F**
Cup A (room-temperature water)			
Cup B (warm water)			
Cup C (slightly warm water)			

Materials

3 plastic cups — thermometer

room temperature water

warm water — slightly warm water

Explain Your Results

4. Interpret Data Compare how warm the water felt with your **measurements.**

5. Draw a Conclusion Discuss why scientists use thermometers to **collect** temperature **data.**

336

UNLOCK THE BIG ?

I will know that scientists collect and interpret data using many different kinds of tools in a safe way.

Words to Know

data	accuracy
precision	inference

Data Collecting

Tornadoes can be very dangerous. In a tornado, winds can gust to more than 100 miles per hour, lift up objects, and cause very serious damage. What makes a tornado form? Scientists have done a great deal of research to try to understand the causes of tornadoes, but there is still a lot to learn in order to predict when tornadoes will happen.

In order for scientists to be able to predict tornadoes more successfully, they need to collect large amounts of data. **Data** are information from which a conclusion can be drawn or a prediction can be made.

For example, scientists can collect data about the air temperature before a tornado forms. These data can be connected to information they already know about other weather patterns during that time. It is important that each type of data is collected consistently and recorded in a useful way. Scientists can find relationships among data and possibly make predictions about how a tornado forms.

1. **Decide** You collect data about the type of weather your town has been experiencing. Can you use the data to draw conclusions about all other areas in the state? Explain.

....

....

....

2. (Circle) what scientists need to do to understand how tornadoes form.

Doppler radar towers track weather patterns and help scientists collect data to predict future storm patterns.

Precision and Accuracy

When collecting data, scientists try to control their experiments. This means they avoid having things happen that might interfere with good data collection. Data from a controlled experiment are consistent and precise.

Precision is the ability to consistently repeat a measurement. **Accuracy** is the ability to make a measurement that is as close to the actual value as possible. Look at the targets in the example below. In science, valid data are data measured with precision and accuracy.

This target shows high precision because the marks are very close to one another. It shows low accuracy because the marks are not at the center of the target.

This target shows high accuracy because the marks are close to the center of the target. It shows low precision because the marks are not very close to one another.

3. **Demonstrate** Draw marks on the target to the right to represent data that are both accurate and precise.

4. **Text Features**
What does the yellow highlighting tell you about the words on this page?

Tools

Scientists use many different kinds of tools to collect data. The tool used depends on the task. You can use tools to help you see things that you normally could not see. If something is very small or very far away, a tool can help you see it in more detail.

Tools also help you measure things and gather information. You can measure volume, temperature, length, distance, mass, time, and more with the proper tools. Tools can help you gather information and analyze your data. Scientists share their findings. Because they do, tools can help you find information collected by others.

5. Describe Underline four things that tools help you do.

6. Infer Why should you look at a graduated cylinder at eye level when reading the scale?

....

....

7. Infer Scientists use tools other than the ones on this page. What tool could help you gather information, analyze data, and find information collected by others?

....

A *microscope* makes objects appear much larger.

You can use a balance *to measure mass.*

You use a thermometer *to measure temperature. Many thermometers have both Fahrenheit and Celsius scales.*

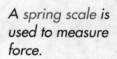

A spring scale *is used to measure force.*

You can use a stopwatch *or* timer *to measure elapsed time.*

Scientists use a meterstick *to measure length and distance.*

A calculator *helps you analyze data easier and faster than you could with paper and pencil.*

A graduated cylinder *is used to measure volume.*

Safety

Scientists know they must work safely when doing experiments. You need to be careful when doing science activities too. It is important to keep yourself and other people safe. Care must be taken to make sure all living organisms, including plants and animals, are handled properly. Follow these safety rules.

8. Explain Why might it be important to ask questions after your teacher gives instructions?

Tie long hair back and avoid wearing loose clothing.

Wear safety goggles when needed.

Never taste or smell any substance unless directed to do so by your teacher.

Listen to the teacher's instructions. Ask questions.

Use chemicals carefully.

Help keep the plants and animals that you use safe.

Read the activity carefully before you start.

Handle sharp items and other equipment carefully.

Organize Data

When scientists use tools to make observations, they collect data. In order to be useful, data must be organized. Organizing data allows a scientist to more easily recognize patterns that may be present. Data can be organized in many ways, including tables, graphs, charts, and graphics.

Tables and Graphs

One way that scientists organize data is by using a table. Look at the table below. It shows that scientists have collected data on the frequency of tornadoes in various states and have organized the information.

Once the information has been organized into a table, it may be displayed in a graph, such as the bar graph below. Graphs can help scientists see mathematical relationships in their data. The information in both the table and the graph is the same, but it is shown in different ways.

9. Compute Use data in the table to complete this bar graph.

10. Infer Based on the table and graph, what might land descriptions tell you about tornadoes and where they are most likely to occur?

....

....

....

....

....

....

....

Number of Tornadoes This Year for Selected States

State	Number of Tornadoes	Land Description
Florida	55	flat
Indiana	22	flat
Louisiana	27	flat
New York	7	hilly
Oregon	2	hilly

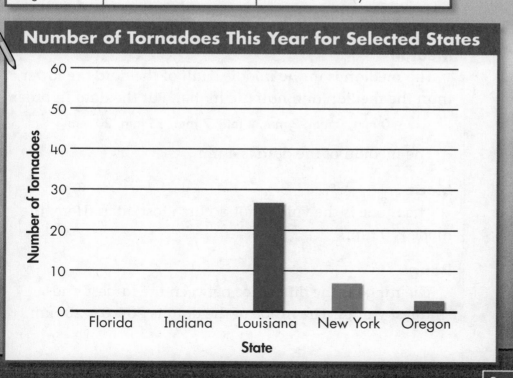

Number of Tornadoes This Year for Selected States

Estimate and Measure

Scientists estimate and measure. Estimate the length, width, or height of an object in your classroom. Measure the object with a meterstick or metric ruler. Make a chart to record your data. Do this with 5 objects in the room. Compare. Did your estimates get more accurate with practice?

11. **Calculate** Look at the table on the previous page. What is the median number of tornadoes for the five states in the table and graph? What is the mean?

Interpret Data

When scientists interpret data, they look at the information they have collected by using tools safely to observe, measure, and estimate. Then they try to find patterns in that data. Patterns may help them make predictions. Weather forecasts are predictions that may help people better prepare for severe storms.

Scientists use values such as the mean, median, mode, and range when they interpret data. These values can help scientists determine the quality and usefulness of data. This analysis may help scientists decide whether they have enough information or whether they should collect more data.

Mean

The mean is the average. You find the mean by adding the data together and then dividing by the number of data. Rainfall measurements were taken daily for one week and the following data were obtained:

> 0 mm, 4 mm, 15 mm, 7 mm, 20 mm, 3 mm, 0 mm

mean = sum of data ÷ number of data

Step 1: Find the sum.

$$0 + 4 + 15 + 7 + 20 + 3 + 0 = 49$$

Step 2: Divide the sum by the number of data to find the mean.

$$49 \div 7 = 7$$

The mean of the data is 7 mm.

Median

The median is in the middle. Half of the data are lower than the median and half are higher. Put the data in order:

> 0 mm, 0 mm, 3 mm, 4 mm, 7 mm, 15 mm, 20 mm

The median of the data is 4 mm.

Mode

The mode is the value that occurs most often. Here, the mode is 0 mm.

Range

The range is the difference between the largest and smallest values. The range of the data is 20 − 0 = 20 mm.

Make Inferences

Science deals with observations and facts. Imagine that you hear a dog barking in the distance. This is a scientific observation because anyone listening to and looking at the dog would agree that the dog is barking. Data and observations are facts. For example, the statement *Dogs bark* is a fact.

Scientific observations are different from opinions. An opinion is a personal belief and is not always based on facts. An example of an opinion in this case would be *The dog is a bad dog.* A scientist uses facts and observations to draw conclusions and make inferences. An **inference** is a conclusion based on observations. An example of an inference is *The dog is barking because it sees a rabbit.* In science, for a conclusion to be valid, it must be based on observations and sound reasoning, not on opinion.

12. Infer Look at this picture of a dog. Write a statement that is an observation. Write a statement that is an inference.

....

....

....

Got it?

13. Describe Why is it important to organize data with consistency and precision?

....

....

....

....

14. How are data used in science?

....

⬜ **Stop!** I need help with ....

⏸ **Wait!** I have a question about ....

▶ **Go!** Now I know ....

Lesson 4

How do scientists support their conclusions?

Tell what you can conclude about these birds' beaks based on your observations.

Inquiry Explore It!

Which towel absorbs the most water?

☐ **1.** Pour 100 mL of water into a cup. **Measure** carefully. Wad up one Brand A towel. Dip it completely into the cup and remove it. Measure and **record** the water left in the cup.

☐ **2.** Repeat twice using the same brand of towel.

☐ **3.** Repeat Steps 1 and 2 with each of the other brands.

Paper Towel Testing

Trial	Water Left in Cup (mL)		
	Brand A	Brand B	Brand C
1			
2			
3			
Total			

Explain Your Results

4. Draw a Conclusion
Which towel absorbed the most?

....

5. How did carrying out repeated trials help you trust your conclusions?

....

....

Materials

plastic cup

graduated cylinder

3 sheets each of 3 different brands of paper towel

water

For each trial, dip your towel the same way.

UNLOCK
THE BIG
?

I will know how scientists draw conclusions and support them using evidence.

Word to Know

evidence

Draw and Defend Conclusions

After analyzing the information that has been collected, scientists draw conclusions about what they have discovered. Scientists defend those conclusions by using the observations they made during their investigations. Sometimes, different conclusions can be drawn from the same set of data. Other scientists may question the methods that the scientists used to draw their conclusions, and the evidence from the investigations must be researched and reviewed.

For example, the behavior of some types of birds is not well known. Scientists must continue to collect and interpret data in order to understand the different behavior of the birds, such as their migration patterns, diet, and shelter preferences. Scientists have drawn conclusions about these bird behaviors, but the scientists' conclusions must be defended with appropriate scientific observations.

1. Give an Example
What is one way a scientist may defend a conclusion? **Underline** a statement in the text to support your answer.

....

....

These scientists are collecting data about bird behavior by placing identification bands around the birds' legs.

Evidence

One way for scientists to ensure that their work is valid is to share their results with others. Each of their investigations must be replicable, or repeatable, by other scientists. In addition, the conclusions that the scientists drew about their experiments must be based on evidence. **Evidence** is a set of observations that make you believe that something is true. When scientists have testable experiments that are based on evidence, they are able to give their results to other members of the scientific community.

During a scientific investigation, evidence may show results that are unexpected. The evidence may not support a scientist's hypothesis. However, this does not mean the experiment was not useful. The unexpected findings can lead to a new understanding of a scientific concept or cause scientists to experiment further.

Sometimes, scientists may misinterpret evidence from an investigation. They may come to an incorrect conclusion. This is why it is important for scientists to communicate with and accept feedback from one another.

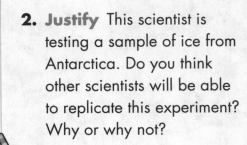

2. **Justify** This scientist is testing a sample of ice from Antarctica. Do you think other scientists will be able to replicate this experiment? Why or why not?

....

....

....

....

....

....

This scientist may be able to use his data as evidence to support his hypothesis.

Lightning Lab

Coin Flip
Scientists gather evidence to make valid conclusions. How often do you think a coin will come up heads? Flip a coin ten times. How often did it come up heads? Have your partner repeat your experiment. Did the results change? Draw a conclusion and explain it.

Review and Retest

Scientists must describe exactly what they did in an experiment and how they did it. This allows other scientists working in the same field to replicate the experiment to see if the results are the same. They may also ask questions about the experiment and point out problems.

In science, communication is important. Scientists must describe their procedures and report their findings honestly. They must answer questions. Although some variation in results is acceptable, the results from different scientists should be similar. If results are not consistent, then the experiment must be done again.

3. **List** two things these scientists may be talking about. **Underline** a statement in the text that supports your answer.

Got it?

4. **Contrast** Explain the difference between an observation and an inference.

5. **UNLOCK THE BIG ?** **Evaluate** Why is it important that scientists' conclusions are based on evidence?

◻ **Stop!** I need help with

⏸ **Wait!** I have a question about

▶ **Go!** Now I know

Inquiry Investigate It!

How does a banana slice change over time?

As you carry out this investigation, practice the inquiry skills you have learned.

Follow a Procedure

☐ **1.** Place a whole banana slice in a cup.

☐ **2.** Use a spoon to cut another banana slice into 4 pieces. Place the pieces in a second cup.

☐ **3.** Put another banana slice into a third cup. Mash this slice with a spoon.

Materials

3 banana slices

3 plastic cups

plastic spoon

Be careful! **Wash your hands when finished.**

Inquiry Skill

Scientists begin by asking a question. Then they make careful observations and record data accurately. They use their data to help make **inferences.**

4. Observe the slices when you place them in the cup and each hour for 3 hours.
Record your observations in the chart.

Changes to Banana Slices over Time			
Time	Observations		
	Whole Slice	Cut-Up Slice	Mashed Slice
When placed in cup			
After 1 hour			
After 2 hours			
After 3 hours			

Analyze and Conclude

5. Communicate Examine your data. Identify a simple pattern you **observed.**

....

....

6. Make an **inference** to explain about the pattern you identified.

....

....

7. UNLOCK THE BIG ? How can investigating cut bananas help scientists learn about other fruits?

....

....

....

Do the math!

Interpret Graphs

In science, graphs are often used to analyze, interpret, and display data. By looking at a graph, a scientist can visualize any trends, or patterns, that might be present. Scientists are able to support the conclusions they draw from data by using graphs.

Example

The students at Oakview School want to find out what things are most popular to collect among boys and girls. They asked 50 boys and 50 girls to choose their favorite collectible. Look at the double-bar graph.

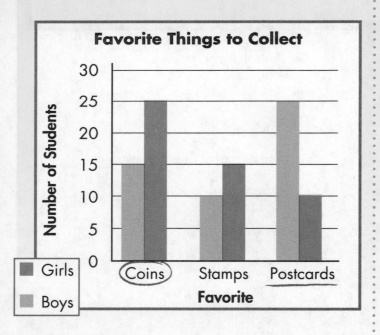

Favorite Things to Collect

1 **Circle** the most popular collectible among girls.

2 **Underline** The most popular collectible among boys.

Practice

Parents at Oakview School want to buy books for the library. They asked 30 fifth-graders to come into the library to choose their favorite type of book to read: science fiction, biography, or nonfiction. Look at the bar graph.

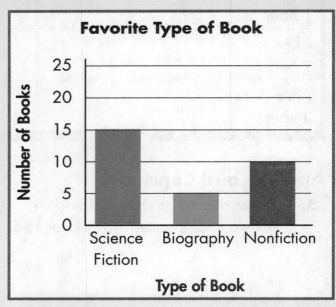

Favorite Type of Book

3 **Circle** the most popular type of book.

4 **Analyze** The parents decide to buy more biography books because they think those are better for the students. Is this decision based on fact or opinion? Explain.

....

....

....

....

Vocabulary Smart Cards

hypothesis
observation
experiment
variable
control group
procedures
data
precision
accuracy
inference
evidence

Play a Game!

Cut out the Vocabulary Smart Cards.

Work with a partner. Choose a card.

Say one word you can think of that is related to that vocabulary word in some way. It might be an example.

Have your partner guess the word. How many clues did it take to guess the correct word?

variable

variable

hypothesis

If… then… because…

hipótesis

control group

grupo de control

observation

observación

procedures

procedimientos

experiment

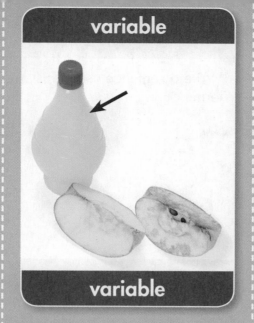

experimento

statement of what you think will happen during an investigation

Write three related words.

....

....

....

enunciado de lo que crees que ocurrirá en una investigación

---

something that can change in a test

Write a sentence using this term.

....

....

....

algo que puede cambiar durante una prueba

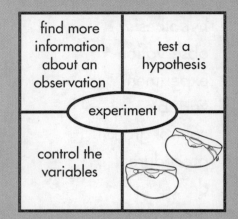

find more information about an observation | test a hypothesis

experiment

control the variables

Make a Word Square!

Choose a vocabulary word and write it in the center of the square. Fill in the squares with related ideas, such as a definition, a characteristic, an example, or something that is not an example.

---

something you find out about objects, events, or living things using your senses

Write a sentence using this term.

....

....

algo que descubres con tus sentidos sobre los objetos, sucesos o seres vivos

---

a standard against which change is measured

Write a sentence using this term.

....

....

....

....

estándar que se usa para medir un cambio

---

the use of scientific methods to test a hypothesis

Write three related words.

....

....

....

uso de métodos científicos para poner a prueba una hipótesis

---

step-by-step instructions for completing a task

Give an example of a procedure you have followed.

....

....

....

instrucciones paso por paso para realizar una tarea

inference

The dog is barking because it sees a rabbit.

inferencia

data

datos

evidence

evidencia

precision

precisión

accuracy

exactitud

Card 1

information from which a conclusion can be drawn or a prediction can be made

Write the singular form of this word.

....

....

....

información de la cual se puede sacar una conclusión o hacer una predicción

Card 2

a conclusion based on observations

Use any form of this word in a sentence.

....

....

....

....

conclusión basada en observaciones

Card 4

the ability to consistently repeat a measurement

Name the adjective form of this word.

....

....

capacidad de repetir una medición de manera consistente

Card 5

observations that make you believe something is true

Write a sentence using this word.

....

....

....

observaciones que te hacen creer que algo es cierto

Card 7

ability to make a measurement that is as close to the actual value as possible

Name the adjective form of this word.

....

....

capacidad de hacer una medición que se aproxime tanto como sea posible al valor verdadero

Lesson 1

What do scientists do?

- Scientists define a problem and try to find answers.
- Scientists make hypotheses and observations.
- Scientists draw conclusions based on their investigations.

Lesson 2

How do scientists investigate?

- Scientists use many different types of scientific investigations.
- Scientists use models, surveys, and sampling to gather data.
- Scientific methods are organized steps for doing an investigation.

Lesson 3

How do scientists collect and interpret data?

- Scientists collect data with tools.
- Scientists organize data using tables and graphs.
- Scientists interpret and draw conclusions from the data they collect.

Lesson 4

How do scientists support their conclusions?

- Scientists use facts, not opinions, when drawing conclusions.
- Scientific investigations should be based on evidence.
- Other scientists must be able to replicate scientific investigations.

Lesson 1

What do scientists do?

1. **Vocabulary** What is an observation?
   A. something that helps you measure
   B. something that has been made for the first time
   C. using the senses to gather information
   D. new ideas or new understandings

2. **Demonstrate** Why do scientists make hypotheses before beginning scientific investigations?

....

....

....

Lesson 2

How do scientists investigate?

3. The Wright brothers' airplane, *Flyer,* had a wingspan of 12 m. You build a model with a wingspan of 10 cm. How many times larger is *Flyer* than your model?

....

4. **Communicate** Explain why a control group is important in an experiment.

....

....

Lesson 3

How do scientists collect and interpret data?

5. **Analyze** Suppose you are doing a presentation for your class about the daily growth of a bean plant over the course of a month. Would you use a chart, a table, or a graph to help explain your results to your class? Explain your answer.

....

....

....

....

6. **Text Features** Use the following paragraph to answer the question.

> In order for scientists to be able to predict tornadoes more successfully, they need to collect large amounts of **data.** Data are information from which a conclusion can be drawn.

Why is the word *data* highlighted in yellow?

....

....

....

Lesson 4

How do scientists support their conclusions?

7. Identify How do scientists use evidence in their investigations?

....

....

....

....

....

8. Write About It Why is it important that scientists communicate?

....

....

....

9. Identify You watch your neighbors as they leave their apartment building. They have suitcases with them. They all get into the car and drive away. You think they are going on vacation. Is your thought a fact or an inference? Explain.

....

....

....

10. APPLY THE BIG ? **What is science?**

....

Explain why scientists will do exactly the same experiments that other scientists have done.

....

....

....

....

....

....

....

....

....

....

....

....

....

....

Part 1
Benchmark Practice

Science,
Engineering,
and
Technology

Read each question and choose the best answer.

1 _____ are observations from which a conclusion can be drawn.

A Predictions
B Inventions
C Data
D Discoveries

2 Which statement about a hypothesis is <u>not</u> true?

A A hypothesis is an explanation of what you think will happen.
B A hypothesis can be tested.
C A hypothesis is written as a question.
D A hypothesis may be a true statement.

3 Which statement about opinions is true?

A They are beliefs or value judgments.
B They are a valuable tool used by scientists.
C They are supported by research.
D They can be used to help write a hypothesis.

4 You are testing to see if music helps plants grow better. You divide the plants into four groups.

Plant Groups	
Group	Music Type
A	jazz
B	classical
C	rock
D	none

What is group D called?

A the model group
B the control group
C the population group
D the experimental group

5 Why is it important for scientists to repeat the investigations of other scientists?

_____

_____

_____

_____

There are different types of flight simulators. This flight simulator is a full-cockpit simulator.

STEM

Flight Simulators

How could you learn to fly an airplane without flying? You could use a flight simulator! What is a flight simulator? It is computer technology that simulates, or duplicates, a realistic impression of flying without actually flying. A flight simulator gives a pilot practice in different scenarios. These scenarios include bad weather, crashing, landing, and taking off. Engineers use technology to develop accurate scenarios. Without accurate scenarios, pilots and companies might not know how they or their technology would respond in an emergency.

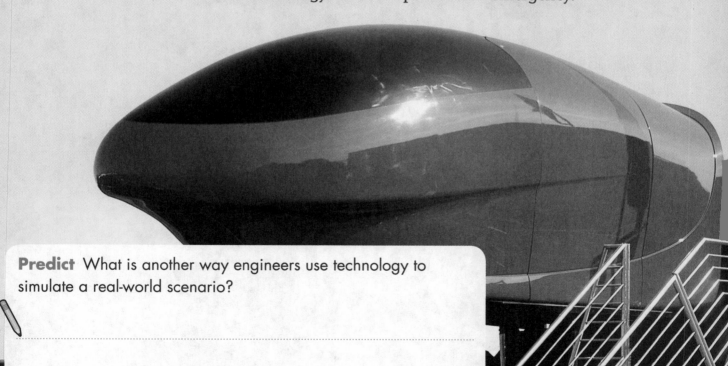

Predict What is another way engineers use technology to simulate a real-world scenario?

....

....

....

What can robots do?

Design and Function

Try It! How can you design a strong glue?

STEM Activity Is Your Arm a Simple Machine?

Lesson 1 What is technology?

Lesson 2 How does technology mimic living things?

Lesson 3 What is the design process?

Investigate It! How can you make and redesign a model of a robotic arm?

Science, Engineering, and Technology

Design It! How much weight can a model arm support?

Robots are designed to do many different tasks. This robot assists shoppers in finding and carrying their groceries. Other robots help people who cannot walk get in and out of their wheelchairs.

Predict What do you think robots will be used for in the future?

....

....

THE BIG ? How does technology affect our lives?

How can you design a strong glue?

☐ **1.** List 3 properties of a strong glue.

....

☐ **2. Observe** the properties of each mixture. **Record.**

Mixture	Properties
Cornstarch and water	
Flour and water	
Gelatin and water	

Materials

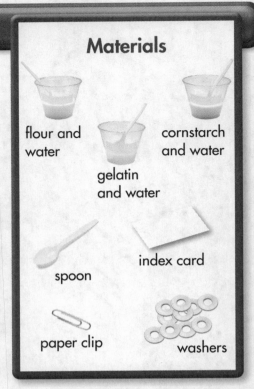

flour and water

cornstarch and water

gelatin and water

spoon

index card

paper clip

washers

☐ **3. Design** a glue that will hold the most weight by combining up to 2 spoonfuls of each mixture.

☐ **4. Test** your glue. Spread it at the bottom of an index card. Pull out the large end of a paper clip to make a hook. Press the small end into the glue. Let the glue dry overnight.

☐ **5.** Hold the card. Hang washers on the hook until the paper clip pulls off the card. Record your results.

Mixture	Spoonfuls	Number of Washers Held
Cornstarch and water		
Flour and water		
Gelatin and water		

Inquiry Skill
Recording your observations on a chart can help you make **inferences.**

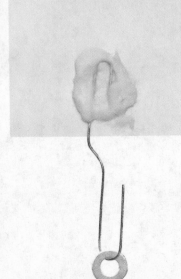

Explain Your Results

6. **UNLOCK THE BIG ?** Compare you results with other groups.

Infer Did different quantities of starting materials result in glue with different properties? Explain.

....

....

⊙ Main Idea and Details

- Learning to find **main ideas** and **details** can help you understand and remember what you read.
- Details can help you to infer the main idea of the article.

Technology and Our Homes

Technology can be found throughout our homes and is used in many ways. Technology makes it easier to do many things in the home. Thermostats can maintain or change the temperature inside the home. Dishwashers get dishes and eating utensils clean. We use technology for entertainment purposes too. Televisions, video games, and MP3 players are all technology. The way people keep and store food has been improved by technology. Refrigerators and freezers offer a healthy way of keeping food fresh for longer periods of time. Even plastic containers offer airtight storage to keep food fresher.

Practice It!

Use the graphic organizer below to list the main idea and details from the article above.

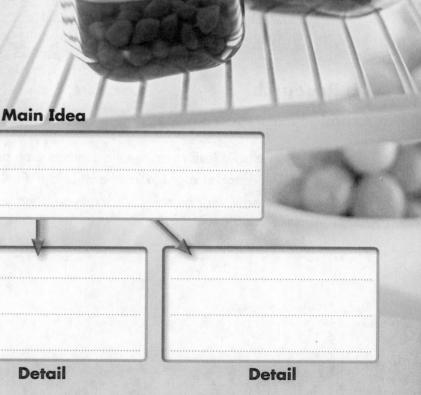

Main Idea

Detail   **Detail**   **Detail**

Is Your Arm a Simple Machine?

The structure of our bodies allow us to do work. Our arms, for example, are levers. A lever is a simple machine that uses a bar that moves around a fulcrum, or pivot point, to do work. The fulcrum in your arm is the elbow, the place where your arm bones meet. Muscles pull on the bones to bend, straighten, and rotate the arm at this joint. Engineers that make artificial arms must understand how the arm works.

To explain sports safety to your school's teams, the physical education teacher has asked you to design a model of an artificial arm and describe how it functions as a system of levers.

Identify the Problem

☐ **1.** What problem will your model help solve? _____

_____

_____

☐ **2.** Why is there a need to solve this problem? _____

_____

_____

Do Research

Examine diagrams of a human arm in the bent and straightened positions.

☐ **3.** With your elbow resting on a solid surface such as your desk or a table, pick up a weight. Bend and straighten your arm again. Feel the muscles as you bend your arm. **Describe** how your muscles work as you bend your arm. _____

_____

_____

_____

4. **Examine** the diagrams of different classes of levers. **Describe** how your arm is like different levers as it bends and straightens.

_____

_____

_____

Go to the materials station(s). **Examine** the materials, and think about how each one may or may not be useful in building a model of an artificial arm. Leave the materials where they are.

5. What are your design constraints? _____

_____

_____

Develop Possible Solutions

6. **Describe** two different ways you could combine some of the materials to solve the problem. _____

_____

_____

Choose One Solution

7. **Draw** your model arm and **describe** how you will build it.

_____

_____

_____

☐ **8. List** the material(s) you will use for your model arm. _____

_____

_____

Design and Construct a Prototype

Gather the materials you need for your model arm and a metric ruler. **Build** your model of an artificial arm.

☐ **9.** Use the metric ruler to **measure** the lengths of the materials you are using in your design. **Round** your measurements to the nearest centimeter. **Record** your measurements. _____

_____

_____

_____

Test the Prototype

Test your design. Bend and straighten your model arm. **Observe** the ways it moves like a human arm and the ways it does not.

Communicate Results

☐ **10.** How closely does your model arm move like a human arm? **Describe** your results, and then share them with your classmates. _____

_____

_____

_____

_____

_____

Evaluate and Redesign

☐ **11.** What changes could you make to your model to make it move more like a human arm?

_____

_____

_____

☐ **12.** What features of an artificial limb do you think would be most useful to people who have one? _____

_____

_____

_____

_____

_____

What is technology?

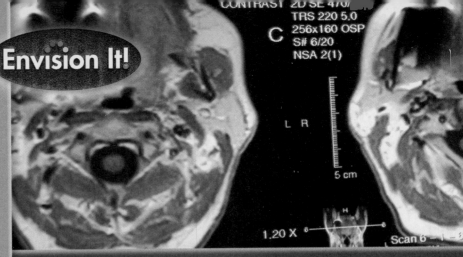

Tell how you think this kind of image can help doctors.

Inquiry Explore It!

Which transport system works best?

☐ **1.** Examine *Possible Water Transport Systems*.

☐ **2. Predict** which systems will always work, which will never work, and which will trap some water.

☐ **3.** Test your predictions. Set up each system. Pour a half cup of water into the funnel. **Observe** the flow of the water.

Explain Your Results

4. In what direction does water flow best through a system?

5. Examine the different **designs,** your **predictions,** and your results. Find a rule that explains the results you **observed.**

Materials

newspaper

plastic tube

empty cup and cup with water

funnel

Possible Water Transport Systems

Put down newspaper before you begin.

Repeat each test. This will help make your results more reliable.

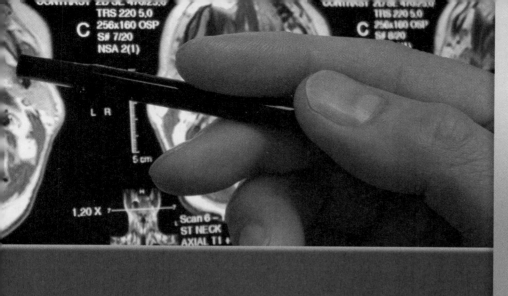

I will know how technology solves problems and provides solutions.

Words to Know

technology
microchip

Problems and Solutions

People constantly gain knowledge and make new discoveries. These discoveries and knowledge often result in technology that makes tasks easier, faster, or more efficient. **Technology** is the knowledge, processes, and products that solve problems and make work easier. Many years ago, illnesses were treated with few medicines. Over time, people began to learn the causes of some illnesses. This allowed people to develop better ways of treating and preventing disease.

Technology has improved people's lives, but it has also caused problems. Medical products and other technologies help people stay healthy. However, new medicines may cause unanticipated side effects.

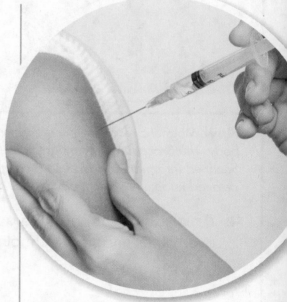

Vaccines were discovered by Edward Jenner in 1796.

1. ◉ **Main Idea and Details** Use the graphic organizer below to list two details and the main idea found in the last paragraph of the text.

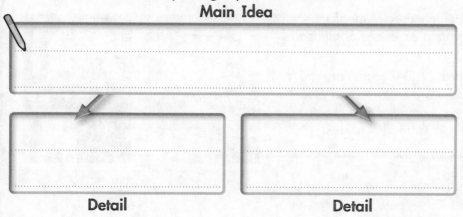

Main Idea

Detail   Detail

2. **Apply** What problem did this technology in the picture above solve?

Tools in Medicine

Technology has contributed to the scientific knowledge of medicine. Since the late 1800s there have been many advances in medical technology.

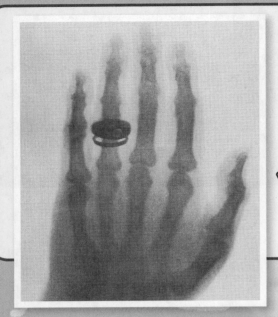

Then *William Röntgen took this X ray of his wife's hand in 1895. It is one of the first X rays used in medicine. X rays allowed doctors and scientists to see things inside a living thing. An X ray is a wave with very high energy. It can go though materials light rays cannot. The harmful effects of exposure to large amounts of X-ray radiation were not known until later.*

3. Infer What features can you recognize? What are the dark oval areas?

....

....

Now *Magnetic resonance imaging (MRI) produces images of the body. The procedure uses magnetic fields and radio wave pulses. Scanned information is fed into a computer. The result is a highly-detailed image. MRI technology does not use harmful radiation.*

4. Analyze What are two advantages of MRI over other imaging technologies?

....

....

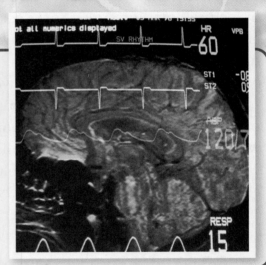

Now *X rays are still very useful and widely used in medicine. Care is taken to keep exposure to radiation as low as possible for both the patient and the technician.*

Now *CT (computed tomography) scans, or CAT scans, are made with a series of X rays. The X-ray images are cross section "slices" of the body. The information is fed into a computer. The process produces an image that can be viewed in three dimensions.*

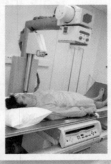 

X-ray machine   *CT scanner*

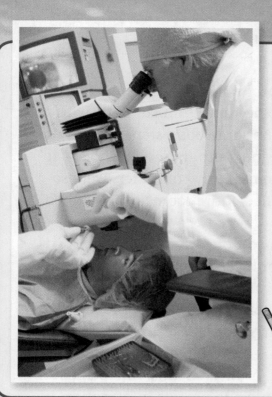

Then *This antique scalpel has a wooden handle. Wood cannot be sterilized to remove germs. The idea that germs cause disease was not widely accepted in this country until the 1890s.*

Now *Surgeons still use scalpels, but they are made of steel and plastic. These scalpels can be sterilized easily to remove germs. However, today there is another option. Lasers produce light waves that are concentrated on a tiny spot. Laser scalpels are able to cut through skin and other soft tissue.*

antique scalpel

5. CHALLENGE Weaker lasers are found in everyday life. Give an example where a laser might be used.

_____

_____

Then *Doctors used stitches, also called sutures, to hold wounds closed until they healed. Some sutures are made with a material that dissolves into the body and does not need to be removed.*

Now *Researchers are developing a glue to hold wounds together. The idea for glue came from animals called mussels that live in the ocean and can bond, or stick, to things underwater. Sutures are still preferred for some procedures, but one day doctors may be able to use glue during surgery.*

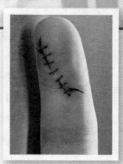

stitches   glue

6. **Predict** Do you think surgical glue or sutures are better at keeping water out of wounds?

_____

_____

_____

At-Home Lab

Design Solutions
Cut out pictures from magazines of three different technologies that help people. Write a short paragraph about who would use each technology.

UNIVAC (Universal Automatic Computer) was built in the United States in 1951. It was the first electronic computer. UNIVAC took up a space of 943 cubic feet.

Today, microchips are used in computers, cars, mobile phones, and video games. Some microchips are the width of a fingernail and others as wide a strand of hair.

7. **Infer** How did the invention of the microchip change computers?

....

....

....

....

....

Computer Technology

Early Computers

Computer technology began in the 1930s and 1940s. These early computers replaced mechanical parts with electrical parts, but used the same basic steps as today's computers—input, processing, output, and feedback—to solve mathematical problems. Early computers were so large that most of them filled entire rooms and weighed thousands of pounds.

The large size and high cost of early computers made them impractical for most people. Computer manufacturers became aware of the need for smaller, faster, and less expensive computers. One of the most important developments in computer technology was the microchip. A **microchip** is a small piece of a computer that contains microscopic, or tiny, circuits. Microchips make it possible for computers to process information very quickly. They also made the cost of a computer much lower because it became less expensive to manufacture computers.

World Wide Web

In the 1980s, computer technology was used to solve another problem. A British computer scientist wanted to make it easier for physicists to communicate with each other. The result was the World Wide Web. The World Wide Web is a computer-based network of information sources. It was first developed for use by the European Organization for Nuclear Research. The first version of the Web was completed in 1990. Today, a person using a computer can search through the Web to find information about practically anything.

8. **Explain** How has the World Wide Web improved communication and research?

....

....

....

Computers Today

Before computer technology, people spent months doing work that one of today's computers does in seconds. A computer only takes a few moments to process tasks such as calculating workers' salaries or figuring out how to steer a rocket. However, some tasks take even computers a long time to complete. Powerful supercomputers or computer networks often help out with very complex tasks.

The invention of the computer has led to many other technologies. Computers can be used with many tools and devices. Several kinds of microscopes, telescopes, thermometers, and cameras use computers. They help people find and record accurate information or results. Computer and other technologies can be found in schools. Students can easily find information for research using the Internet. DVD players and interactive whiteboards help present information in new ways.

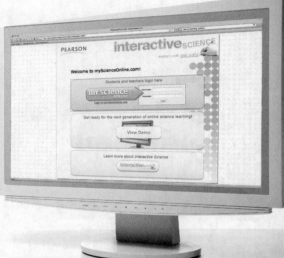

9. ◉ **Main Idea and Details**
Underline the main idea in the second paragraph.

Got it?

10. **UNLOCK THE BIG ?** **Identify** What are three additional technologies that you can benefit from?

....

....

11. **Analyze** Name a technology that has changed quickly. Name a technology that has changed more slowly.

....

....

⬛ **Stop!** I need help with ....

⏸ **Wait!** I have a question about ....

▶ **Go!** Now I know ....

How does technology mimic living things?

Envision It!

How can this device help someone speak?

my planet diary

Did You Know?

Robotics is the study, design, construction, and use of robots. New Lutheran Hospital in Fort Wayne, Indiana is using robotics to help save lives. The Sensei X Robotic Catheter System looks like a thin, flexible tube. The design allows it to go into areas of the heart that are hard for doctors to reach. A video camera connects to the robot. This allows doctors to see inside a patient's body. The video camera also helps doctors control the robot's movement.

What is the need for robotics in the medical field?

....

....

....

During surgery, the doctor uses a joystick to control movements of the Sensei X.

UNLOCK THE BIG ?

I will know how some technology can mimic the muscular and skeletal systems.

Words to Know

prosthetic limb

Technology and the Human Body

The human body is an amazing structure. Engineers sometimes use scientific knowledge of how the body works to develop technologies. Some of the technologies help people whose bodies do not function as they should. Some technologies do tasks that are too dangerous for people.

Technologies that have moving parts can be like the human body. A robot is one of these technologies. Robots can have a body structure and movable joints, which are similar to the human skeletal and muscular systems. Robotic technologies use an electrical energy source to help them move. The human body uses energy from food to help it move. Robots have a sensor system and a computer to control movements. In the human body, the brain and nervous system help to control movement.

1. **Explain** How do you think this robot is like you?

....

....

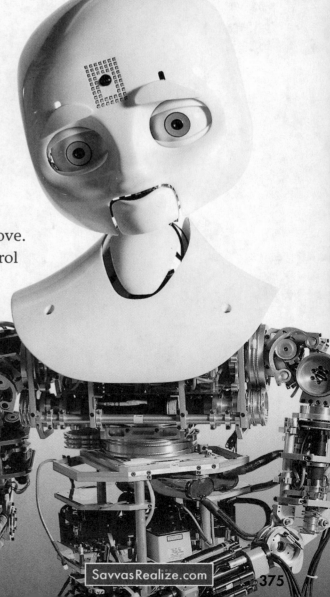

Nexi is a social robot developed by engineers at Massachusetts Institute of Technology.

Even though these prosthetic legs look different than real legs, they allow this woman the ability to run.

2. Compare How are this runner's prosthetic legs similar to the legs of the other runners?

_____

_____

_____

Prosthetic Limbs

Robotic technology that mimics movements of the human body is also used to make a prosthetic limb move. A **prosthetic limb** is an artificial arm, hand, leg, or foot that replaces a missing one. Modern prosthetic limbs can be controlled by electrical signals from the brain.

Past prosthetic hands had few fingers and could not do many things. Today, they have a thumb and four fingers that are controlled individually. These prosthetic hands can turn a key, pick up small objects, and hold a glass.

Current prosthetic legs and feet allow their users to walk and even run. As technology advances, prosthetic legs and feet work more like real legs and feet. The latest prosthetic limbs also look more like real limbs.

3. **Summarize** How do prosthetic limbs help people?

....

....

Each finger on this prosthetic hand can be moved separately. This woman can do many everyday things that she could not do without a prosthetic hand.

At-Home Lab

Technology Walk
Walk around your neighborhood with an adult. Observe any ways in which technology mimics living things. Record these observations in your science notebook.

Animals and Technology

Some technologies mimic the muscular and skeletal systems of animals. These systems help animals to move in different ways. The wings and tails of birds help the birds fly. Fish have muscular and skeletal systems that help them swim.

Airplanes have parts that mimic the wings and tails of birds. Like the wings and tails of birds, airplane wings and tails can be adjusted to control how the airplane moves. Some robots can also fly. The robotic bat flaps its wings and flies like a bat. It can search collapsed buildings and other areas people cannot get to. Some robots used to explore the ocean have parts that mimic the muscular and skeletal systems of fish.

Scientists use robotic animals to study the behavior of real animals. A robotic squirrel makes noise and moves its tail like a real squirrel. It can be placed in an area where real squirrels live. A real squirrel may wiggle its tail and make noises at the robotic squirrel. Scientists can use this information to learn how squirrels communicate with one another.

Robotic bats have movements similar to a real bat. They can access places too small or dangerous for people to access.

4. **Predict** Why do scientists use robotic squirrels to help study real squirrels?

....

....

....

Robotic squirrels can help scientists study the behavior of real squirrels. This robotic squirrel can make sounds and wiggle its tail like a real squirrel.

Nanobots

How can you build a robot that is only a few billionths of a meter long? Scientists hope to be able to build these tiny robots using nanotechnology. Scientists have found ways to move one atom at a time. They hope to be able to use this technology to build tiny robots, or nanobots, that can perform all kinds of tasks.

One idea is to use nanobots inside the human body. Nanobots may be able to deliver medications better than current methods. Scientists are also researching how to make a nanobot that can remove cholesterol from the walls of arteries.

5. Generate How do you think nanobots might be useful?

....

....

....

....

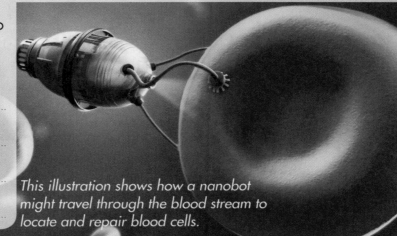

This illustration shows how a nanobot might travel through the blood stream to locate and repair blood cells.

Got it?

6. **UNLOCK THE BIG ?** How does one kind of technology mimic human muscular and skeletal systems?

....

....

7. Hypothesize Why do you think engineers build robots that mimic human or animal systems?

....

....

....

⬜ **Stop!** I need help with ....

⏸ **Wait!** I have a question about ....

▶ **Go!** Now I know ....

What is the design process?

Explain how you think people design new technologies.

Explore It!

How can the design of a model arm help you learn about how your arm works?

☐ **1. Make a model** of an arm as shown.

☐ **2.** Pull on Yarn A. **Observe.** Pull on Yarn B. Observe.

☐ **3.** Bend the arm pieces together. What happens to the yarn?

Materials

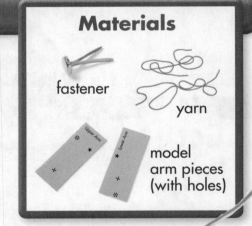

fastener

yarn

model arm pieces (with holes)

Explain Your Results

4. Communicate In your model, what do the yarn, the cardboard, and the fastener represent?

....

....

5. Draw a Conclusion How can people use models to help them learn about the human body?

....

....

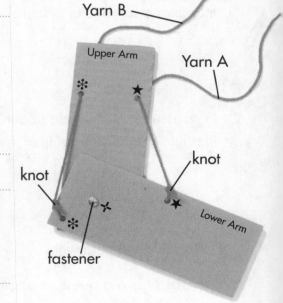

Yarn B

Yarn A

Upper Arm

knot

knot

fastener

Lower Arm

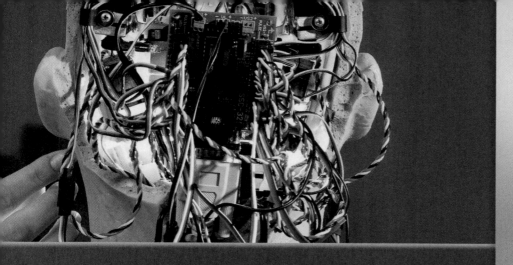

Words to Know

design process
prototype

Design Process

Technology helps to solve many of the problems we have. We use technology in our homes, schools, and offices. There are technologies for constructing buildings, communicating with others, transporting people and products, and so much more.

Who makes all this technology? People all over the world develop technologies. You may be surprised to know that even students your age develop new technologies. An engineer is a person who designs new technologies. People work in many different fields to apply scientific knowledge to everyday life. People use the design process to develop new technologies. The **design process** is a set of steps for developing products and processes that solve problems.

1. (Circle) what a person who designs technology is called.

2. **Predict** Why is it important to use the design process when developing new technologies?

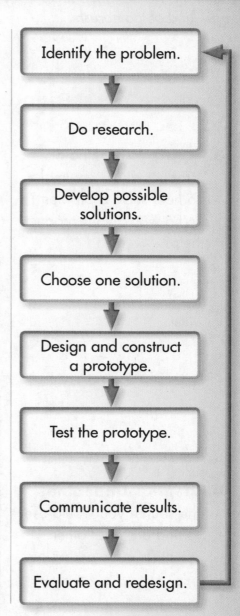

Identify the problem.

Do research.

Develop possible solutions.

Choose one solution.

Design and construct a prototype.

Test the prototype.

Communicate results.

Evaluate and redesign.

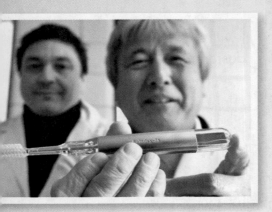

Dr. Kunio Komiyama is an engineer in the field of dentistry. He designed a new kind of toothbrush.

3. Apply What kind of product would you make to help solve a problem? Who would your product help?

....

....

....

....

....

4. Identify Underline the source you would use to find out what other scientists are working on.

Steps of the Design Process

While some engineers may use different steps or use them in a different order, they all have an end goal of finding a solution to a problem.

Identify the problem.

The first step in the design process is to identify a need or problem. All technology comes from the need for a solution to a problem. It is important in this step to determine who would be helped by the solution. For example, a toothbrush that cleans teeth with less effort could potentially help everyone reduce cavities and gum problems.

Do research.

Research is another important step in the design process. In order to make or improve on existing technology, scientists need to know what technology already exists. Scientific journals, magazines, the Internet, informational books, and encyclopedias can be helpful as you study ways to solve a design problem. Sometimes the best way to find the information you need is to interview an expert.

Engineers designing a new toothbrush might research how the shape of the handle affects how people brush their teeth. Engineers should also know how different bristle materials affect teeth.

Develop possible solutions.

Using what they learned in their research, scientists and engineers think of ways to improve an existing technology. Each possible solution should be carefully planned. Charts and diagrams can be used to communicate the design solution to others.

5. Interpret Look at the drawing below. What information can you find in the drawing?

....

....

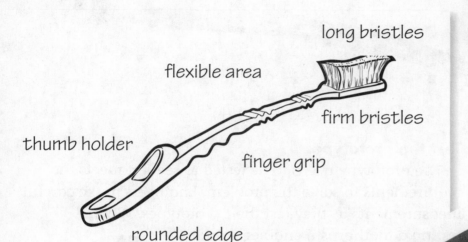

long bristles

flexible area

firm bristles

thumb holder

finger grip

rounded edge

This toothbrush uses advanced technology. It works very well, but it costs more than other toothbrushes.

Choose one solution.

It is important to choose wisely the one solution you will build. Making many solutions may take too much time. The cost of making the solution can also affect your decision. For example, if the toothbrush works very well, but is very expensive, people may not buy it.

6. Identify (Circle) two things that may affect which design solution you choose to build.

7. Explain Why do engineers build prototypes of their design solutions?

....

....

....

....

....

8. Infer What do you think this toothbrush is made of? Why do you think the engineers used those materials?

....

....

....

....

....

....

9. Interpret What do you think is one important thing that must be done when making a test to evaluate a prototype?

....

....

....

....

Design and construct a prototype.

The next step is to build a version of the solution, called a **prototype.** It is used to test the solution. It is important to identify the kinds of materials you use to build your prototype. The properties of the materials you use affect the function of your prototype. You will need a strong, flexible material for parts that bend. If you do not want the part to bend you should use a rigid material. You will also need to identify the tools you use to build your prototype.

toothbrush prototype

Test the prototype.

The prototype needs to be tested to see if it meets the requirements to solve the problem. Engineers make careful measurements as they test their prototypes. When testing a toothbrush, engineers might measure how much plaque is left on the teeth after brushing for one minute. These measurements help the engineers evaluate how well the prototype works.

Testing a toothbrush is important to make sure it works for everyone that will be using it.

Communicate results.

Throughout the design process it is important to document your work. Document means to record what you learn. Documentation helps you communicate with others. If you are working in a company, you will need to communicate your process and design to managers, salespeople, and many others. Often others will need to repeat your tests to verify the results. They will need to know your test procedures and the specifics of your design. The people who you share your design with may be able to offer advice on how to improve your idea.

Your design solution can be communicated in many ways. Labeled diagrams can show the size and shape of the parts of your product. Graphic organizers can be used to show how parts are put together. You will also need a list of materials and tools used to make each part. Tables, charts, and graphs can help you communicate the results of your tests.

Evaluate and redesign.

Using the results of your tests and feedback from others, you can evaluate how well your design solved the problem. This information can help you redesign your product to make it work better. You may need to make minor adjustments or choose a completely new solution.

10. Infer Why do you think an engineer might redesign a prototype?

11. Predict What might happen if you fail to document your design?

12. Evaluate Look at the redesigned prototype below. It has improvements such as a better handle. Work with a partner. Tell why you think the handle is a better design.

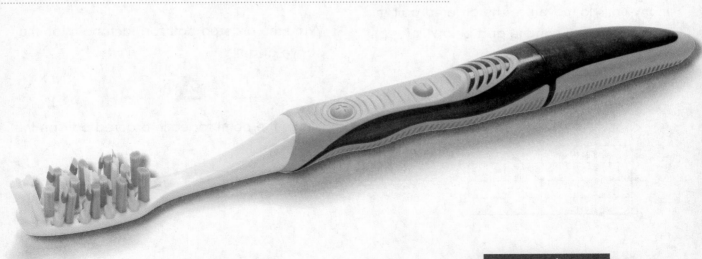

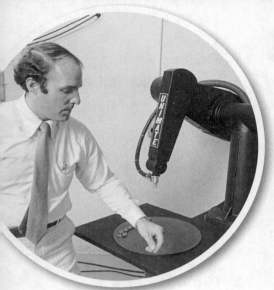

PUMA, an industrial programmable robot, was introduced in 1980. It had all the characteristics of a human arm.

Designing Robotic Arms

Engineers use the design process to develop robotic arms. Robotic arms are designed and built to mimic the movement of human arms.

The first robotic arm used in a factory was developed by George Devol. The robotic arm picked up and stacked metal parts that were too hot for workers to handle. George Devol and his partner, Joseph Engelberger, called the robotic arm, the *Unimate*.

The *Unimate* had a "shoulder" but no "elbow." Devol and Engelberger continued to redesign the robotic arm. They developed a new robotic arm with an "elbow" that allowed it to perform more tasks. Today's robotic arms can move in many different directions.

13. Compare How do you think the picture on the right might be better than the PUMA robotic arm?

Do the math!

Ordered Pairs

The computer that controls robot movement uses a coordinate grid system. An ordered pair is used to identify a point on a coordinate grid. The x-coordinate, or the first number, tells how many units to move to the right. The y-coordinate, or second number, tells how many units to move up. The ordered pair that identifies Point D on the grid below is (2, 5).

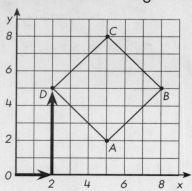

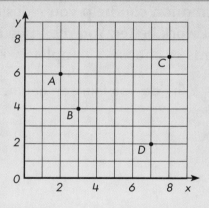

Write the ordered pair for each point on the above grid.

1 A _____   **2** B _____

Name the point for each ordered pair on the above grid.

3 (7, 2) _____   **4** (8, 7) _____

14. Identify Label the parts of the robotic arm that are like the parts of a human arm.

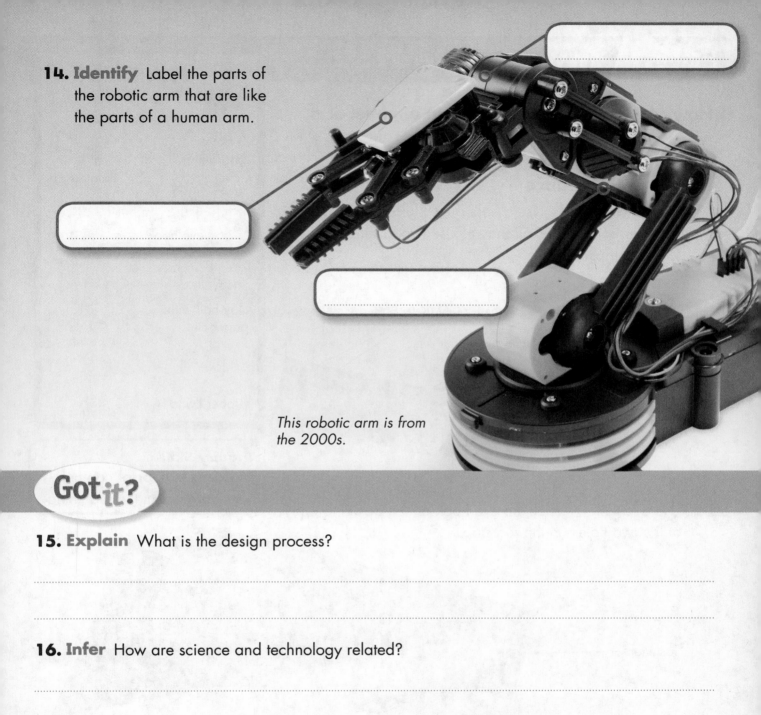

This robotic arm is from the 2000s.

Got it?

15. Explain What is the design process?

....

....

16. Infer How are science and technology related?

....

....

⬛ **Stop!** I need help with ....

⏸ **Wait!** I have a question about ....

▶ **Go!** Now I know ....

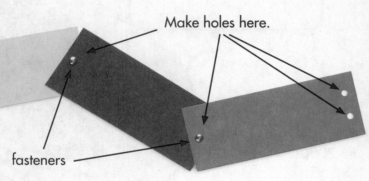

Inquiry ▸ Investigate It!

How can you make and redesign a model of a robotic arm?

Follow a Procedure

☐ **1. Make a Model** Use a hole punch to make holes in 3 poster board strips as shown. Use two fasteners to join the strips together.

Make holes here.

fasteners

☐ **2.** Use a fastener. Attach the eye hook on the dowel to one of the two holes on the red strip.

fastener

paper clip

Materials

3 poster board strips

metric ruler

hole punch

dowel with eye hook

3 fasteners

clay ball with paper clip

large paper clip

rubber band

string

Inquiry Skill
Making a model can help you learn about the real thing.

3. Bend a large paper clip into an S shape.
   Put the top of the S through the other hole in the red strip.

4. Use the robotic arm. Try to pick up the objects listed in the chart.
   Record the number of tries you need. Use up to 5 tries for each object.

5. **Redesign** your model of a robotic arm. Repeat Step 4.

Objects Chart

Objects	Number of Tries	
Clay ball with paper clip		
Paper clip		
Rubber band		
String		

Analyze and Conclude

6. **Communicate** What **design** change did you make to your **model**?

....

....

7. **UNLOCK THE BIG ?** Describe two ways in which the model is not like a
   real robotic arm.

....

....

....

Move this end of the poster board back and forth.

Hold the dowel with one hand so it does not move.

Denim Insulation

Are you wearing your favorite pair of jeans right now? When they wear out, they could serve another purpose. The surprise is that they might end up in someone's attic or walls—as insulation.

More than half the energy used in your home goes toward keeping it cool in summer and warm in winter. A good way to save money and use less energy is to insulate. One of the newest technologies is a process that turns denim cloth into fiber insulation.

Denim scraps and old denim jeans are processed into fibers. The fibers are treated with borate, which makes the product fire retardant and resistant to mold. About 500 pairs of jeans are needed to make the insulation for an average home. The insulation itself is 100 percent recyclable. Jeans are no longer just blue. They are also "green"!

APPLY THE BIG Q What steps did scientists use to determine the insulating properties of denim?

390

Vocabulary Smart Cards

technology
microchip
prosthetic limb
design process
prototype

Play a Game!

Cut out the Vocabulary Smart Cards.

Work with a partner. One person puts the cards picture-side up. The other person puts the cards picture-side down.

Take turns matching each word with its definition.

design process

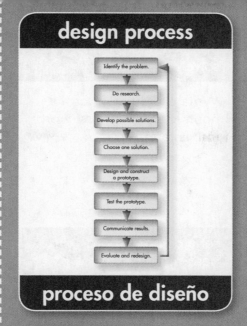

proceso de diseño

technology

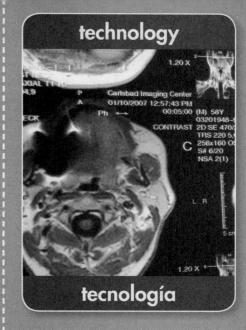

tecnología

prototype

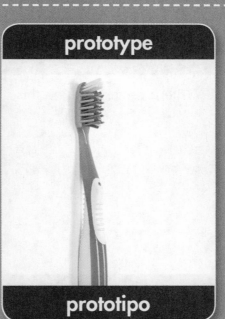

prototipo

microchip

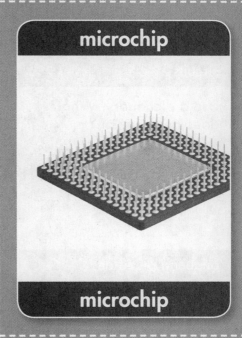

microchip

prosthetic limb

prótesis

the knowledge, processes, and products that solve problems and make work easier

Name three technologies that begin with the same letter of the alphabet.

....

....

conocimiento, procesos y productos que se usan para resolver problemas y facilitar el trabajo

---

a set of steps for developing products and processes that solve problems

Write a definition for the noun form of the first word in this term.

....

....

serie de pasos para desarrollar productos y procesos que resuelven problemas

---

Interactive Vocabulary

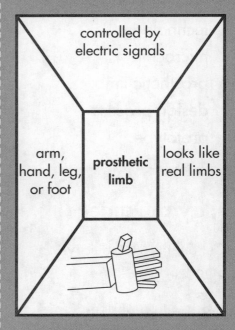

controlled by electric signals

arm, hand, leg, or foot

prosthetic limb

looks like real limbs

Make a Word Frame!

Choose a vocabulary word and write it in the center of the frame. Write or draw details about the vocabulary word in the spaces around it.

---

a small piece of a computer that contains microscopic circuits

Use a dictionary. What does *micro-* mean?

....

....

pequeña pieza de computadora que contiene circuitos microscópicos

---

a version of a solution to a problem

Write a sentence using this word.

....

....

....

versión de la solución de un problema

---

an artificial arm, hand, leg, or foot that replaces a missing one

Write a sentence using this word.

....

....

brazo, mano, pierna o pie artificial que reemplaza el miembro o la parte que falta

---

....

....

....

....

392

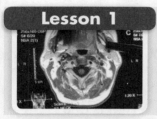

Lesson 1

What is technology?

- Technology is the knowledge, processes, and products that solve problems and make work easier.
- Medical technologies help us live longer and healthier lives.

Lesson 2

How does technology mimic living things?

- Many people use prosthetic limbs to help them do everyday tasks.
- Some technologies mimic the way animals move.

Lesson 3

What is the design process?

- The design process is a set of steps for developing products and processes that solve problems.
- Engineers build and test prototypes of their designs.

Lesson 1

What is technology?

1. **Write About It** Describe a technology you use every day and the problem it solves.

....

....

....

....

2. **Vocabulary** Technology is the _____ that solve problems and make work easier.
   A. materials, skills, and processes
   B. knowledge, processes, and skills
   C. knowledge, people, and ideas
   D. skills, materials, and people

3. **Explain** What problem does an X-ray machine solve?

....

....

....

....

Lesson 2

How does technology mimic living things?

4. **Give an Example** What is one technology that mimics the human muscular and skeletal systems?

....

....

5. **Main Idea and Details** Use the following paragraph to answer the question below.

> Robotic arms can have different end effectors. An end effector is the attachment that is put on the end of the robotic arm. An end effector may be a claw that can pick things up and place them. Other end effectors include a welding tool and a drill.

What is the main idea of this paragraph?

....

....

6. **Infer** What kind of animal might a robot that explores the ocean mimic?

....

....

....

Lesson 3

What is the design process?

7. Suppose a robot arm can put a toy together five times as fast a person. If a person can make 56 toys in 8 hours, how many toys can the robot make in the same amount of time?

....

....

8. Apply How would an engineer use the design process to build a car that uses less gas?

....

....

....

....

....

9. Vocabulary The design process is a set of steps for _____.
  A. developing a product or process
  B. doing an experiment
  C. drawing a diagram
  D. researching a product or process

10. APPLY THE BIG ? How does technology affect our lives?

....

Tell how a technology has affected human life.

....

....

....

....

....

....

....

....

....

....

....

....

....

....

Part 2
Benchmark Practice

Science,
Engineering,
and
Technology

Read each question and choose the best answer.

1 One similarity between a modern computer and an older computer is that _____

A they weigh the same.

B they both use input and output.

C they have the same price.

D both use microchips.

2 Before developing possible solutions, an engineer usually _____

A communicates his or her results.

B makes sure the prototype has been tested.

C identifies a problem and does research.

D evaluates and chooses a design.

3 Which of these technologies did <u>not</u> exist before 1900?

A surgical glue

B surgical stitches

C X-rays

D scalpels

4 A prototype is a _____

A set of choices for solving a problem.

B finished product that can be packaged.

C nanobot.

D version of the solution to a problem.

5 Suppose you are on a team that is designing a prosthetic eye for a patient with vision loss. What features would be useful in a prosthetic eye?

....

....

....

....

....

Infrared Technology

My World

Big World

Do you remember the last time you got your temperature taken at the doctor's office? Perhaps the doctor used a thermometer that uses infrared technology.

The word *infrared* describes a type of light energy that people cannot see. Infrared energy is often thought of as light energy from a heat source. You cannot see infrared energy, but you can use tools to measure it.

NASA developed technology that uses a special tool to measure the infrared energy that comes from Earth and outer space. These tools are on satellites that orbit Earth and on probes that travel through space. Infrared technology is useful because infrared radiation can pass through areas of dust and gas. The information can give scientists clues about clouds on Earth as well as clues about the formation of planets and stars.

APPLY THE BIG ? What sort of experiment might you be able to plan that involves using an infrared thermometer?

....

....

....

How much weight can a model arm support?

An arm must be able to raise and lower objects of different weights. The arm also needs to support the weight it picks up. You must make a model arm that will be able to pick up different weights. The model arm will be used to pick up a cup holding 25 gram cubes. You will repeat the test by adding 25 gram cubes to the cup each time. Your testing is over when your arm bends the wrong way.

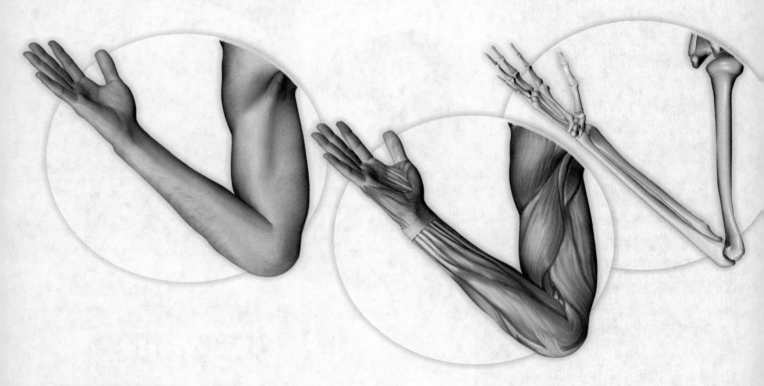

Identify the problem.

☐ **1.** Identify the task your **model** arm will perform.

Possible Materials

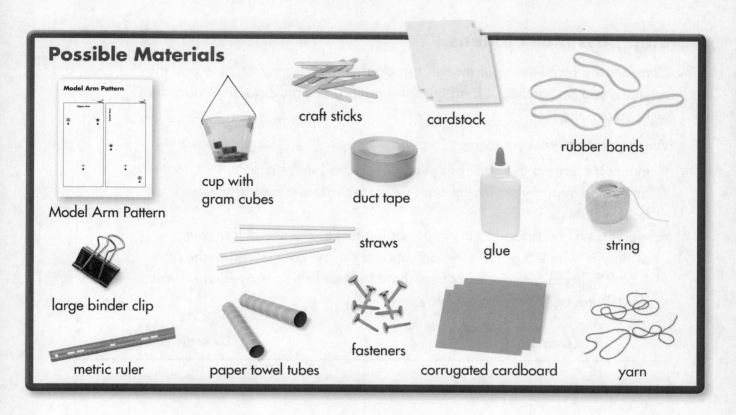

Model Arm Pattern

cup with gram cubes

craft sticks

cardstock

rubber bands

duct tape

glue

string

large binder clip

straws

metric ruler

paper towel tubes

fasteners

corrugated cardboard

yarn

Do research.

2. Consider the tasks you have identified. Research **design** solutions others have created to perform those tasks. Brainstorm ideas with others. List three solutions others have used or suggested.

Develop possible solutions.

3. Consider the problems your model arm **design** needs to overcome and the solutions you researched. Using this information, design 2 possible arms that will perform the task.

When you **test** your prototype:

- mount the arm to the back of the chair using a binder clip.
- attach the cup to your model arm. Consider where a real arm would hold weights.
- weights will be added to the cup. For the first trial you will test your prototype with 25 grams. The arm should be level at the end of the lift.
- Add 25 grams to the cup. Repeat the test. Your testing is over when your model arm bends the wrong way.

Design A	Design B

Choose one solution.

4. Choose one **design** to build and **test.** Tell which design you chose. Explain why you chose that design.

Design and construct a prototype.

☐ **5.** Draw the **design** you will use to make a prototype.

☐ **6.** List the materials you used in your prototype.

....

....

....

Test the prototype.

☐ **7.** Start with 25 grams in the cup. **Record** if the arm passes or fails. A pass is when the arm lifts the cup. A fail is when the arm bends the wrong way.

☐ **8.** Add 25 grams to the cup. Repeat your **test.** Continue testing by adding 25 grams to the cup. Keep repeating your test until the arm fails.

Testing Results

Trial	Load (grams)	Pass or Fail
1	25	
2	50	
3	75	
4	100	
5	125	

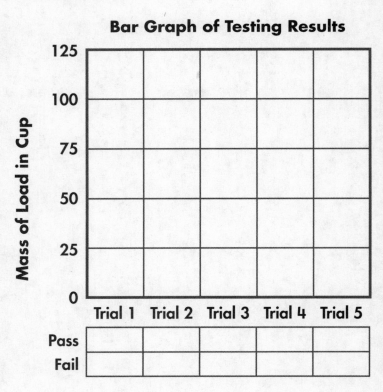

Bar Graph of Testing Results

Mass of Load in Cup: 0, 25, 50, 75, 100, 125

	Trial 1	Trial 2	Trial 3	Trial 4	Trial 5
Pass					
Fail					

Communicate results.

☐ **9.** Which parts of your **design** worked well in your prototype? Use your test results and your **observations** to support your **conclusions.**

....

....

☐ **10.** Which parts of your design could be improved?

....

....

....

....

Evaluate and redesign.

11. Evaluate what did and did not work in your prototype.
Use what you learned from testing to **redesign** your prototype.

Write or draw your design changes.

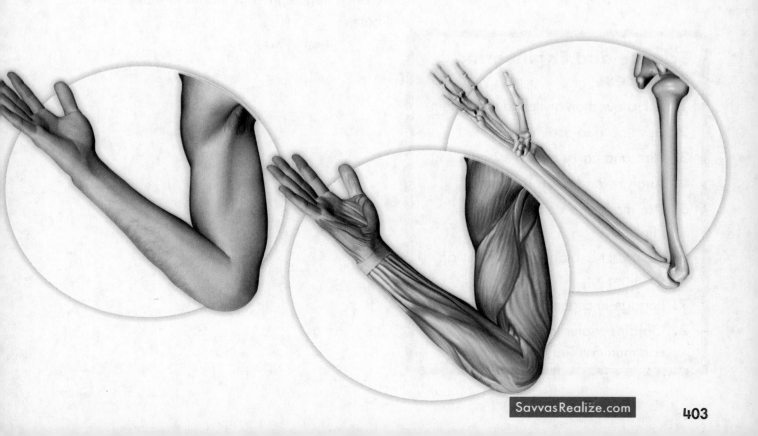

Make a Graph

Test a rubber ball, a table-tennis ball, and a marble to see which bounces the highest. Remember to identify and control all the variables. Measure the height of each bounce. Make a graph of your results. Share your results with your class.

Write a Story

Think of a technology that might be invented in the future. Write a story about how using the technology will affect the lives of people. Describe what the technology will be and what it will do.

Make a Model

Make a model of an animal. Design a way to make the legs, wings, or fins of your model move like the animal you chose. Test how your model works. Redesign your model to make it work better.

Science and Engineering Practices

1. Ask a question or define a problem.

2. Develop and use models.

3. Plan and carry out investigations.

4. Analyze and interpret data.

5. Use math and computational thinking.

6. Construct explanations or design solutions.

7. Engage in argument from evidence.

8. Obtain, evaluate, and communicate information.

Measurements

Metric and Customary Measurements

The metric system is the measurement system most commonly used in science. Metric units are sometimes called SI units. SI stands for International System. It is called that because these units are used around the world.

These prefixes are used in the metric system:

kilo- means *thousand*
1 kilometer = 1,000 meters

milli- means *one thousandth*
1,000 millimeters = 1 meter, or 1 millimeter = 0.001 meter

centi- means *one hundredth*
100 centimeters = 1 meter, or 1 centimeter = 0.01 meter

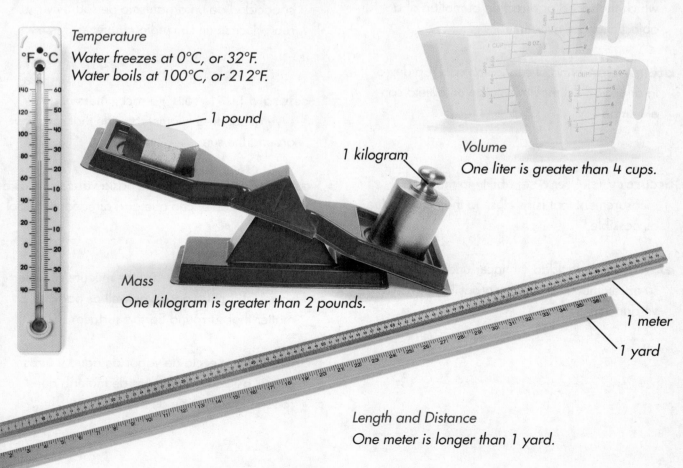

1 liter

1 cup

Temperature
Water freezes at 0°C, or 32°F.
Water boils at 100°C, or 212°F.

1 pound

1 kilogram

Volume
One liter is greater than 4 cups.

Mass
One kilogram is greater than 2 pounds.

1 meter

1 yard

Length and Distance
One meter is longer than 1 yard.

Glossary

The glossary uses letters and signs to show how words are pronounced. The mark ′ is placed after a syllable with a primary or heavy accent. The mark ′ is placed after a syllable with a secondary or lighter accent.

To hear these vocabulary words and definitions, you can log on to the digital path's Vocabulary Smart Cards.

Pronunciation Key

a	in hat	ō	in open	sh	in she
ā	in age	ȯ	in all	th	in thin
â	in care	ô	in order	ŦH	in then
ä	in far	oi	in oil	zh	in measure
e	in let	ou	in out	ə	= a in about
ē	in equal	u	in cup	ə	= e in taken
ėr	in term	ū	in put	ə	= i in pencil
i	in it	ü	in rule	ə	= o in lemon
ī	in ice	ch	in child	ə	= u in circus
o	in hot	ng	in long		

A

acceleration (ak sel′ ə rā′ shən) the rate at which the speed or direction of motion of an object changes over time

aceleración ritmo al cual cambia la rapidez o la dirección del movimiento de un objeto con el tiempo

accuracy (ak′ yər ə sē) ability to make a measurement that is as close to the actual value as possible

exactitud capacidad de hacer una medición que se aproxime tanto como sea posible al valor verdadero

adaptation (ad′ ap tā′ shən) a characteristic that increases an organism's ability to survive and reproduce in its environment

adaptación característica que aumenta la capacidad de un organismo de sobrevivir y reproducirse en su medio ambiente

asteroid (as′ tə roid′) a rocky mass up to several hundred kilometers wide that revolves around the sun

asteroide masa rocosa de hasta varios cientos de kilómetros de ancho que gira alrededor del Sol

atmosphere (at′ mə sfir) the mixture of water vapor and other gases, as well as particles of matter that surround Earth's surface

atmósfera mezcla de vapor de agua y otros gases, así como partículas de materia que rodean la superficie de la Tierra

atom (at′ əm) the smallest part of an element that still has the properties of the element

átomo la partícula más pequeña de un elemento, que todavía tiene las propiedades de ese elemento

atomic theory (ə tom′ ik thē′ ər ē) the idea that everything is made of small particles

teoría atómica la idea de que la materia está formada por partículas pequeñas

axis (ak′ sis) an imaginary line around which an object spins

eje línea imaginaria en torno a la cual gira un objeto

balanced (bal′ ənsd) describes equal forces that combine to act on an object in opposite directions

balanceadas describe fuerzas iguales que se combinan y actúan sobre un objeto en direcciones opuestas

barometric pressure (bar′ ə met′ rik presh′ ər) the pushing force of the atmosphere

presión atmosférica fuerza que ejerce la atmósfera

biosphere (bī′ ə sfir) the part of Earth in which all living things are found

biosfera la parte de la Tierra donde están todos los seres vivos

cellular respiration (sel′ yə lər res′ pə rā′ shən) the process by which cells break down sugar to release energy

respiración celular proceso mediante el cual las células descomponen el azúcar para obtener energía

chemical change (kem′ ə kəl chānj) a change of one or more types of matter into other types of matter with different properties

cambio químico cambio de uno o más tipos de materia a otros tipos de materia con propiedades diferentes

circulation (sėr′ kyə lā′ shən) movement of air that redistributes heat on Earth

circulación movimiento del aire que redistribuye el calor en la Tierra

climate (klī′ mit) the average of weather conditions over a long time

clima promedio de las condiciones del tiempo durante un período largo

comet (kom′ it) a frozen mass of different types of ice and dust orbiting the sun

cometa masa helada de distintos tipos de hielo y polvo que orbita el Sol

competition (kom′ pə tish′ ən) the struggle among organisms for the same limited resources

competencia lucha entre organismos por los mismos recursos limitados

compound (kom′ pound) a type of matter made of two or more elements

compuesto tipo de materia formada por dos o más elementos

condensation (kon′ den sā′ shən) the process in which a gas turns into a liquid

condensación proceso en el que un gas se convierte en líquido

conservation (kon′ sər vā′ shən) an attempt to preserve or protect an environment from harmful changes

conservación intento de conservar o de proteger el medio ambiente de cambios dañinos

constellation (kon′ stə lā′ shən) a group of stars that forms a pattern

constelación grupo de estrellas que forma una figura

consumer (kən sü′ mər) organism that cannot make its own food

consumidor organismo que no puede hacer su propio alimento

contact force (kon′ takt fôrs) a force that requires two pieces of matter to touch

fuerza de contacto fuerza que requiere que dos porciones de materia se toquen

control group (kən trōl′ grüp) a standard against which change is measured

grupo de control estándar que se usa para medir un cambio

— D —

data (dā′ tə) information from which a conclusion can be drawn or a prediction can be made

datos información de la cual se puede sacar una conclusión o hacer una predicción

decomposer (dē′ kəm pō′ zər) organism that gets its energy by breaking down wastes and dead organisms

descomponedor organismo que obtiene su energía descomponiendo desechos y organismos muertos

deposition (dep′ ə zish′ ən) process of laying down materials, such as rocks and soil

sedimentación proceso por el cual materiales como rocas y partículas de suelo se asientan

design process (di zīn′ pros′ es) a set of steps for developing products and processes that solve problems

proceso de diseño serie de pasos para desarrollar productos y procesos que resuelven problemas

dwarf planet (dwôrf plan′ it) a large, round object that revolves around the sun but has not cleared the region around its orbit

planeta enano cuerpo grande y redondo que orbita el Sol, pero que no ha despejado la zona que rodea su órbita

elevation (el′ ə vā′ shən) height above sea level

elevación altura sobre el nivel del mar

environment (en vī′ rən mənt) all of the conditions surrounding an organism

medio ambiente todas las condiciones que rodean a un ser vivo

erosion (i rō′ zhən) the movement of materials away from a place

erosión movimiento de materiales que se alejan de un lugar

evaporation (i vap′ ə rā′ shən) the changing of a liquid to a gas

evaporación cambio de líquido a gas

evidence (ev′ ə dəns) observations that make you believe something is true

evidencia observaciones que te hacen creer que algo es cierto

exoskeleton (ek′ sō skel′ ə tən) a hard skeleton on the outside of the body of some animals

exoesqueleto esqueleto duro en el exterior del cuerpo de algunos animales

......

experiment (ek sper′ ə mənt) the use of scientific methods to test a hypothesis

experimento uso de métodos científicos para poner a prueba una hipótesis

......

extinct species (ek stingkt′ spē′ shēz) a species that has no more members of its kind alive

especie extinta especie de la que ya no queda vivo ningún miembro

---

food chain (füd chān) a series of steps by which energy moves from one type of living thing to another

cadena alimentaria serie de pasos mediante los cuales la energía pasa de un ser vivo a otro

food web (füd web) a diagram that combines many food chains into one picture

red alimentaria diagrama que combina varias redes alimentarias en una sola imagen

......

force (fôrs) a push or pull that acts on an object

fuerza empujón o jalón que se le da a un objeto

......

friction (frik′ shən) the force that results when two materials rub against each other or when their contact prevents sliding

fricción fuerza que resulta al frotar un material contra otro o cuando el contacto entre ambos impide el deslizamiento

---

gas (gas) a substance without a definite volume or shape

gas sustancia que no tiene ni volumen ni forma definidos

......

gravity (grav′ ə tē) the force of attraction between any two objects

gravedad fuerza de atracción entre dos cuerpos cualesquiera

hail (hāl) frozen precipitation that forms in layers

granizo precipitación congelada que se forma en capas

humidity (hyü mid′ ə tē) the amount of water vapor in the air

humedad cantidad de vapor de agua en el aire

hydrosphere (hī′ drə sfir) all the waters of Earth

hidrosfera toda el agua de la Tierra

hypothesis (hī poth′ ə sis) statement of what you think will happen during an investigation

hipótesis enunciado de lo que crees que ocurrirá en una investigación

inertia (in ėr′ shə) the tendency of an object to resist any change in motion

inercia tendencia de un cuerpo a resistirse a cualquier cambio de movimiento

inference (in′ fər əns) a conclusion based on observations

inferencia conclusión basada en observaciones

inner planet (in′ ər plan′ it) any of the four closest planets to the sun

planeta interior cualquiera de los cuatro planetas más cercanos al Sol

latitude (lat′ ə tüd) a measure of how far a place is from the equator

latitud medida de la distancia entre un objeto y el Ecuador

liquid (lik′ wid) a substance that has a definite volume but no definite shape

líquido sustancia que tiene un volumen definido pero no una forma definida

lithosphere (lith′ ə sfir) the solid, rocky layer of Earth

litosfera capa rocosa y sólida de la Tierra

mass (mas) the amount of matter in a solid, liquid, or gas

masa cantidad de materia que tiene un sólido, líquido o gas

metamorphosis (met′ ə môr′ fə sis) the process of an animal changing form during its life cycle

metamorfosis proceso en el cual cambia la forma de un animal durante su ciclo de vida

microchip (mī′ krō chip) a small piece of a computer that contains microscopic circuits

microchip pequeña pieza de computadora que contiene circuitos microscópicos

mixture (miks′ chər) different materials placed together, but each material keeps its own properties

mezcla unión de materiales diferentes en la cual cada material mantiene sus propiedades

molecule (mol′ ə kyül) the smallest particle of a compound that still has the properties of that compound

molécula la partícula más pequeña de un compuesto, que todavía tiene las propiedades de ese compuesto

moon (mün) a natural object that revolves around a planet

luna satélite natural que orbita un planeta

non-contact force (non kon′ takt fôrs) a force that acts at a distance

fuerza sin contacto fuerza que actúa a distancia

observation (əb′ zər vā′ shən) something you find out about objects, events, or living things using your senses

observación algo que descubres con tus sentidos sobre los objetos, sucesos o seres vivos

orbit (ôr′ bit) the path an object takes as it revolves around a star, planet, or moon

órbita el camino que sigue un objeto al girar alrededor de una estrella, un planeta o una luna

outer planet (out′ ər plan′ it) any of the four planets in our solar system beyond Mars

planeta exterior cualquiera de los cuatro planetas de nuestro sistema solar que quedan más allá de Marte

photosynthesis (fō′ tō sin′ thə sis) the process in which plants make a sugar called glucose

fotosíntesis proceso en el que las plantas producen un azúcar llamado glucose

physical change (fiz′ ə kəl chānj) a change in some properties of matter without forming a different kind of matter

cambio físico cambio en algunas de las propiedades de la materia sin que se forme un nuevo tipo de materia

planet (plan′ it) a large, round object that revolves around a star and has cleared the region around its orbit

planeta cuerpo grande y redondo que orbita una estrella y que ha despejado la zona que rodea su órbita

pollution (pə lü′ shən) any substance that damages the environment

contaminación cualquier sustancia que le hace daño al medio ambiente

precipitation (pri sip′ ə tā′ shən) water that falls from clouds as rain, snow, sleet, or hail

precipitación agua que cae de las nubes en forma de lluvia, nieve, aguanieve o granizo

precision (pri sizh′ ən) the ability to consistently repeat a measurement

precisión capacidad de repetir una medición de manera consistente

predator (pred′ ə tər) a consumer that hunts and eats another animal

predador consumidor que atrapa a otro animal y se lo come

prey (prā) any animal that is hunted by others for food

presa cualquier animal que es cazado por otros para alimentación

procedures (prə sē′ jərz) step-by-step instructions for completing a task

procedimientos instrucciones paso por paso para realizar una tarea

producer (prə dü′ sər) organism that makes its own food for energy

productor organismo que hace su propio alimento para obtener energía

prosthetic limb (pros the′ tik lim) an artificial arm, hand, leg, or foot that replaces a missing one

prótesis brazo, mano, pierna o pie artificial que reemplaza el miembro o la parte que falta

prototype (prō′ tə tīp) a version of a solution to a problem

prototipo versión de la solución de un problema

R

revolution (rev′ ə lü′ shən) one full orbit around the sun

traslación una órbita completa alrededor del Sol

rotation (rō tā′ shən) one whole spin of an object on its axis

rotación una vuelta completa de un objeto en torno a su eje

S

shadow (shad′ ō) an area of partial darkness where light has been blocked by an object

sombra región de oscuridad parcial donde la luz ha sido bloqueada por un objeto

sleet (slēt) frozen raindrops

aguanieve gotas de lluvia congeladas

solar flare (sō′ lər flâr) an explosive eruption of waves and particles into space

fulguración solar erupción explosiva de ondas y partículas emitidas hacia el espacio

solid (sol′ id) a substance that has a definite shape and volume

sólido sustancia que tiene una forma y un volumen definidos

solution (sə lü′ shən) a mixture in which substances are spread out evenly and will not settle

solución mezcla en la cual una sustancia se dispersa de manera uniforme en otra sustancia y no se asienta

space probe (spās prōb) a spacecraft that gathers data without a crew

sonda espacial nave espacial sin tripulantes que recoge datos

technology (tek nol′ ə jē) the knowledge, processes, and products that solve problems and make work easier

tecnología conocimiento, procesos y productos que se usan para resolver problemas y facilitar el trabajo

temperature (tem′ pər ə chər) a measure of how fast the particles in an object are moving

temperatura medida de la rapidez con que se mueven las partículas de un objeto

variable (vâr′ ē ə bəl) something that can change in a test

variable algo que puede cambiar durante una prueba

volume (vol′ yəm) the amount of space an object takes up

volumen el espacio que ocupa un objeto

water cycle (wȯ′ tər sī′ kəl) repeated movement of water through the environment in different forms

ciclo del agua movimiento repetido del agua en formas distintas a través del medio ambiente

weather (weŦн′ ər) the state of the atmosphere

tiempo atmosférico estado de la atmósfera

Index

A

Acceleration, 67, 85–88
  mass and, 70–72
  motion and, 67
Accuracy, 337, 338, 351–354
Activities
  At-Home Lab, 30, 36, 64, 111, 122, 128, 168, 208, 221, 227, 292, 330, 371, 378
  Explore It!, 16, 22, 28, 34, 66, 74, 78, 114, 120, 126, 158, 174, 216, 224, 230, 236, 264, 276, 284, 290, 328, 336, 344, 368, 380
  Go Green, 69, 156, 176, 240, 325, 383
  Investigate It!, 1, 40–41, 53, 82–83, 101, 132–133, 143, 178–179, 197, 242–243, 257, 296–297, 315, 348–349, 361, 388–389
  Lightning Lab, 13, 20, 25, 38, 76, 80, 118, 162, 213, 234, 267, 272, 282, 287, 342, 346
  Try It!, 1, 2, 53, 54, 101, 102, 143, 144, 197, 198, 257, 258, 315, 316, 361, 362
Adaptation, 115, 135–136, 141
  animals, 120–125
  behavioral, 124–125
  environmental change and, 170
  mutations, 115–116
  plants, 114–117
  structural, 122–123
Aerogels, 51
Air, 34
  circulation, 222–223
  composition of, 218
  resistance, 62, 64
  temperature, 178–179, 219, 225, 226
  water in, 205
Air pressure
  high and low, 218–220
  weather and, 212
  winds and, 222
Air resistance, 68
Airplane, 378
Airplane engines, 93
Alaska, 210
Alligators, 159
Altocumulus clouds, 228
Aluminum, 10
Amphibian metamorphosis, 128–129

Analyze, 21, 65, 186, 324, 326, 350, 356, 370, 373
Anemometer, 220
Animals
  adaptations, 120–125
  circulation and respiration, 112
  eggs of, 109, 111
  endangered species, 180
  life cycles, 122, 126–131
  migration and hibernation, 125, 180
  physical characteristics, 122
  reproduction, 111
  response to environmental change, 121
  survival of, 168, 170, 172, 173
  technology and, 378
  transporting seeds, 109
Apples, 38, 332, 333, 334
Apply, 119, 187, 207, 272, 369, 382, 395
Apply It! activities
  How is motion affected by mass?, 94–97
  How can salt affect the hatching of brine shrimp eggs?, 190–193
  How does the speed of a meteorite affect the crater it makes?, 308–311
Archery, 71
Arctic Ocean, 213
Area, estimating, 209
Arm, human
  model of, 364–367, 380
  robotic, 386–389
Ash, 37
Asteroid belt, 278, 291
Asteroids, 291
At-Home Lab
  Design Solutions, 371
  Does Gravity Affect You?, 64
  Falling Water, 330
  Growing Up, 128
  Long Ago, 168
  Meteor Shower, 292
  Mixed-Up Foods, 30
  Parts and the Whole, 111
  Rainmaker, 227
  Running Hot and Cold, 221
  Swimming Birds, 122
  Technology Walk, 378
  Twin Balloons, 36
  Watering Can, 208
Atlantic ghost crabs, 124
Atlantic Ocean, 213
Atmosphere, 212
  carbon dioxide in, 4
  composition of, 218

  Earth, 211
  Earth's moon, 281
  Jupiter's, 286
  Mercury's, 279
  moons of planets, 295
  Neptune's, 288
  outer planets, 285
  Saturn's, 287
  sun, 272
  Uranus's, 288
  Venus's, 280
Atom, 9, 12–13, 43–46
Atomic theory, 9, 12, 43–46
Average, 342
Axis, 265, 266, 268, 299–302
Axis of rotation, 266, 268

B

Balance, 18
Balance, pan, 339
Balanced forces, 75, 76
Balloon rocket, 56–59, 82–83
Balloons, 36, 56
Bar graph, 279, 350
Barometer, 218, 219
Barometric pressure, 212, 217, 245–250
  high and low, 218–220
  winds and, 222
Bat, robotic, 378
Batteries, 175
Beaches, 238
Bears, 160, 164
Bees, 127
Behavioral adaptations, 121, 124–125
Benchmark Practice, 50, 92, 140, 188, 254, 306, 358, 396
Big Dipper, 274, 275
Big Question
  Answer the Big Question, 91, 253
  Apply the Big Question, 49, 139, 187, 189, 305, 307, 357, 390, 395
  Chapter Opener, 1, 53, 101, 143, 197, 257, 315, 361
  Review the Big Question, 42, 47, 89, 90, 137, 185, 251, 252, 303, 304, 355, 356, 393, 394
  Unlock the Big Question, 2, 9, 15, 16–17, 21, 22–23, 27, 28–29, 33, 34–35, 39, 54, 60–61, 65, 66–67, 73, 74–75,

78–79, 83, 108–109, 113,
114–115, 119, 120–121, 125,
126–127,131, 133, 141, 144,
150–151, 158–159, 166–167,
173, 174–175, 179, 204–205,
209, 210–211, 216–217, 223,
224–225, 229, 230–231, 235,
236–237, 241, 243, 258,
264–265, 270–271, 276–277,
284–285, 289, 290–291, 295,
297, 316, 322–323, 328–329,
336–337, 343, 344–345, 349,
362, 368–369, 373, 374–375,
379, 380–381, 389

Big World My World
    Infrared Technology, 397
Biography
    Darwin, Charles, 141
    Newton, Isaac, 84
Biosphere, 211, 215
Birds
    beaks, 120, 141, 344–345
    color patterns, 108
    endangered species, 180
    as predators, 159
Black bears, 160, 164
Blimp, 16–17
Blue-ringed octopus, 121
Boats, 70
Bogs, 144
Boiling points, 26
Bowling ball, 69
Broad-bodied chaser dragonfly, 131
Bromine, 13
Bumper cars, 73
Butter, 23, 36
Butterfly, 126–127, 130

Calcium, 10
Calculate, 15, 91, 214, 268, 292,
    294, 342
Calculator, 339
Callisto, 286
Canada geese, 125
Candles, 36, 38
Canyon, 282
Carbon, 12–13
Carbon dioxide
    in the atmosphere, 4, 178–179,
    212, 281
    in cellular respiration, 156
    in photosynthesis, 154–155

Carbon dioxide trap, 4–7
Careers. *See* Science Careers
Carnivore, 160, 162–163
Cars, 330
    inertia and, 68–69
    motion of, 67
Cassini, 289
Categorize, 31
Caterpillar, 112
Cause and effect, 80, 103, 109,
    117, 125, 167, 238, 280, 293
Ceiling fan, 222–223
Cells, in plant leaves, 152
Cellular respiration, 151, 156,
    181–184
Celsius scale, 20, 339
Cement, 42
Chapter Review, 48–49, 90–91,
    138–139, 186–187, 252–253,
    304–305, 356–357, 394–395
Charon, 294
Chemical change, 35, 37–39,
    43–46
Cherry trees, 116
Chicago River, 28–29
Chips, computer, 372
Chlorine, 14
Chlorophyll, 154–155
Chloroplasts, 154–155
Choose, 73
Chromosphere, 272
Cicada, 110
Circle graph, 213
Circulation (air), 217, 222–223,
    245–250
Circulatory system, 112–113
Cirrus clouds, 228
Classify, 30, 49, 159, 161, 169,
    229, 316
Cleaner shrimp, 165
Climate, 168, 231–235, 245–250
    bodies of water and, 234
    elevations' effect on, 235
    latitude's effect on, 232–233
    weather and, 231
Clouds, 225–228
    formation of, 27, 206, 221, 224,
    225
    on Neptune, 288
    types of, 228–229
    on Venus, 280
Coconuts, 117
Cocoon, 126–127
Coin flip, 346
Collect data, 102, 336, 337
Color

as characteristic of matter, 17
    chemical change, 37
Comet, 291, 293, 299–302
Communicate, 22, 41, 66, 78, 158,
    198, 224, 230, 243, 349, 356,
    380, 389
Communication, 347
Compare, 25, 48, 70, 113, 138,
    212, 227, 288, 376, 386
Compare and contrast, 3, 9, 13,
    19, 23, 35, 37, 116, 123, 124,
    127, 130, 139, 157, 165, 259,
    265, 267, 285, 295, 304
Competition, 164, 167, 170,
    181–184
Complete metamorphosis, 130
Compose, 325
Compost pile, 189
Compound, 9, 14–15, 43–46
Compute, 75, 213, 341
Computed tomography (CT)
    scan, 370
Computer model, 330
Computer technology, 372–373
Conclude, 38, 65, 238
Conclusions, scientific, 327, 333,
    344–347
Concrete, 42
Condensation, 27, 36, 198, 205–
    208, 224, 245–250
Conservation, 175, 177, 181–184
Constellation, 271, 274, 299–302
Consumer, 159, 160, 181–184
Contact force, 61, 62, 85–88
Continental drift, 168
Continents, 214
Contrast, 14, 113, 286, 347
Control group, 329, 332, 351–354
Cooking oil, 23
Coordinate grid, 386
Copper, 3
Corona, 272
Coyote, 162
Crabs, 124
Craters, 279, 281, 291, 292
Critical Thinking Skills
    analyze, 21, 186, 324, 326,
    350, 356, 370, 373
    apply, 119, 187, 207, 272,
    369, 382, 395
    calculate, 15, 214, 268, 292,
    294, 342
    categorize, 31
    cause and effect, 80, 109, 117,
    125, 167, 238, 280, 293
    choose, 73

classify, 30, 49, 159, 161, 169, 229
communicate, 356
compare, 25, 48, 70, 113, 138, 212, 227, 288, 376, 386
compare and contrast, 3, 9, 13, 19, 23, 35, 37, 116, 123, 124, 127, 130, 139, 157, 165, 259, 265, 267, 285, 295, 304
compose, 325
compute, 213, 341
conclude, 38, 65, 238
contrast, 14, 113, 286, 347
decide, 173, 337
demonstrate, 222, 338, 356
describe, 8, 17, 27, 37, 48, 119, 128, 131, 154, 157, 165, 177, 186, 221, 233, 269, 275, 283, 322, 327, 335, 339, 343
determine, 208
diagram, 111, 129
draw, 112, 220, 223
draw conclusions, 199, 217, 226, 235, 253, 327
evaluate, 331, 335, 347, 385
exemplify, 214
explain, 15, 26, 49, 63, 67, 73, 81, 90, 91, 108, 131, 151, 167, 170, 187, 215, 241, 253, 266, 269, 274, 283, 291, 295, 304, 327, 335, 340, 372, 375, 384, 387, 394
fill in the blank, 154
find out, 18
generalize, 212
generate, 379
give an example, 11, 160, 168, 227, 330, 333, 345, 394
group, 289
hypothesize, 125, 175, 176, 240, 379
identify, 10, 65, 127, 130, 131, 139, 151, 153, 156, 157, 212, 215, 225, 228, 241, 253, 269, 272, 273, 304, 332, 357, 373, 382, 383, 387
infer, 2, 13, 20, 28, 31, 32, 39, 41, 71, 77, 80, 81, 83, 102, 115, 122, 124, 130, 138, 152, 171, 172, 175, 176, 209, 223, 231, 234, 237, 239, 267, 274, 275, 278, 282, 288, 339, 341, 343, 372, 384, 385, 394
interpret, 11, 27, 90, 332, 383, 384
justify, 138, 233, 346
label, 111
list, 10, 12, 21, 252, 347

main idea and details, 55, 61, 68, 90, 144, 163, 186, 208, 363, 369, 373, 394
predict, 1, 33, 48, 53, 66, 71, 82, 101, 102, 138, 143, 187, 197, 198, 213, 219, 230, 242, 243, 257, 279, 304, 315, 323, 325, 329, 359, 361, 368, 371, 378, 381, 385
recognize, 25, 271
sequence, 118, 162, 205, 211, 229, 283, 305
show, 235
solve, 180
suggest, 29, 69, 117, 169, 217
summarize, 39, 48, 177, 221, 226, 271, 275, 305, 333, 377
support, 29, 186, 232
synthesize, 90, 91, 205
text features, 317, 323, 333, 338, 356
vocabulary, 48, 49, 90, 138, 186, 252, 304, 356, 394, 395
Crystals, xxxvi–1, 8
CT (CAT) scan, 370
Cumulonimbus clouds, 228

Dactyl, 291
DART station, 244
Darwin, Charles, 141
Data, 337–339, 351–354
    collecting, 337
    interpreting, 342
    organizing, 341
    precision and accuracy, 338
    tools, 322–323, 339
Decide, 173, 337
Decomposer, 159, 161, 162, 181–184
Deer, 162
Deltas, 238
Demonstrate, 222, 338, 356
Denim insulation, 390
Dependent variable, 332
Deposition (weathering), 236–241, 245–250
Desalination, 204
Describe, 8, 17, 27, 37, 48, 119, 128, 131, 154, 157, 165, 177, 186, 221, 233, 269, 275, 283, 322, 327, 335, 339, 343
Design, 362, 368, 389

Design It! activity
    How much weight can a model arm support?, 398–403
Design process, 380–385, 391–392
    communicate results, 7, 59, 106, 149, 202, 262, 320, 366
    design, construct, and test prototypes, 6, 58–59, 106, 148, 202, 262, 320, 366, 384
    develop and choose possible solutions, 5–6, 57–58, 105, 147, 201, 261, 319–320, 365, 383
    documentation of, 385
    evaluate and redesign, 7, 59, 106–107, 149, 203, 263, 321, 367, 385
    glue, 362
    identify the problem, 4, 56, 104, 146, 200, 260, 318, 364, 383
    models, 380
    research, 4, 56, 104, 146, 200, 260, 318–319, 364–365, 382
    steps in, 381–385
    for technology, 381
    toothbrush, 382–385
Determine, 76, 208
Devol, George, 386
Dew, 27, 206
Diagram, 76, 111, 129
Diamonds, 13
Distance, 339
Do the Math!, 48, 186, 252, 305, 356, 395
    Analyze a Bar Graph, 279
    Analyze Data, 152
    Calculate Rates, 239
    Estimating Area, 209
    Interpret Graphs, 350
    Line Graphs, 219
    Ordered Pairs, 386
    Ranges, 26
    Read a Circle Graph, 213
    Read a Graph, 164
    Subtracting Fractions, 172
    Using Formulas, 72
Dodo, 123
Dogs, 61, 343
Doppler radar, 337
Dragonfly, 131
Draw, 32, 76, 79, 112, 220, 223
Draw conclusions, 120, 133, 158, 178, 179, 199, 216, 217, 226, 235, 236, 253, 316, 327, 344, 380

Dust storms, 282
DVD (digital video disc), 373
Dwarf planet, 291, 294, 299–302

Earth, 264–265
　aging of, 214
　asteroids hitting, 291
　atmosphere of, 212, 218, 281
　biosphere of, 215
　erosion and deposition on,
　　237–241
　gravity, 267
　hydrosphere of, 213
　lithosphere of, 214
　moon of, 257, 281, 295
　orbit of, 278
　rotation and revolution of,
　　266–267
　seasons, 268–269
　stars seen from, 273–275
　sun and, 265–269, 271
　as a system, 211
Ecosystem, 143–180; 181–184. *See
also* Environment; Environmental
changes
　changes in, 166–173
　energy roles in, 160–161
　food chains and webs, 162–163
　human impact on, 169,
　　174–177
　interactions in, 159–167
　local, 144
　niches in, 164
　roles in, 164
　symbiosis in, 165
Eggs, 111, 130
Electric forces, 65
Electrons, 12
Elements, 10–13
　compounds, 14–15
　metals, 10
　nonmetals and semimetals, 11
Elevation, 231, 235, 245–250
Elliptical orbit, 267
Endangered species, 180
Energy
　in ecosystems, 160–161
　from food, 159
　light, 79–80, 397
　stored and used in plants,
　　156–157
　thermal, 4

Energy sources
　fossil fuel, 4
　sun, 79, 151
Engelberger, Joseph, 386
Engines, 93
Environment, 181–184. *See also*
Ecosystem
　pollution of, 175
　regulation and conservation, 177
Environmental changes, 166–173.
　See also Ecosystem
　adaptation to, 170–171
　effect on animals, 121
　human activities causing, 169,
　　175–177
　natural causes, 168
　organisms causing, 169, 175
　pollution, 175
　survival of, 172–173
Envision It!, 8–9, 16–17, 22–23,
　28–29, 34–35, 60–61, 66–67,
　74–75, 78–79, 108–109,
　114–115, 120–121, 126–127,
　150–151, 158–159, 166–167,
　174–175, 204–205, 210–211,
　216–217, 224–225, 230–231,
　236–237, 264–265, 270–271,
　276–277, 284–285, 290–291,
　322–323, 328–329, 336–337,
　344–345, 368–369, 374–375,
　380–381
Epidermis tissue of plants, 152–153
Equator, 222, 232
Erosion, 236–241
Escalator, 67
Estimate, 76, 209, 342
Europa, 286
**European Organization for Nuclear
　Research,** 372
Evaluate, 331, 335, 347, 385
Evaporation, 26, 36, 198,
　206–208, 245–250
Evidence, 345, 346, 351–354
Exemplify, 214
Exoskeleton, 109–110, 135–136
Experiment, 329, 332–333,
　351–354
Experiments. *See* At-Home Lab;
　Explore It!; Go Green!; Investigate
　It!; Lightning Lab; Try It!
Explain, 15, 26, 49, 63, 67, 73,
　81, 90, 91, 108, 131, 151,
　167, 170, 187, 215, 241, 253,
　266, 269, 274, 283, 291, 295,
　304, 327, 335, 340, 372, 375,
　384, 387, 394

Explore It!, 16, 22, 28, 34, 66, 74, 78,
　114, 120, 126, 158, 174, 216,
　224, 230, 236, 264, 276, 284,
　290, 328, 336, 344, 368, 380
Extinct species, 121, 123, 135–136
Extinction, 123

Fahrenheit scale, 20, 339
Farming
　environmental changes, 169
　soil conservation, 238
　soil erosion, 241
Feather, 64
Fertilization, 111
Field Trip
　Green Bank Observatory, 307
　NASA's Space Centers, 93
Fields, 241
Fill in the blank, 154, 162, 170,
　206, 266
Finches, 123, 141
Find out, 18
Fireballs, 292
Fish reproduction, 111
Fishing sinker, 25
Flea, 55
Flight simulator, 359
Flooding, 238
Flowers, 111
Flying dragon, 121
Flying squid, 120–121
Fog, 228
Food
　made by plants, 151, 152
　movement through plants, 152,
　　162–163
Food chain, 159, 162, 181–184
Food web, 159, 163, 181–184
Forces, 61–65, 85–88, 339
　acceleration and, 70–72
　balanced, 76
　combined, 75
　contact, 62–63
　electric and magnetic,
　　65, 74
　equal and opposite, 56, 73,
　　74–75
　friction, 62, 63
　gravity, 61, 64, 76,
　　85–88, 218, 225, 238, 239,
　　267, 278

motion and, 66–73
net, 76
non-contact, 64–65
Forest fire, 168, 170–171
Formulas, 72
Fossil fuels, 4
Fractions, subtracting, 172
Freezing, 25, 36
Fresh water, 213
Friction, 61, 62, 63, 68, 85–88
Frogs, 108–109, 128–129, 173
Frost, 206
Fulcrum, 364
Fulgurite, 199
Full-cockpit simulator, 359

Galaxy, 258
Galileo, 286, 287
Galileo probe, 289
Ganymede, 286
Garlic-mustard plant, 176
Garter snake, 109
Gas giants, 284–289
Gases, 23–27, 43–46
in the atmosphere, 212, 218, 281
formed in chemical change, 37
nonmetals as, 11
properties, 17–21
in stars, 271
in water, 32
water vapor, 205
Gazelle, 74–75
Gecko, 122
Generalize, 212
Generate, 379
Genes
mutations, 115–116
plant, 115
Giant stars, 271
Giant tubeworms, 322
Gills, 112
Give an example, 11, 160, 168, 227, 330, 333, 345, 394
Glaciers
erosion and deposition by, 238, 239
melting, 210
Glass frog, 108–109
Glow sticks, 38

Glue, 371
Go Green
Blown Over, 240
Bright Invention, 325
Carry Less, Save Gas, 69
Green Design, 383
Make a Brochure, 176
Trees and Your Community, 156
Go Green!
Aerogels, 51
Create a Compost Pile, 189
Denim Insulation, 390
Gold, 12
Graduated cylinder, 19, 339
Graphite, 13
Graphs, 341
bar, 280, 350
circle, 213
line, 219
Grasses, 162, 170, 238
Gravity, 61, 64, 85–88
air pressure and, 218
balanced forces, 76
erosion and deposition by, 238, 239
planetary orbits and, 267, 278, 281
on planets, 280
precipitation and, 225
weight and, 64, 280
Great Red Spot, 286
Green Bank Observatory, 307
Green slime, 35
Groundwater, 207, 213
Group, 289
Gulf Stream, 234

Hail, 225, 226, 245–250
Hailstones, 226
Heat, 37
Helium, 286, 287, 288
Herbivore, 160
Hibernation, 125
Hot air balloon, 219
Humans' effect on the environment, 169, 175–177
Humidity, 217, 221, 245–250
Hummingbird, 161
Hurricane, 168, 242–243
Huygens, 289
Hydrogen, 286, 287, 288

Hydrosphere, 211, 213, 245–250
Hydrothermal vents, 322
Hygrometer, 221
Hypothesis, 323, 325, 329, 333, 351–354
Hypothesize, 125, 175, 176, 240, 379

Ice, 206
Ice crystals, 225–226
Ichthyologist, 134
Ida, 291
Identify, 10, 65, 127, 130, 131, 139, 151, 152, 156, 157, 212, 215, 225, 228, 241, 253, 269, 272, 273, 304, 332, 357, 373, 382, 383, 387
Incomplete metamorphosis, 131
Independent variable, 332
Indian Ocean, 213
Indoor-plant waterer, 146–149
Inertia, 67, 68, 85–88
Infer, 2, 13, 20, 28, 31, 32, 39, 41, 71, 76, 80, 81, 83, 102, 115, 122, 124, 130, 138, 152, 171, 172, 175, 176, 209, 223, 231, 234, 237, 239, 267, 274, 275, 278, 282, 288, 339, 341, 343, 372, 384, 385, 394
Infer (Inquiry Skill), 74, 120, 144, 174, 264, 276, 297, 328, 348, 362
Inferences, 343, 362
Infrared technology, 397
Inline skates, 63
Inner planets, 277–283, 285, 295, 299–302
Inquiries. *See* At-Home Lab; Explore It!; Go Green!; Investigate It!; Lightning Lab; Try It!
Inquiry Skills
calculate, 91
classify, 316
collect data, 102, 336
communicate, 22, 41, 66, 78, 158, 198, 224, 230, 243, 349, 380, 389
compute, 75
design, 362, 368, 389

draw conclusions, 120, 133, 158, 178, 179, 216, 236, 316, 344, 380
infer, 2, 28, 34, 40, 41, 74, 83, 102, 114, 120, 144, 174, 264, 276, 297, 328, 348, 349, 362
interpret data, 2, 126, 179, 328, 336
investigate, 66
make and use models, 54, 120, 198, 236, 258, 284, 290, 296, 297, 380, 388
measure, 284, 336, 344
observe, 16, 22, 28, 34, 54, 74, 78, 82, 83, 158, 224, 230, 236, 258, 264, 276, 284, 290, 297, 362
predict, 1, 53, 66, 82, 101, 102, 143, 197, 198, 230, 242, 243, 257, 315, 361, 368
record data, 2, 40, 83, 114, 120, 126, 133, 174, 178, 198, 216, 297, 328, 336, 344, 349, 362, 389
redesign, 389
test, 362

Insects, 159
Instincts, 124
Interactive Vocabulary
    Make a Word Frame!, 44, 246, 392
    Make a Word Magnet!, 182
    Make a Word Pyramid!, 86
    Make a Word Square!, 352
    Make a Word Wheel!, 136, 300
Interpret, 11, 27, 90, 332, 383, 384
Interpret data, 2, 126, 179, 328, 336
Investigate, 66
Investigate It!, 1, 40–41, 53, 82–83, 101, 132–133, 143, 178–179, 197, 242–243, 257, 296–297, 315, 348–349, 361, 388–389
Investigations, scientific, 329–335, 348–349
    control group, 332
    models, 329, 330
    steps in, 332–333
    surveys and sampling, 331
Io, 286, 295
Iron filings, 30
Iron oxide, 282

Jellyfish blooms, 102
Jenner, Edward, 369
Jet engines, 93
Jet stream, 220
Journal, weather, 255
Jupiter, 278, 284–287, 295, 298
Justify, 138, 233, 346

Kite, 260–263
Komiyama, Kunio, 382
Kudzu, 164

Label, 111
Lakes and ponds, 213
Landforms
    arch, 236–237
    effect on climate, 235
    winds' interaction with, 220
Larva, 130
Lasers, 371
Latitude, 231, 232–233, 245–250
Lead, 25
Leaf, 151–157
    cells and tissues of, 152–153
    cellular respiration in, 156–157
    photosynthesis in, 154–155
Leaf-cutting ants, 55
Learned behaviors, 124
Lemons, 38, 332, 333
Length, 339
Let's Read Science!, 3, 55, 103, 145, 199, 259, 317, 363
Lettuce, 151
Lever, 364
Lichen, 168
Life cycles, 126–131
    of animals, 122
    of butterfly, 126–127
    of plants, 116
Light
    as energy, 79–80

    as evidence of chemical change, 37
    infrared technology, 397
    planets and, 277
    sources of, 79
Lightning, 168, 199, 212, 280
Lightning Lab
    Balancing Act, 76
    Bodies of Water Near You, 213
    Climate Zones, 234
    Coin Flip, 346
    Comparing Apples and Lemons, 38
    Day and Night, 267
    Do I Need a Thermometer?, 20
    Estimate and Measure, 342
    Letters and Atoms, 13
    Making Shadows, 80
    Measuring Shadows, 272
    Model Planets, 282
    Reading in the Dark, 287
    Wandering Ice, 25
    You in the Food Chain, 162
    You Light Up My Leaf, 118
Lions, 124, 204–205
Liquid, 23–27, 43–46
    immiscible, 17
    properties, 17–21
    in solutions, 32
List, 10, 12, 21, 252, 347
Lithosphere, 211, 214, 245–250
Little Dipper, 274
Living things, 108–113. *See also* Animals; Plants
    in the biosphere, 215
    physical structures, 108–113
    on Earth, 281
Locusts, 169
Lulin, 293
Lungs, 112

Machine, 364
Magnetic forces, 65
Magnetic resonance imaging (MRI) scan, 368–369, 370
Magnetism separating mixtures, 30
Magnets, 65, 74
Main idea and details, 55, 61, 68, 90, 145, 163, 186, 208, 363, 369, 373, 394

Make and use models, 54, 120, 198, 236, 258, 284, 290, 296, 297, 380, 388

Malachite, 3

Manatees, 325

Mangrove tree, 115

Maple tree, 109

Mariner 10, 279

Mars, 278, 282–283, 295

Marsh, 145

Mass, 18, 43–46
acceleration and, 70–72
inertia and, 68
matter and, 9
measurement of, 339
of the sun, 271

Matter, 9–15
atoms, 12–13
chemical changes, 37–39
elements, 10–13
evaporation and condensation, 26–27
freezing and melting, 25, 208
measuring, 2
physical changes, 35–36
properties of, 17–21
states of, 22–27
volume of, 339

Mean, 342

Measure, 284, 336, 344

Measurement, 342
force, 72, 339
length and distance, 339
mass, 339
temperature, 339
time, 339
volume, 339

Median, 342

Medical technology, 369–371, 379

Melting, 25, 36, 198, 208

Melting point, 36

Mercury (element), 10

Mercury (planet), 259, 278, 279

Metals, 10

Metamorphosis, 126–131, 135–136
amphibian, 128–129
complete, 130
incomplete, 131

Meteor Crater, 292

Meteor showers, 292, 293

Meteorites, 279, 281, 292

Meteoroids, 290, 292

Meteorologist, 217

Meteors, 292

Meterstick, 339

Methane, 288

Microchip, 369, 372, 391–392

Microscope, 339

Migration, 125, 180

Milk, 36

Millipede, 167

Minerals in lithosphere, 214

Mitochondrion, 156

Mixture, 28–31, 43–46
separating, 28, 30–31, 40–41

Mode, 342

Models, 330. *See also* Make and use models
arm, 380
drawings, 104

Molds, 158

Molecule, 9, 15, 43–46

Moles, 171

Moon (of Earth), 256–257, 281, 295

Moons of planets, 288
Jupiter's, 286, 295, 299–302
Neptune's, 288
Pluto's, 294

Moose, 160

Moray eel, 165

Motion
acceleration, 67–68, 85–88
balanced forces and, 76
force and, 61–73
Newton's laws of, 56, 68–75
uniform, 67

Mountains
effect on climate, 235
effect on weather, 220

MRI scan, 368–369, 370

Mushrooms, 161

Muskrat, 145

Mussels, 176, 371

Mutations, 115–116

My Planet Diary
Connections, 108, 204
Did You Know?, 374
Discovery, 150
Fun Facts, 8, 166, 210, 322
Misconception, 60, 270

Nanobots, 379

NASA
infrared technology, 397
satellites, 180
Space Centers, 93

National Radio Astronomy Observatory, 307

Natural selection, 116, 122–123

Neon, 11

Neptune, 259, 279, 288, 294

Net force, 76

Neutrons, 12

New Lutheran Hospital, 374

Newton (N), 61, 72

Newton, Isaac, 84

Newton's first law of motion, 68–69

Newton's second law of motion, 70–72

Newton's third law of motion, 56, 73, 74–75

Niche, 164

Nitrogen, 212, 218, 281

Non-contact force, 61, 64–65, 85–88

Nonmetals, 11

Nonnative species, 176–177

North Atlantic Drift, 234

North Star, 274

Nymph, 131

Oak trees, 162

Observation, 323, 326, 329, 344, 345, 347, 349, 351–354

Observe, 16, 22, 28, 34, 54, 74, 78, 82, 83, 114, 126, 132, 144, 158, 198, 224, 230, 236, 258, 264, 276, 284, 290, 297, 328, 349, 362, 368, 380

Ocean currents, 234, 238

Ocean vents, 322

Ocean waves, 238

Oceans, 213
temperature and circulation, 234

Octopus, 121

Oil pollution, 51

Okapi, 122

Omnivore, 160, 162

Opportunity, 283

Orbit, 265, 267, 277, 278, 281, 291, 295, 299–302
of Pluto, 294

Ordered pairs, 386

Organisms. *See also* Animals; Plants
energy in food chains and food webs, 162–163
energy relationships among, 162–163

energy roles of, 160–161
Ornithologist, 134
Outer planets, 284–289, 295, 299–302
Ovary, 111
Overhunting, 177
Owls, 123
Oxygen, 11, 218
in the atmosphere, 212, 281
in cellular respiration, 156
in photosynthesis, 154–155
respiration and circulation, 112–113

Pacific Ocean, 213
Painted bunting, 108
Palisade tissue, 152–153
Pan balance, 339
Papaya trees, 116
Paper, 35, 37
Paper helicopter, 54
Paper towels, 344
Paperbark maple tree, 109
Parachute, 62
Parasites, 165
Peat, 145
Performance-Based Assessment, 98–99, 194–195, 312–313, 404
Photosphere, 272
Photosynthesis, 37, 112, 151, 154, 181–184
Physical change, 35–36, 43–46
Pioneers 10 & 11, 289
Pistil, 111
Planet, 277, 299–302
diameters of, 284
dwarf, 294
finding, 298
inner, 277–283
light reflected off, 277
orbits of, 267, 277, 278, 281
outer, 284–289
rotation of, 299–300
Planets. *See* Inner planets; Outer planets
Plants
adaptations, 114–117
air quality improvement, 169
energy source, 151
in food chains and food webs, 163

food made by, 151
forest fire's effect on, 170
genetic mutations, 116
leaves, 112, 113, 151–157
life cycles of, 116
needs of, 114–115
prevention of erosion, 238
reproduction, 111
respiration, 112
seeds, 109, 111
stems, 110, 113
stomata, 112
succession, 118, 119
survival of, 172
vascular, 113
Plasma, 24
Pluto, 294
Polar ice caps, 282
Polar zones, 232–233
Polaris, 274
Pollen tube, 111
Pollution, 51, 175, 181–184, 325
Population, 167
Prairie food chain, 162
Precipitation, 205, 206–208, 219, 221, 225–227, 245–250
Precision, 337, 338, 351–354
Predator, 124, 159, 181–184
Predict, 1, 33, 48, 53, 66, 71, 82, 101, 102, 138, 143, 187, 197, 198, 213, 219, 230, 242, 243, 257, 279, 304, 315, 323, 325, 329, 359, 361, 368, 371, 378, 381, 385
Predictions, weather, 242–243
Prey, 159, 181–184
Prickly pear cactus, 117
Problems, 369
Problem-solving, 323
Procedures, 329, 334, 351–354
Producer, 159, 160, 181–184
Prominence, solar, 272
Prosthetic limb, 375–377, 391–392
Protons, 12
Prototype, 381, 384, 391–392
A-frame tent, 104–107
artificial arm, 364–367
balloon rocket, 56–59
carbon dioxide trap, 4–7
indoor-plant waterer, 146–149
kite, 260–263
water filtration system, 200
wind vane, 318
PUMA robot, 386
Pupa, 130

Questionnaires, 331
Questions, scientific, 316, 323

Race cars, 63
Radiation, 271, 273, 370
Rain
in the atmosphere, 212
erosion and deposition by, 238–239
as form of precipitation, 221, 226–227
formation of, 206
mountains' effect on, 220, 235
Range, 342
Reading Skills. *See* Target Reading Skills
Recognize, 25, 271
Record data, 2, 40, 83, 114, 120, 126, 133, 174, 178, 198, 216, 297, 328, 336, 344, 349, 362, 389
Red Planet, 282
Redesign, 389
Reference material, 324
Regulation, environmental, 177
Reproduction, 111
Research, scientific, 324
Reservoir, 245–250
Respiration, 112–113
Resurrection plants, 172
Review, scientific, 347
Revolution, 265, 267, 299–302
Rings of outer planets, 285, 287, 288
Rings of Saturn, 287
Rings of Uranus, 288
Ripening, 39
Rivers and streams
erosion and deposition by, 238–239
fresh water in, 213
Robotic arm, 386–389
Robotics, 374–379
Robots, 360–361, 375
Rockets
equal and opposite forces, 56
motion of, 82
power of, 93

Rocks
erosion and deposition of, 237–241
in lithosphere, 214

Röntgen, William, 370

Rotation, 265, 299–302
of Earth, 266
of Jupiter, 286
of planets, 296–297
of Uranus, 288

Rubber, 35–36

Runoff, 206–208

S

Safety rules, 340

Salt, 14, 16, 204

Salt marsh, 163

Sampling, 331

Sand, 16, 30

Sand dunes, 240

Sand sculpture, 9

Sandhill crane, 180

Satellite, 281

Saturn, 278, 287, 295

Scalpel, 371

Scavenger, 160

Science, 322–349
conclusions, 327, 333, 345–347
control group, 332
data, 337–339
evidence, 346
experiments, 329, 332–333
hypotheses, 325, 333
investigations, 329, 331–333, 335, 348–349
observations, 326, 329, 344–347, 349
procedures and records, 334–335
research, 324
reviewing and retesting, 347
safety rules, 340
scientific questions, 316, 323
technology, 368–373
tools, 322–323, 339

Science Careers
zoologist, 134

Science in Your Back Yard
Keep a Weather Journal, 255
Planet Hunting, 298
Sidewalks & Playgrounds, 42

Screen filter, 30

Sea turtle, 326

Sea urchin, 122

Seasons
on Earth, 168, 268–269
on Mars, 282

Sediments, 238–239

Seedling, 111

Seeds, 111
dispersal of, 109
fire's effect on, 170
growth of, 132–133
temperature's effect on, 102

Semimetals, 11

Sensei X Robotic Catheter System, 374

Separating mixtures, 28, 30–32, 40–41

Sequence, 118, 162, 205, 211, 229, 283, 305

Sequoia trees, 171, 231

Shadow, 85–88, 272
light source producing, 79
size and shape change, 78, 80–81

Shark egg, 111

Shooting stars, 292

Show, 235

Shrimp, 165

Silicon, 11

Simple machines, 364–365

Skeleton, 111

Skull, 110

Sleet, 226, 245–250

Slime, green, 35

Smell, 37

Snakes, 109

Snow, 227

Snowboarder, 66–67

Snowflakes, 224–225

Snowshoe hare, 125

Sodium, 14

Soil, 174
erosion and deposition of, 237–241
in lithosphere, 214
on Mars, 282

Sojourner, 283

Sol, 282

Solar flare, 271, 272–273, 299–302

Solar system, 265
asteroids, 291
comets, 293
dwarf planet, 294
Earth, 265–269
inner planets, 276–283
meteoroids, 290

meteors, 292
moons, 295
outer planets, 277, 284–289
sun, 265–269, 270–273

Solid, 23–25, 43–46
formed in chemical change, 37
mass and weight, 18
properties of, 17–21
in solutions, 32

Solubility, 33

Solute, 32

Solution, 32–33, 43–46

Solutions to problems, 369, 372

Solve, 180

Solvent, 32

South America, 235

Southern Ocean, 213

Space probe, 68, 277, 279, 280, 283, 289, 299–302

Species
extinct, 123
nonnative, 176

Speed, 67
force and, 61

Spinach, 151

Spiracles, 112

Spiral galaxy, 258

Spirit, 283

Spitzer Space Telescope, 287

Spongy tissue, 152–153

Spring scale, 339

Squirrel robot, 378

Stamen, 111

Stars, 270–271
apparent motion of, 275
constellations, 274

STEM
Flight Simulators, 359
Predicting Tsunamis, 244
Tracking Migrations, 180

STEM activities
Breathe Deeply, 260–263
Come in Out of Nature!, 104–107
Filter It Out!, 200–203
Is Your Arm a Simple Machine?, 364–367
Let It Self-Water!, 146–149
Trap and Store, 4–7
Watch It Fly!, 56–59
Where's the Wind Going?, 318–321

Stems, 111

Stitches, 371

Stomata, 112

Stopwatch, 339

Storms
 on Neptune, 288
 thunderstorms, 212, 228
Stratus clouds, 228
Structural adaptations, 117, 122–123
Study Guide, 47, 89, 137, 185, 251, 303, 355, 393
Sublimation, 206
Subtracting fractions, 172
Succession, 118
Sugar, 37, 113
 cellular respiration of, 156
 photosynthesis of, 154–155
 storage in plants, 157
Sugar glider, 121
Suggest, 29, 69, 117, 169, 217
Sulfur, 11, 295
Summarize, 39, 48, 177, 221, 226, 271, 275, 305, 333, 377
Summer, 268, 269
Sun, 264–265, 270–271
 characteristics of, 272–273
 Earth and, 256–257, 265–269, 271
 planets' orbits around, 259, 278
Sunlight
 atmosphere blocking, 212, 281
 change with seasons, 268
 concentration of, 264, 268
 at different latitudes, 232
 in photosynthesis, 154–155
 as source of energy, 151
 as source of light, 79
Sunspots, 272
Support, 29, 186, 232
Surgical glue, 371
Surtsey Island, 166
Surveys, 331
Sutures, 371
Swamp, 144
Symbiosis, 165
Synthesize, 90, 91, 205

Table Mountain pine, 171
Table salt, 14
Tables, 341
Tadpoles, 128, 129
Target Reading Skills
 cause and effect, 80, 103, 109, 117, 125, 167, 238, 280, 293

compare and contrast, 3, 9, 13, 19, 23, 35, 37, 111, 116, 123, 124, 127, 130, 139, 157, 165, 259, 265, 267, 285, 295, 304
 draw conclusions, 199, 217, 226, 235, 236, 253
 main idea and details, 55, 61, 68, 90, 145, 163, 186, 208, 363, 369, 373, 394
 sequence, 118, 162, 205, 229, 283, 305
 summarize, 39, 271, 275
 text features, 317, 323, 333, 338, 356
Technology, 368–373, 391–392. *See also* STEM activities
 animals and, 378
 computer, 372–373
 design process, 380–387
 home, 363
 infrared, 397
 medical, 369–371
 nanotechnology, 379
 robotics, 374–379, 386–389
Temperate zones, 232–233
Temperature, 20, 43–46, 336, 339
 air, 4, 34, 178–179, 219, 225, 226
 average monthly, 219
 boiling points, 26
 effect on seed growth, 102
 elevation affecting, 235
 as evidence of chemical change, 38–39
 freezing/melting points, 25
 on Mercury, 279
 ocean, 234
 physical change caused by, 34, 35, 36
 scales, 20
 water bodies affecting, 234
Tent pattern, 104–107
Test, 362
Text features
 black headings, 333
 blue heading, 323
 caption, 317
 heading, 317
 photograph, 323
 picture, 317
 picture of a pencil, 317
 yellow highlight, 317, 338, 356
Texture, 21
Thermal energy. *See also* **Temperature**
 atmosphere blocking, 4

Thermometers, 217, 230, 336, 339, 397
Thunder, 212
Thunderstorms, 228
Tiger swallowtail butterfly, 130
Timer, 339
Tissues in plant leaves, 152
Titan, 289, 295
Tomatoes, 39
Tombaugh, Clyde, 294
Tools, 322–323, 339, 370–371
Toothbrush design, 382–385
Tornado, 337, 341
Tortoise beetles, 55
Trade winds, 222
Transport system, water, 368
Trees, 154
 cherry, 116
 maple, 109
 oak, 162
 papaya, 116
 prevention of erosion, 241
 sequoia, 171, 231
 Table Mountain pine, 171
Triton, 288
Tropical zone, 232–233
Trucks, 70
Try It!, 1, 2, 53, 54, 101, 102, 143, 144, 197, 198, 257, 258, 315, 316, 361, 362
Tsunami, 244
Tubeworm, 322

Uniform motion, 67
Unimate robotic arm, 386
UNIVAC (Universal Automatic Computer), 372
Universal solvent, 32
Uranus, 278, 288

Vaccines, 369
Valley
 U-shaped, 239
 V-shaped, 238
Variable, 329, 332, 351–354
 control group, 332
 dependent/independent, 332

Vascular, 113
Veins, 152–153
Venus, 278, 280, 298
Venus's–flytrap, 117
Viking I, 283
Vocabulary
    acceleration, 67, 85–88
    accuracy, 337, 338, 351–354
    adaptation, 115, 134–135
    asteroid, 291, 299–302
    atmosphere, 211, 212, 245–250
    atom, 9, 12, 43–46
    atomic theory, 9, 12, 43–46
    axis, 265, 266, 299–302
    balanced, 75, 76, 85–88
    barometric pressure, 217, 218, 245–250
    biosphere, 211, 215, 245–250
    cellular respiration, 151, 156, 181–184
    chemical change, 35, 37, 43–46
    circulation, 217, 222, 245–250
    climate, 231, 245–250
    comet, 291, 293, 299–302
    community, 181–184
    competition, 167, 170, 181–184
    compound, 9, 14–15, 43–46
    condensation, 205, 206, 245–250
    conservation, 175, 177, 181–184
    constellation, 271, 274, 299–302
    consumer, 159, 160, 181–184
    contact force, 61, 62, 85–88
    control group, 329, 332, 351–354
    data, 337, 351–354
    decomposer, 159, 161, 181–184
    deposition, 237
    design process, 381, 391–392
    dwarf planet, 291, 294, 299–302
    ecosystem, 181–184
    elevation, 231, 235, 245–250
    environment, 167, 181–184
    erosion, 237
    evaporation, 205, 206, 245–250
    evidence, 345, 346, 351–354
    exoskeleton, 109, 111, 135–136
    experiment, 329, 351–354
    extinct species, 121, 123, 135–136
    food chain, 159, 162, 181–184
    food web, 159, 163, 181–184
    force, 61, 85–88
    friction, 61, 62, 85–88

    gas, 23, 24, 43–46
    gravity, 61, 64, 85–88
    habitat, 181–184
    hail, 225, 226, 245–250
    humidity, 217, 221, 245–250
    hydrosphere, 211, 213, 245–250
    hypothesis, 323, 325, 351–354
    inertia, 67, 68, 85–88
    inference, 337, 343, 351–354
    inner planet, 277, 299–302
    latitude, 231, 232, 245–250
    liquid, 23, 24, 43–46
    lithosphere, 211, 214
    mass, 17, 18, 43–46
    metamorphosis, 127, 135–136
    microchip, 369, 372, 391–392
    mixture, 29, 43–46
    molecule, 9, 15, 43–46
    moon, 277, 281, 299–302
    non-contact force, 61, 64, 85–88
    observation, 323, 326, 351–354
    orbit, 265, 267, 299–302
    outer planet, 285, 299–302
    photosynthesis, 151, 154, 181–184
    physical change, 35, 43–46
    planet, 277, 299–302
    pollution, 175, 181–184
    population,167
    precipitation, 205, 206, 245–250
    precision, 337, 338, 351–354
    predator, 159, 181–184
    prey, 159, 181–184
    procedures, 329, 334, 351–354
    producer, 159, 160, 181–184
    prosthetic limb, 375, 377, 391–392
    prototype, 381, 384, 391–392
    revolution, 265, 267, 299–302
    rotation, 265, 266, 299–302
    shadow, 79, 85–88
    sleet, 225, 226, 245–250
    solar flare, 271, 272, 299–302
    solid, 23, 24, 43–46
    solution, 29, 32, 43–46
    space probe, 277, 279, 299–302
    technology, 369, 391–392
    temperature, 17, 20, 43–46
    variable, 329, 332, 351–354
    volume, 17, 19, 43–46
    water cycle, 205, 206, 245–250
    weather, 217, 245–250
Vocabulary (Critical Thinking), 48, 49, 90, 138, 186, 252, 304, 356, 394, 395

Volcanic islands, 166
Volcanoes, 168, 272, 295
Volume, 19, 24, 43–46, 339
    combining/mixing and, 2
Voyagers 1 & 2, 289

Water
    absorption, 344
    in air, 205
    in cellular respiration, 156
    in cement, 42
    dissolved gases in, 32
    on Earth, 281
    erosion and deposition by, 238–239
    evaporation and condensation, 26–27, 198, 206–208
    friction of, 62
    molecules, 15
    movement through plants, 152
    in photosynthesis, 154–155
    pollution of, 325
    states of, 23–27
    temperature and, 234
    transport systems, 368
    as universal solvent, 32
Water cycle, 198, 205, 206–208, 245–250
Water filtration system, 200
Water lily, 117
Water loss, 152
Water purification system, 200
Water vapor, 36
    in the atmosphere, 206–208, 218, 221
    cloud formation, 225
    precipitation and, 226
Waves (ocean), 238
Wax, 36
Weather, 168, 217–229, 245–250, 336–337, 342
    air circulation, 222–223
    air temperature, 219
    barometric pressure, 218
    climate compared to, 231
    clouds, 206, 221, 225–229
    high and low pressure, 219–220
    humidity, 221
    precipitation, 206–208, 221, 225–227, 235
    weather maps, 216–217
    winds, 220, 222

Weather forecasts, 216, 242–243, 244

Weather journal, 255

Weather vane, 220

Weathering, 238

Weight
    as characteristic of matter, 18
    combining/mixing and, 2
    gravity and, 64, 280

Wetlands, 145

Wind
    in the atmosphere, 212
    effect on ocean currents, 234
    erosion and deposition by, 240–241
    interaction with landforms, 220

    on Mars, 282
    movement from high to low pressure areas, 222
    names of, 318
    on Venus, 280

Wind tunnel, 330

Wind vane, 318

Windsurf, 210–211

Winter, 268, 269

Wood, 110

Wood frog, 173

World Wide Web, 372

Worms, 189

Write about it, 186, 225, 252, 289, 357, 394

X rays, 370

Zebra mussels, 176

Zookeepers, 134

Zoologist, 134

Credits

Staff Credits

The people who made up the *Interactive Science* team—representing core design digital and multimedia production services, digital product development, editorial, manufacturing, and production—are listed below.

Geri Amani, Alisa Anderson, Jose Arrendondo, Amy Austin, Lindsay Bellino, Jennifer Berry, Charlie Bink, Bridget Binstock, Holly Blessen, Robin Bobo, Craig Bottomley, Jim Brady, Laura Brancky, Chris Budzisz, Mary Chingwa, Sitha Chhor, Caroline Chung, Margaret Clampitt, Karen Corliss, Brandon Cole, Mitch Coulter, AnnMarie Coyne, Fran Curran, Dana Damiano, Nancy Duffner, Susan Falcon, Amanda Ferguson, David Gall, Mark Geyer, Amy Goodwin, Gerardine Griffin, Chris Haggerty, Laura Hancko, Jericho Hernandez, Autumn Hickenlooper, Guy Huff, George Jacobson, Marian Jones, Abigail Jungreis, Kathi Kalina, Chris Kammer, Sheila Kanitsch, Alyse Kondrat, Mary Kramer, Thea Limpus, Dominique Mariano, Lori McGuire, Melinda Medina, Angelina Mendez, Claudi Mimo, John Moore, Phoebe Novak, Anthony Nuccio, Jeffrey Osier, Rachel Pancare, Dorothy Preston, Julianne Regnier, Charlene Rimsa, Rebecca Roberts, Camille Salerno, Manuel Sanchez, Carol Schmitz, Amanda Seldera, Sheetal Shah, Jeannine Shelton El, Geri Shulman, Greg Sorenson, Samantha Sparkman, Mindy Spelius, Karen Stockwell, Dee Sunday, Dennis Tarwood, Jennie Teece, Lois Teesdale, Michaela Tudela, Oscar Vera, Dave Wade, Melissa Walker, Tom Wickland, James Yagelski, Tim Yetzina, Diane Zimmermann

Illustrations

vi-vii, 1, 47, 49-50, 53, 89, 91-92, 98 ©Aleksi Markku/ Shutterstock; viii-ix, 101, 143, 145-146, 149, 185, 187-188, 194 ©Jens Stolt/Shutterstock; x-xi, 197, 251, 253-254, 257, 303, 305-306, 313 Leonello Calvetti/ Getty Images; xii-xiii, 332, 373, 375-376, 379, 393, 394-95, 192 ©James Thew/Shutterstock; xi, 239, 277-278, 306, 317, 319 Robert (Bob) Kayganich; 116 Big Sesh Studios; 117, 119, 159-160 Jeff Mangiat; 118 Peter Bollinger; 12, 24, 26, 43, 45, 62-63, 66-67, 70, 85, 89, 169, 176-177, 189, 195, 230, 234-235, 241, 244-245, 259, 260, 280 Precision Graphics; 172-173, 197 Adam Benton; 218-221, 228-229, 257, 259, 263, 313 Studio Liddell; 61, 85 June Melber

Photographs

Photo locators denoted as follows: Top (T), Center (C), Bottom (B), Left (L), Right (R), Background (Bkgd)

COVER: Brent Landreth/Alamy